A Baptist Democracy

MERCER
UNIVERSITY PRESS

Endowed by
TOM WATSON BROWN
and
THE WATSON-BROWN FOUNDATION, INC.

A Baptist Democracy

Separating God and Caesar in the Land of the Free

Lee Canipe

MERCER UNIVERSITY PRESS
MACON, GEORGIA

MUP/P427

© 2011 Mercer University Press
1400 Coleman Avenue
Macon, Georgia 31207
All rights reserved

First Edition

Books published by Mercer University Press are printed on acid-free paper that meets the requirements of American National Standard for Information Sciences—Permanence of Paper for Printed Library Materials.

Portions of chapter five have been reprinted from the *American Baptist Quarterly*, Vol. XXI, No. 4, pp. 415-431, with the permission of the American Baptist Historical Society, Atlanta, GA, 30341.

Mercer University Press is a member of Green Press Initiative (greenpressinitiative.org), a nonprofit organization working to help publishers and printers increase their use of recycled paper and decrease their use of fiber derived from endangered forests. This book is printed on recycled paper.

Library of Congress Cataloging-in-Publication Data

Canipe, Lee, 1970-
 A Baptist democracy : separating God and Caesar in the Land of the Free / Lee Canipe. -- 1st ed.
   p. cm.
 Includes bibliographical references (p.   ) and index.
 ISBN 978-0-88146-239-5 (pbk. : alk. paper)
 1. Democracy--Religious aspects--Baptists--History of doctrines--20th century. 2. Church and state--United States--History of doctrines--20th century. 3. Baptists--United States--Doctrines--History--20th century. 4. United States--Church history--20th century. 5. Rauschenbusch, Walter, 1861-1918. 6. Mullins, Edgar Young, 1860-1928. 7. Truett, George W. (George Washington), 1867-1944. I. Title.
 BX6237.C36 2011
 261.7--dc22
                                                        2011002052

*This work is dedicated
to the glory of
God,
and in honor of my wife,
Hilary*

Contents

Acknowledgments	viii
Introduction	1
1: The Transformation of Freedom in Baptist Thought	14
2: Walter Rauschenbusch and the Democratic Kingdom of God	52
3: E. Y. Mullins and the "Baptist Empire" of American Democracy	88
4: George Truett and the Baptist Apology for American Democracy	127
5: Baptists and the Subtle Snares of Freedom	153
Conclusion	170
Bibliography	181
Index	197

Acknowledgments

I am responsible for the content of this book. Any errors that appear in the following pages, whether they be errors of fact, errors of interpretation, or errors of judgment, are mine and mine alone.

The flaws in this book should be charged to my account. Credit for the rest, however, must be rightly and properly shared. Indeed, at no point here can I plausibly claim to have accomplished anything of merit exclusively through my own efforts. As this book has progressed from idea to reality, I have, at every step along the way, been blessed by the generous encouragement and wise counsel of people who know a lot more than I do. They have guided my research, clarified my thinking, challenged my assumptions, polished my prose, and saved me from making the kind of mistakes—both big and small—that scholars more seasoned than I are careful to avoid. I am sincerely and profoundly grateful for their investment in me and my work.

More than anyone else, Barry Hankins helped to nurture the ideas from which this book developed. His suggestions invariably strengthened my arguments and streamlined my writing. It is my good fortune to have had him as a mentor. He remains a trusted and graciously accessible source of advice and guidance.

William Brackney, Derek Davis, and Barry Harvey read earlier versions of my work and offered their constructive criticism. They gave liberally of their time and professional expertise, and their insights considerably elevated the quality of this finished product. I am grateful also to Dwight Allman, who tutored me in political theory. I consider myself very fortunate to have had the opportunity to learn from these outstanding scholars.

A number of gracious individuals provided me with welcome and much-needed assistance in locating archival photographs for use in this book. Many thanks to Jason Fowler, of the James P. Boyce Centennial Library at Southern Baptist Theological Seminary; Taffey Hall, of the Southern Baptist Historical Library and Archives; and Lindsey Walker, of the A. Webb Roberts Library at Southwestern Baptist Theological Seminary. I am indebted **also** to John DiLustro for his technical support and computer skills, and to South Moore for his assistance in compiling the index.

Portions of chapters two and five originally appeared as journal articles. I am grateful to Ian Randall, editor of the *Baptist Quarterly*, and to Robert Johnson, editor of the *American Baptist Quarterly*, for kindly granting me permission to include material from their respective journals in this book.

Thanks also to Marc Jolley of Mercer University Press, both for his confidence in this project and for his help in bringing it to fruition. At various stages in the publication process, I received good counsel from Curtis Freeman, Rob Nash, Philip Thompson, and Scott Walker. Their spot-on advice was and is greatly appreciated.

Some additional words of gratitude are in order. I came to faith in Jesus Christ largely due to the kind and patient ministry of men and women at the First Baptist Church of Greensboro, North Carolina. I was baptized in that church and, years later, was ordained to the ministry by that congregation. My Baptist heritage is a gift I have received from these saints. I am grateful as well to the good people of Murfreesboro Baptist Church in Murfreesboro, North Carolina, for calling me to serve as their pastor. They have been a constant source of encouragement and have generously given me the time and space to pursue my own research and writing interests. It is both a joy and a privilege to serve the Lord in the company of this congregation.

I also have the benefit of being part of an academic community located just down the street from my church. J Brabban and Danny Moore of Chowan University have been kind enough to provide me with an office on campus. Rachel Peterson at the university's Whitaker Library, meanwhile, has answered my every interlibrary loan request (and there have been many) with remarkable grace and speed.

Bill and Crystal Leathers have been wonderful cheerleaders throughout the process of writing this book; for many reasons, I am fortunate to be their son-in-law. My parents, Chris and Sandra Canipe, have blessed me with both the freedom to succeed and the security to fail. Their support of me—and of this book—cannot be exaggerated. I stand upon their shoulders, and those of their parents as well; whatever I am or shall become is but a partial discharge of the debt I owe them all for their sacrificial love.

Above all, however, I am grateful for my wife, Hilary. Not only is she the mother of my daughter, Helen, and my sons, Watt and Peter, but she serves as a daily reminder to me that God is good. Her faith in me is contagious and has carried me further than I could ever have gone alone. It is altogether fitting, then, that this book be dedicated to her and to the glory of God.

Lee Canipe
Murfreesboro, North Carolina

Walter Rauschenbusch, c. 1905

Walter Rauschenbusch, c. 1915

E. Y. Mullins, c. 1902. *Courtesy of the Southern Baptist Historical Library and Archives.*

E. Y. Mullins, c. 1926.
Courtesy of the James P. Boyce Centennial Library at Southern Baptist Theological Seminary.

E. Y. Mullins, J. B. Gambrell, and D. G. Whittinghill (L-R) outside of St. Mark's Cathedral in Venice during a visit to encourage European Baptists in the aftermath of World War I. The Southern Baptist Convention commissioned this visit at its annual meeting in 1920. *Courtesy of James P. Boyce Centennial Library at Southern Baptist Theological Seminary.*

George W. Truett, c. 1918, in uniform as a member of the Young Men's Christian Association delegation of ministers providing encouragement and pastoral support for American sailors and soldiers during World War I. *Courtesy of the A. Webb Roberts Library at Southwestern Baptist Theological Seminary.*

(Above) An aerial photograph of the Southern Baptist Theological Seminary campus, c. 1926, near the end of E.Y. Mullins' tenure as president. *Courtesy of the Southern Baptist Historical Library and Archives.*

(Below) Attendees of the Baptist World Alliance (BWA) regional conference in Riga, Latvia in October, 1926. E. Y. Mullins, then president of the BWA, is seated fourth from the left in the first row of seated individuals. George W. Truett is two seats down from Mullins' left. *Courtesy of James P. Boyce Centennial Library at Southern Baptist Theological Seminary.*

George W. Truett, c. 1920.
Courtesy of the A. Webb Roberts Library at Southwestern Baptist Theological Seminary.

George W. Truett and messengers to the 1920 Southern Baptist Convention, on the steps of the United States Capitol building in Washington, DC. Truett is standing on the right in the center of the photograph. J. B. Gambrell is on the left. *Courtesy of the Southern Baptist Historical Library and Archives.*

The First Baptist Church of Dallas, Texas, c. 1925. *Courtesy of the Southern Baptist Historical Library and Archives.*

Introduction

Why is "The Star-Spangled Banner" in the *Baptist Hymnal*?

This question is not an easy one to answer. Given the Baptists' traditional insistence upon the separation of church and state, a Baptist hymnbook would certainly seem to be an unlikely home for a national anthem. After all, as J. M. Dawson, the first executive director of the staunchly separationist Baptist Joint Committee on Public Affairs, wrote in 1956, "church-state separation for the Baptists is bound up with their conception of Christianity."[1] And yet, there it is on page 635 of the 1991 edition of the *Baptist Hymnal*: "The Star-Spangled Banner." How, then, does the American national anthem's presence in the hymnal square with the Baptist notion that church and state belong to separate realms, have separate concerns, and address separate realities? Could it be that Baptists somehow identify with the American state in a way that allows them to sing their devotion to it in practice even as they proclaim their distance from it in principle?

It's not just the national anthem. The hymnal also contains "America, the Beautiful," "My Country 'Tis of Thee," and other patriotic standards that celebrate the United States and its professed ideals of freedom and equality for all. Some of these patriotic hymns have been in Baptist worship books since at least 1921. "My Country 'Tis of Thee," in fact, appeared in the very first Southern Baptist hymnal, published in 1850.[2] It has been said that hymnals, more so than sermons, creeds, or confessions of faith, reflect what Christians *really* believe.[3] If this argument is true—if

---

[1] J. M. Dawson, *Baptists and the American Republic* (Nashville TN: Broadman Press, 1956) 99.

[2] See *Handbook to the Baptist Hymnal* (Nashville TN.: Convention Press, 1992) 191, 198, 209-210. *Kingdom Songs* (1921) was the first Baptist hymnbook to include "The Star-Spangled Banner" and "America, the Beautiful." *The Baptist Psalmody* (1850) was the first self-consciously Southern Baptist hymnal.

[3] Harry Eskew and Hugh T. McElrath, *Sing With Understanding: An Introduction to Christian Hymnology* (Nashville TN: Broadman Press, 1980) 59. "The basic beliefs of most Christians have been formed more by the hymns they sing than by the preaching they hear

hymns do, in fact, offer the most accurate glimpses of popular faith and theology—then the presence of patriotic songs in the *Baptist Hymnal* suggests that, on a visceral level, Baptists in the United States are much more comfortable than they admit with the idea that church and state might indeed share common, sacred ground in the hearts and minds of Christian believers.

The American novelist F. Scott Fitzgerald once observed that "the test of a first-rate intelligence is the ability to hold two opposed ideas in the mind at the same time, and still retain the ability to function."[4] The strange juxtaposition of church and state in Baptist thought represents an ongoing—and protracted—experiment in defense of Fitzgerald's thesis. Since the early days of the American republic, Baptists have sent mixed messages about how Christians should relate to the state. On the one hand, Baptists have been very clear in their belief that the affairs of church and state do not (and should not) overlap. Quoting Matthew 22:21, they have insisted that Caesar and God properly receive tribute in their rightful (and separate) domains, a doctrine that sequesters spiritual concerns away from more worldly matters.[5] According to John Leland, an active Baptist campaigner for religious liberty in the years following the American Revolution, "the government has no more to do with the religious opinions of men than it has to do with the principles of mathematics."[6] This being the case, Baptists in the United States have traditionally greeted any hint of confusion between the boundaries of

---

or the Bible study they pursue," write Eskew and McElrath. Hymns, they believe, serve as musical bearers of theology at the grass-roots level, both shaping and reflecting the particular religious convictions of Christian churches.

[4]F. Scott Fitzgerald, "The Crack-Up," in *The Crack-Up*, ed. Edmund Wilson (New York: New Directions Publishing Company, 1945) 69.

[5]See James E. Wood, Jr., "Biblical Foundations of Church-State Relations," in *Church and State in Scripture, History, and Constitutional Law*, eds. James E. Wood, Jr., E. Bruce Thompson, and Robert T. Miller (Waco TX: Baylor University Press, 1958) 33. Cf. New Testament scholar Richard Hays writes that Jesus' "answer" to the Pharisees should be understood more as claim about God's sovereignty over *all* creation than as a definitive statement about how his followers should relate to Caesar. See Hays, *The Moral Vision of the New Testament: A Contemporary Introduction to New Testament Ethics* (San Francisco: Harper Collins, 1996) 127.

[6]John Leland, "The Rights of Conscience Inalienable," in *The Writings of John Leland*, ed., L.F. Greene (New York: G. W. Wood, 1845; reprint, New York: Arno Press, 1969) 184.

church and state, such as the use of public tax money to support religious endeavors, with loud and sustained opposition.

On the other hand, Baptists have also been among the most ardent and patriotic supporters of the American state. "Nothing is more plain," wrote the same John Leland who flatly denied the existence of any connection between religion and government, "than that the Almighty has set up the government of the United States in answer to the prayers of all the saints, down from the first proclamation of the gospel."[7] From the beginning of the new republic, Baptist enthusiasm for the fledgling United States has revolved around the nation's professed commitment to freedom, democracy, and separation of church and state. As America stands for freedom, Baptists have stood with America and proudly defended the country's ideals as their own.

Where, then, does the truth of the matter lie for Baptists? Do they believe in a rigorous separation of church and state, or in a harmonious relationship between the two? The short answer is: both. While Baptists in America have traditionally insisted that the *institutions* of church and state remain separate, they have, at the same time, also recognized a complementary convergence of the two on moral grounds, particularly around the idea of freedom.

***

It is difficult to exaggerate the extent to which this notion of freedom has shaped the collective imagination of Baptists in America—specifically, white Baptists who live, work, and worship in the South. When the Southern Baptist Convention's fragile theological and cultural consensus fell apart in the early 1980s, the proposition that freedom represented a supremely distinctive Baptist virtue—above and beyond all others—took on added resonance for the self-described "moderate"

---

[7] John Leland, "Miscellaneous Essays," in *The Writings of John Leland*, 410. To celebrate Jefferson's election as president in 1800, Leland directed the citizens of Cheshire, Connecticut, in producing a mammoth, 1,235-pound cheese that he personally delivered to the White House. The crust of the cheese was emblazoned—again, at Leland's behest—with the motto, "Rebellion to tyrants is obedience to God." See Daniel L. Driesbach, "Mr. Jefferson, a Mammoth Cheese, and the 'Wall of Separation Between Church and State': A Bicentennial Commemoration," *Journal of Church and State* 43 (2002): 725-745.

Baptists who suddenly found themselves on the outside looking in at a denominational structure they once dominated.[8] In the two decades of Baptist battles that followed, the Southern Baptist conservatives positioned themselves as stalwart defenders of the Bible's authority as God's holy, inerrant word. The moderates, meanwhile, chose to take their stand as principled fighters for freedom in all its various Baptist forms.[9] Among these theologically moderate Baptists, the idea of freedom in and of itself quickly became an article of faith—a conviction perhaps best reflected in (but by no means limited to) the work of historian Walter Shurden, who tended to describe Baptists' religious identity in terms of radical autonomy, personal choice, and individual freedom.[10] The essence of the moderate argument was clear enough: history is on our side. The freedom of autonomous, individual believers to take personal responsibility for their spiritual welfare, moderates insisted, had always been the defining characteristic of the Baptist tradition and it remained a normative conviction for *all* true Baptists. As

---

[8] Bill J. Leonard has argued that the real surprise was not that the Southern Baptist consensus failed, but rather that it lasted as long as it did. For an excellent account of the rise and fall of this theological and cultural consensus, see Leonard, *God's Last and Only Hope: The Fragmentation of the Southern Baptist Convention* (Grand Rapids MI.: Eerdmans Publishing Company, 1990).

[9] For a good account of the intramural conflict in the Southern Baptist Convention, see Nancy Ammerman, *Baptist Battles: Social Change and Religious Conflict in the Southern Baptist Convention* (New Brunswick NJ: Rutgers University Press, 1990). See also David Morgan, *The New Crusades, the New Holy Land: Conflict in the Southern Baptist Convention, 1969-1991* (Tuscaloosa AL.: University of Alabama Press, 1996). For a concise look at how moderates interpreted the denominational split, see Walter Shurden, *Not a Silent People: Controversies That Have Shaped Southern Baptists* (Macon GA.: Smyth and Helwys, 1995) 83ff. Barry Hankins provides a solid, scholarly interpretation of the conservative position in *Uneasy in Babylon: Southern Baptist Conservatives and American Culture* (Tuscaloosa AL.: University of Alabama Press, 2002).

[10] Shurden, a prolific author, has written numerous books and articles on the Baptist understanding of freedom. A short, representative sample of his work can be found in "How We Got That Way: Baptists on Religious Liberty and the Separation of Church and State," in *Proclaiming the Baptist Vision: Religious Liberty*, ed. Walter B. Shurden (Macon GA: Smyth and Helwys, 1997) 13-31. His *The Baptist Identity: Four Fragile Freedoms* (Macon GA: Smyth and Helwys, 1993) has become the standard moderate account of what Baptists believe and why they believe it.

the title of one moderate Baptist publication boldly stated during the denominational conflict, being Baptist, in fact, *meant* freedom.[11]

Within a tradition as broad and diverse at the Baptists, however, such an assertion remains open to debate. Some scholars, for example, point to the early Baptists in seventeenth-century England who understood themselves in theological terms not as a collection of free, autonomous individuals but, rather, as a community of Christian believers gathered by the Holy Spirit and called to share both a life of discipleship and a set of distinctive religious practices such as baptism and the Lord's Supper.[12] From this perspective, the prevailing moderate Baptist understanding of freedom owes much more to the philosophical ideas of the Enlightenment that continue to shape modern American life—that is, the conviction that individuals should be morally and politically free to choose both their own identities and their own destinies—than it does to historic Baptist theology.[13] In other words, instead of presenting a radical alternative to the ways of the world—as the prototypical Baptists John Smyth and Thomas Helwys attempted to do in the early seventeenth century—a Baptist religious identity that emphasizes individual freedom above all else runs the risk of offering little more than a spiritualized echo of an American democratic culture that emphasizes individual freedom above all else.

***

---

[11] Alan Neely, ed., *Being Baptist Means Freedom* (Charlotte NC: Southern Baptist Alliance, 1988).

[12] For a concise account of this argument, see "Re-Envisioning Baptist Identity: A Manifesto for Baptist Communities in North America," *Perspectives in Religious Studies* 24 (1997) 303-310. The document reflects the work of a handful of theologians and pastors who announced their desire to "revision" Baptist identity along more communal and sacramental lines, a task they considered consistent with the early Baptist heritage in seventeenth-century England. In doing so, they pointedly questioned the role of freedom, particularly as described by moderates such as Shurden, in shaping Baptist identity. See also Curtis Freeman, "Can Baptist Theology Be Revisioned?" *Perspectives in Religious Studies* 24 (1997): 273-302; and "A New Perspective On Baptist Identity," *Perspectives in Religious Studies* 26 (1999): 59-65.

[13] See Barry Harvey's description of the Enlightenment ideas and assumptions that facilitated a "Cartesian shift" in modern Western thought in *Another City: An Ecclesiological Primer for a Post-Christian World* (Harrisburg PA: Trinity Press International, 1999) 95-111.

The history of religion in America suggests that this is not a groundless fear. Observers have long noted the influence of democratic ideals in shaping religious culture in the United States. Alexis de Tocqueville, one of the earliest students of American culture (and still perhaps the most insightful), wrote in 1835 that religion in the new republic "is mingled with all the habits of the nation and all the feelings of patriotism, whence it derives a peculiar force."[14] This ambiguous, but undeniable, relationship between Christianity and democracy in the United States especially intrigued Tocqueville, who noted that "religion in America takes no direct part in the government of society, but it must be regarded as the first of their political institutions; for if it does not impart a taste for freedom, it facilitates the use of it."[15] Despite the formal separation of church from state, it seemed to Tocqueville that the two shared a common interest in protecting and perpetuating democratic freedom in the United States—and that each relied on the other to keep up its end of the bargain. Not only did America's republican institutions protect religion, he wrote, but religion was "indispensible to the maintenance of republican institutions" in the new nation.[16] There was in the United States, it seemed, a kind of implicit *quid pro quo* between church and state.

The continued interplay between religion and politics in America has only served to strengthen the force of Tocqueville's insights.[17] Throughout the nineteenth century, writes historian Martin Marty, "the free individual in American republicanism paralleled the free Christian

---

[14] Alexis de Tocqueville, *Democracy in America*, vol. 2, ed. Phillips Bradley (New York: Alfred A. Knopf, 1945) 3.

[15] Tocqueville, *Democracy in America*, vol. 1, 316.

[16] Ibid.

[17] For an excellent study of the ways in which the radical spirit of political democracy carried over into the religious realm and decisively transformed the nature of Christianity in America, see Nathan Hatch, *The Democratization of American Religion* (New Haven CT: Yale University Press, 1989). Among the better religious histories of the United States are Sydney Ahlstrom, *A Religious History of the American People* (New Haven CT: Yale University Press, 1972); Robert T. Handy, *A History of the Churches in the United States and Canada* (Oxford: Oxford University Press, 1976); and Mark A. Noll, *A History of Christianity in the United States and Canada* (Grand Rapids MI: Eerdmans Publishing Company, 1992).

man of evangelical regeneration." Church and state not only shared a commitment to freedom, he continues, but "the democratic faith and Protestantism alike called people to mission in the world. Both fed each other's sense of destiny."[18] According to evangelical historians Nathan Hatch, George Marsden, and Mark Noll, a good deal of the confusion regarding America's religious identity may be traced back to the Revolutionary era and its thorough mix of patriotic and religious language, in which words such as "liberty" circulated freely between the pulpit and the public square. While the distinctively Christian meaning of these words got lost in translation, the words themselves still retained their religious power, thus lending a gloss of sacred significance to the American political experiment.[19] Old habits die hard, though, and over time, this kind of carelessness has compromised the ability of American Christians to proclaim the gospel of Jesus Christ in all its profundity.[20]

In his study of New England Baptists, historian William McLoughlin reached a similar conclusion, observing that—by the early 1800s—these one-time dissenters had successfully made the transition from persecuted religious outsiders to patriotic, cultural insiders. With this shift in social status came a shift in Baptist self-consciousness. No longer did Baptists in New England consider themselves outside the mainstream of American culture. Instead, wrote McLoughlin, they concluded in the years following the Revolution that "to be a good Baptist one should be a good American, and to be a good American one should be a good Baptist."[21] Baptists in the South experienced a similar conversion, although the prevailing moral and cultural assumptions there always leaned in a distinctively *Southern* (as opposed to a more

---

[18] Martin E. Marty, *Righteous Empire: The Protestant Experience in America* (New York: Dial Press, 1970) 112.
[19] Mark A. Noll, George M. Marsden, and Nathan O. Hatch, *The Search for a Christian America* (Colorado Springs CO: Helmers and Howard, 1989) 82.
[20] Ibid., 119.
[21] William McLoughlin, *Soul Liberty: The Baptists' Struggle in New England, 1630-1833* (New Hanover NH: University Press of New England, 1991) 2.

generally *American*) direction, especially in the years following the Civil War.[22]

Moreover, in the Baptist account of American history, Baptists often assume a pivotal role in shaping the American character itself. According to historian Robert Torbet, Baptists during the Revolutionary era were ardent patriots fighting for the right to worship freely according to the dictates of individual conscience.[23] "In many respects," he wrote, "Baptist support of the patriotic cause was regarded by them as support for the cause of religious liberty."[24] Baptists willingly spilled their blood

---

[22] See Rufus Spain, *At Ease in Zion: Social History of Southern Baptists, 1865-1900* (Nashville TN: Vanderbilt University Press, 1967). See also John Eighmy, *Churches in Cultural Captivity: A History of the Social Attitudes of Southern Baptists* (Knoxville TN: University of Tennessee Press, 1972) 49; and Leonard, *God's Last and Only Hope*, 13. Charles Marsh provides an excellent discussion of how the democratic way in which Baptist congregations govern themselves traditionally encouraged cultural conformity in *God's Long Summer: Stories of Faith and Civil Rights* (Princeton NJ: Princeton University Press, 1997) 82-115. In his examination of contemporary conservative Southern Baptists, meanwhile, Barry Hankins argues that many Baptists now perceive culture as an enemy, rather than an ally, of Christian morality. Unlike Spain's Southern Baptists who were at ease in their culture, Hankins writes, conservative Southern Baptists now "are convinced that American culture has turned hostile to traditional forms of faith and that the South has become more like the rest of the United States than ever before. This being the case, they are seeking to put America's largest Protestant denomination at the head of what they perceive to be a full-scale culture war." See Hankins, *Uneasy in Babylon*, 2.

[23] A prominent exception to this rule was Morgan Edwards, a leading figure among Philadelphia Baptists who adamantly refused to support the American cause. See Robert G. Torbet, *A History of the Baptists* (Valley Forge PA: Judson Press, 1963) 226.

[24] Torbet, *A History of Baptists*, 238. William McLoughlin, however, has challenged the existence of a "simple one-to-one relationship between Baptist religious doctrine and American revolutionary politics." Quakers, Moravians, and other religious sects, he wrote in 1971, shared the Baptists' views on such matters as spiritual equality, congregational polity, and priesthood of the believer, yet they remained silent during the war and, in some cases, refused to fight for the American independence. Democratic religious inclinations, in other words, did not necessarily engender revolutionary sentiments. A more likely explanation for the Baptists' willingness to fight for the patriot cause, McLoughlin suggested, rested in their belief that worldly freedom made spiritual freedom possible. "God's kingdom being not of this world," he wrote, "God's elect has to be free in certain worldly respects to sustain their Christian liberty in certain spiritual respects." See William McLoughlin, *New England Dissent, 1630-1833*, vol. 1 (Cambridge MA: Harvard University Press, 1971) 573-574.

for the revolutionary cause, but their contributions to American democracy did not stop with their heroic efforts on the battlefield.[25] Their example of democratic congregational governance, claimed Torbet, helped influence the nation's political values.[26] Perhaps most importantly, wrote historian Leon McBeth, "Baptists provided many of the ideas undergirding religious liberty, and they spearheaded the public agitation which led to the Bill of Rights. In the past two centuries whenever the First Amendment has been under attack, or up for proposed revision, Baptists have ever been its steadfast defenders."[27]

In a sense, this struggle to secure a constitutional guarantee of religious liberty represents—for many Baptists, at least—*the* defining moment at which their story finally flowed into the larger narrative stream of American history. J. M. Dawson's *Baptists and the American Republic* (1956) perhaps best exemplifies not only the standard Baptist interpretation of the fight for religious liberty, but also what this fight illustrates about the relationship between Baptist religious principles and American political ideals. Since colonial days, Dawson wrote, Baptists had called—with varying degrees of success—for the separation of church and state and a guarantee of religious liberty for all people. Finally, thanks to the political support of like-minded sympathizers Thomas Jefferson and James Madison, Baptists triumphantly realized their goals with the adoption of the First Amendment to the Constitution in 1792. Without the Baptists, Dawson claimed, "in all probability the United States could never have adopted a positive guarantee of separation of church and state with full religious liberty for all."[28] This most cherished pillar of American democracy, he concluded, was primarily a Baptist achievement.

The claim, therefore, that Baptists in America have identified closely with the democratic ideals of the nation is certainly not new. What is new, however, is the realization that the Baptists' habit of articulating their faith in the borrowed language of liberal democracy compromises

---

[25] H. Leon McBeth, *The Baptist Heritage: Four Centuries of Baptist Witness* (Nashville TN: Broadman Press, 1987) 201.
[26] Torbet, *A History of Baptists,* 488.
[27] McBeth, IThe Baptist Heritage, 283.
[28] Dawson, *Baptists and the American Republic*, 117.

their distinctive Christian witness to the world. Insofar as Baptists understand themselves as stubbornly principled dissenters against the tendencies of government to interfere in matters of faith, this loss of theological integrity should be cause for concern. Even more worrisome is the fact that Baptists have largely facilitated such a loss through their own careless language and misplaced priorities. Before Baptists—in particular, theologically moderate Baptists in the South—can recover their distinctive theological bearings, they need to understand how they lost them in the first place.

***

The first quarter of the twentieth century provides a helpful vantage point from which to consider this moral overlap between Baptist theology and American democracy—a phenomenon that, for the sake of convenience, can be called "Baptist democracy."[29] During these years, Americans wore their democratic status proudly and considered themselves to be in the vanguard of a new world order. Democracy, they ardently believed, was the irresistible trend of the future, and the American ideals of freedom and equality seemed to be gaining more currency around the globe everyday.[30] For some, this spirit of democratic optimism contributed to an even more profound conviction that God had called the United States to be not only a political, but a spiritual, blessing to other nations of the world. Describing his decision to annex the Philippines following the Spanish-American War in 1898, for

---

[29] The phrase "Baptist democracy" first came to the author's attention in an essay by Paul Harvey titled "'Yankee faith' and Southern Redemption: White Southern Baptist Ministers, 1850-1890," 167-186, in *Religion and the American Civil War*, eds. Randall Miller, Harry Stout, and Charles Reagan Wilson (New York: Oxford University Press, 1998). In its original usage, the phrase described "a white southern cultural identity founded upon a particular brand of democratic evangelism" (168). Though given a slightly different definition here, the phrase itself is nonetheless a borrowed one for which the author is indebted.

[30] Mark Sullivan, *Our Times: The United States, 1900-1925*, vol. 1 (New York: Scribners, 1926) 1ff. Sullivan's six-volume contemporary history is an invaluable, if lengthy, resource for readers seeking to acquaint themselves with American history, thought, and culture in the first quarter of the twentieth century. It was, wrote Sullivan, an age dominated by the "average man" and his democratic tastes. A nice summary of American life in 1919 may be found in Frederick Lewis Allen, *Only Yesterday: An Informal History of the 1920s* (New York: Harper and Row, 1931) 1-14.

example, President William McKinley told a group of Methodist ministers that, while praying one night, he had realized "there was nothing left for us to do but to take them all and educate the Filipinos and uplift and civilize and Christianize them and by God's grace do the very best we could by them, as our fellow men for whom Christ died."[31] Senator Albert J. Beveridge of Indiana put the matter more bluntly in January 1900. God, he declared, had "marked the American people as His chosen nation to finally lead in the regeneration of the world. This is the divine mission of America, and it holds for us all the profit, all the glory, all the happiness possible to man. We are the trustees of the world's progress, guardians of its righteous peace."[32]

Even the terrible, senseless slaughter of the Great War in Europe seemed to represent an opening for the United States to exercise its benevolent, principled moral authority on behalf of the world's oppressed people. "The world must be made safe for democracy," declared Woodrow Wilson in his war message to a special joint session of Congress on 2 April 1917. "Its peace must be planted upon the tested foundation of political liberty. We have no selfish ends to serve. We desire no conquest, no dominion."[33] Instead, said the president, America must consider it a privilege "to spend her blood and her might for the principles that gave her birth and happiness and the peace which she has treasured. God helping her, she can do no other."[34]

Wilson's rhetoric, filled with soaring phrases and lofty sentiments (and punctuated by a declaration strongly reminiscent of Martin Luther's famous statement to the Diet of Worms), appealed to both the nation's democratic idealism and the belief that God had established it as a "city on a hill" to be a blessing and inspiration to the rest of the world. As historian George Marsden has observed, the patriotic enthusiasm

---

[31] McKinley, as recounted in Charles S. Olcott, *The Life of William McKinley* (Boston: Houghton, Mifflin, and Company, 1910) 2:110-111.
[32] Congress, Senate, Senator Beveridge of Indiana, Speaking for the Joint Resolution on United States policy in the Philippines, S.R. 53, 56th Cong., 1st sess. *Congressional Record* 33, pt. 1 (9 January 1900): 711. The entire speech may be found on 704-712.
[33] Woodrow Wilson, "War Message to Congress," in *The Papers of Woodrow Wilson*, vol. 41, ed. Arthur S. Link (Princeton NJ: Princeton University Press, 1983) 525.
[34] Woodrow Wilson, *Papers*, 526-527.

generated by the war effort reflected an "increasingly popular zeal for an American democratic way of life, a somewhat secularized form of the old ideal of Christian and republican civilization."[35] Along with their fellow Americans and in keeping with the sentiments of their congregations, leaders from across the religious spectrum gladly supported the war effort and the basic goodness of American democracy it symbolized.[36] As Marsden has described it, "the clergy were probably no more or less extreme than most other Americans, which meant that some were cautious about unrestrained nationalism while others endorsed the American cause with abandon. Some of the latter virtually draped the flag over the cross so that one could no longer tell the difference between the two."[37]

In step with the times, Baptists in the United States during these first decades of the twentieth century—both before and after the war—brimmed with confidence that, as the democratic principles of the United States spread throughout the world, so would their Christian message of salvation in Jesus Christ. "In the United States we have a great future as a people if we know how to use our opportunity," claimed a typical editorial from 1915 in the *Baptist World*, a newspaper associated with the Southern Baptist Theological Seminary. "The Baptist message is in full accord with the best aspirations of our day in its struggle toward a real democracy in religion, in government, in education."[38]

Unlike their spiritual forebears who self-consciously lived as dissenters outside of the social mainstream, Baptists between 1900 and 1925 found themselves at home in the world, more often than not reflecting (and sometimes amplifying) many of the era's dominant opinions. It was during these years that three prominent and influential Baptists—Walter Rauschenbusch (1861-1918), a church historian and advocate of Christian social reform; E. Y. Mullins (1860-1928), a theologian and president of the Southern Baptist Theological Seminary;

---

[35] George Marsden, *Religion and American Culture*, 2nd ed. (Fort Worth TX: Harcourt College Publishers, 2001) 187.
[36] Ahlstrom, *A Religious History of the American People*, 884.
[37] Marsden, *Religion and American Culture*, 187.
[38] *The Baptist World*, 7 January 1915, 16.

and George Truett (1867-1944), the pastor of the First Baptist Church of Dallas, Texas, and easily one of the most recognizable preachers in America—all made their most significant contributions to Baptist life in America.

They also participated decisively in the rise of Baptist democracy. What had been a raw, yet passionate, democratic Baptist ethos in the early years of the American republic acquired theological polish and sophistication thanks to the teaching, preaching, and publishing efforts of these three leading Baptists. Rauschenbusch, Mullins, and Truett, in other words, combined the loose, but generally prevalent, assumptions about Baptists and American democracy popularized by men such as John Leland, into a coherent, popularly accessible vision and, in the process, made a last, decisive break with the dissenting heritage of Baptists in America. They made it plain: what America is to politics, Baptists are to religion—God's chosen way for humanity. Or, as George Truett put it in 1911, "the triumph of democracy, thank God, means the triumph of Baptists everywhere."[39]

At one time, dissenting communities of Baptists presented a stark moral alternative to the world. Refusing to allow the state to claim any share of their identity as the people of God, they sharply distinguished the obligations of citizenship from the practices of Christian discipleship. The respective stories of church and state were not, for Baptists, identical. Do Baptists in America still possess the skills of discernment needed to separate the true claims of God from the false claims of Caesar? Sadly, the promises of American democracy may have accomplished what the chains of persecution could not: persuade Baptists to compromise their freedom as Christians. This, ultimately, is the problematic and enduring legacy of Baptist democracy, a legacy decisively shaped by Walter Rauschenbusch, E. Y. Mullins, and George Truett in the first decades of the twentieth century.

---

[39] George Truett, "God's Call to America," in *God's Call to America* (New York: George H. Doran Company, 1923) 19.

1

The Transformation of Freedom in Baptist Thought

Baptist history often seems to function as a kind of denominational Rorschach test: the concerns of the present determine what Baptists see when they look into their past.[1] Take, for example, the idea of freedom as it pertains to Baptist identity. Without question, Baptists have always been champions of freedom.[2] That much has remained constant since 1609, when John Smyth baptized himself and his small congregation of English expatriates living in the Netherlands. What has changed, however, is the way Baptists define the word "freedom"—so much so that when contemporary Baptists claim to share a common understanding of "freedom" with their seventeenth-century ancestors, their assertion stretches the limits of historical accuracy.

The late Cambridge historian Herbert Butterfield once famously described the tendency to fill old wineskins from the past with the new wine of the present as the "whig interpretation of history." People who study the past with direct reference to the present, he wrote in 1963, will tend to see the former exclusively through the lens of the latter. In other

---

[1] Not all Baptist history, of course, is political. Over the last decade, McBeth's *The Baptist Heritage* has become a standard scholarly survey of Baptist history, joining Robert Torbet's *A History of the Baptists* in that category. Both texts offer a thorough account of the Baptist story and may be consulted with confidence by the reader. For a more thematic interpretation of Baptist history, see William H. Brackney, *The Baptists* (New York: Greenwood Press, 1988) which examines the five "vertices" that have shaped Baptist faith and practice through the years: Scripture, polity and ecclesiology, the ordinances, the voluntary nature of religion, and religious liberty. See also Brackney's *Baptist Life and Thought: A Source Book*, rev. ed. (Valley Forge PA: Judson Press, 1998) that serves as a valuable source for primary material and scholarly interpretation of essential Baptist documents.

[2] For a comprehensive review of early English Baptist thought on religious liberty, see H. Leon McBeth, "English Baptist Literature on Religious Liberty" (Th.D. diss., Southwestern Baptist Theological Seminary, 1961).

words, they "will find it easy to say that [they have] seen the present in the past, [they] will imagine that [they have] discovered a 'root' or an 'anticipation' of the 20th century, when in reality [they are] in a world of different connotations altogether, and [they have] merely stumbled upon what could be shown to be a misleading analogy."[3] Following Butterfield's lead, a "whiggish" interpretation of Baptist history might assume that there exists something like a fully-formed notion of "freedom" floating through time intact, passing through the centuries and over an ocean, but never losing its essential integrity as it shaped the thought of such disparate Baptists as Thomas Helwys, Roger Williams, E.Y. Mullins, and Martin Luther King, Jr. According to Butterfield, the fallacy in this perspective resides in the fact that "the immediate juxtaposition of past and present, though it makes everything easy and makes some inferences perilously obvious, is bound to lead to an oversimplification of the relations between events and a complete misapprehension of the relations between past and present."[4] When considering the ways in which Baptists have thought about freedom through the years, it is important to keep Butterfield's warning in mind. The gravitational pull of anachronism is too strong to be safely ignored.

Simply put, as times have changed, so have Baptist understandings of freedom. The faith tradition into which Walter Rauschenbusch, E. Y. Mullins, and George Truett were baptized in the late nineteenth century resembled, in many ways, that of Helwys and his fellow English Baptists of the 1600s. At the most basic level, the practice of believers' baptism and the acknowledgment of biblical authority linked these American Baptists with their seventeenth-century spiritual forebears. By the beginning of the nineteenth century, however, Baptists in the United States such as John Leland had already begun speaking of religious liberty and freedom of conscience in ways that would have seemed strange to the early English Baptists.

---

[3]Herbert Butterfield, *The Whig Interpretation of History* (London: G. Bell and Sons, 1963) 11-12. Interestingly, Butterfield repeatedly uses the example of religious liberty to demonstrate how the whig interpretation of history works. See, for instance, 17-18 and 68-89.
[4]Ibid., 14.

In order to illustrate the shift that occurred in Baptist theology during these years, perhaps the best place to begin is at the beginning, with John Smyth and Thomas Helwys. These two Christians, the first to articulate and apply the principles of what eventually became Baptist Christianity in the early seventeenth century, thought a great deal about the nature (and limits) of freedom. It was central to their understanding of the Christian faith. It was, however, a decidedly different *kind* of freedom than the democratic liberty John Leland celebrated some two hundred years later. Times had indeed changed over the course of two centuries, and Leland's more modern ideas fit comfortably within an American context shaped by the liberal ideals of personal choice, autonomy, and individual rights.[5] As such, they provided the foundation upon which the edifice of Baptist democracy arose in the early 1900s. It was a foundation built with materials that Smyth, Helwys, and their contemporaries would have scarcely recognized.

***

Though especially popular among theologically moderate Baptists, the claim that Baptists have always built their arguments for religious liberty upon a foundation of individual rights seems strangely anachronistic—or, to use Butterfield's term, "whiggish." Consider the times in which distinctively "Baptist" interpretations of the Christian faith first circulated. While early English Baptists like John Smyth (c.1570-1612) and Thomas Helwys (c.1550-c.1615) began publishing their ideas in the first decade of the 1600s, the notion of inalienable "rights" as such did not become widely popular until the latter half of the seventeenth century and the publication of the English philosopher John Locke's *A Letter Concerning Toleration* in 1689. Arguing eloquently for religious toleration as a means to achieve social stability and civility, Locke believed that religious strife would cease if all churches would

---

[5] The word "liberal" is used here (and throughout this book, unless otherwise noted) to denote the philosophical conviction that the best political arrangement is one that, to the greatest degree possible, maximizes individual freedom and protects individual rights. This is the classical understanding of the word "liberal" and needs to be distinguished from its later incarnation in American politics as the opposite of "conservative." The most faithful advocates of truly *liberal* political ideals in twenty-first-century American politics are those who identify themselves as libertarians.

"teach that *liberty of conscience is every man's natural right*... and that nobody ought to be compelled in matters of religion either by law or force."[6] Every individual, he asserted, had "the supreme and absolute authority of judging for himself" the merits of religious truth claims.[7] This right to exercise private judgment lay securely within the domain of conscience, where the individual enjoyed complete freedom to choose his or her religious beliefs. Although they certainly influenced later generations of Baptists, both in England and America, Locke's ideas about religion, tolerance, and liberty of conscience did not appear in public until several decades after the generation of Baptist pioneers had died.[8] Smyth and Helwys knew nothing of John Locke, nor of his arguments for religious toleration. Instead, they lived and wrote during the years that bridged the sixteenth and seventeenth centuries, a time when "liberty of conscience" implied a religious duty, not a natural right.

The difference is significant. Writing centuries before Smyth and Helwys, Augustine (354-430) observed that "man has within himself, independently of any extrinsic source, an infallible means by which, on the most general level, he is able to discriminate between right and wrong. [Conscience] is concerned with future as well as past actions and thus functions not only as a guide but as a witness and a judge."[9] God,

---

[6] John Locke, "A Letter Concerning Toleration," in *"A Letter Concerning Toleration" in Focus*, eds. John Horton and Susan Mendus (New York: Routledge, 1991) 47, emphasis added.

[7] Ibid., 43.

[8] Hugh Wamble, for one, asserts that Baptists in America incorporated Locke's political theory into their theological rationale for religious liberty and individual freedom in "Baptist Contributions to the Separation of Church and State," *Baptist History and Heritage* 20 (July 1985) 10-11. In fairness, it must be noted that the legal and political ideas of Sir Edward Coke (1552-1634) that helped shape Locke's thought, would have been available to educated Englishmen of the early seventeenth century. Coke was an ardent proponent of the English common law as a limitation upon royal prerogative, and he frequently used the language of "rights" to bolster his arguments. Nevertheless, the liberal understandings of religion, tolerance, and liberty of conscience that moderate Baptists often attribute to Smyth and Helwys are found in Locke, not Coke.

[9] Ernest Fortin, "The Political Implications of St. Augustine's Theory of Conscience," in *Classical Christianity and the Social Order*, ed. J. Brian Benestad (Lanham MD: Rowman and

Augustine believed, endows all people with a conscience, and through the exercise of conscience in tandem with human reason, individuals can discern the principles of justice that govern the universe. No one can ignore conscience "or fail to be aware of the fact that by disregarding [it] he behaves in a manner contrary to what he knows to be right."[10] Conscience, for Augustine, was not a kind of innate personal moral sensibility or ethical awareness but, rather, the mechanism by which "the eternal or natural law [of God] to which all men owe obedience at all times under pain of guilt and retribution" exerted its control over individual conduct.[11] Conscience served as a governor, not a liberator, reminding Christians of their obligations to conform themselves in all respects to God's will.

Thomas Aquinas (1224/5-1274), building upon Augustine's definition, noted that conscience consisted of two parts: *synteresis* and *conscientia*. The former served as a repository of moral principles, the innate habit of mind that inclined individuals toward good and away from evil. The latter, meanwhile, represented an exercise of reason that applied these moral principles to specific cases.[12] The Protestant reformers of the sixteenth century echoed this idea even as they rejected the Roman Catholic tradition from which it had emerged. As historian Meg Lota Brown observes, Reformation theologians believed that, while reason and conscience were fallible due to the corrupting influence of sin, "they receive[d] direction from the Holy Spirit and Scripture. With such guides, conscience [was] the Christian's highest guide on earth. To deny church officials jurisdiction over conscience [was] not to leave the individual rudderless or wholly self-directed, since one's final criteria for judgment is God's Word."[13] Martin Luther (1483-1546), writes Reformation historian Randall Zachman, described the conscience "more

---

Littlefield, 1996) 72-73. See Augustine, *Confessions*, trans. Rex Warner (New York: Mentor, 1963) 37.

[10] Ibid., 73. Fortin cites Augustine, *Contra Faustum Manichaeum*, 26.3.

[11] Ibid., 74. Fortin cites Augustine, *De diversis quaestionibus LXXXIII*, 53.2.

[12] Thomas Aquinas, *Summa Theologica*, vol. 3, trans. Fathers of the English Dominican Province (London: R. & T. Washbourne, 1912) 1.79.12-13.

[13] Meg Lota Brown, *Donne and the Politics of Conscience in Early Modern England* (Leiden, The Netherlands: E. J. Brill, 1995) 52.

as a power to receive instruction than as a power of autonomous self-legislation."[14] The conscience, Luther believed, "[was] a capacity for judging good and evil, but it [was] not of itself an infallible source for knowing what is good and what is evil. One can have a true conscience only if one follows true teaching, not if one follows the feeling of conscience."[15] The challenge for Christians lay in ensuring that their consciences were rightly formed in keeping with the teachings of Scripture.

In England, William Perkins (1558-1602) articulated a popular understanding of conscience along these lines.[16] Conscience, he wrote, was "of a divine nature, a thing placed of God in the midst between him and man, as an arbitrator to give sentence."[17] As such, Perkins and his peers generally understood conscience to be the means by which God judged a person's actions. Accordingly, people defied the dictates of their consciences at their own peril. "To all men," wrote Protestant theologian John Abernethy in 1622, "conscience is as a God: sitting in the middle of a man's heart... it accuseth and condemneth; making the heart to be pricked and to smite itself: and like a worm to gnaw the heart, stirring up... fear and our own thoughts to trouble and affray."[18] A

---

[14] Randall C. Zachman, *The Assurances of Faith: Conscience in the Theology of Martin Luther and John Calvin* (Minneapolis: Fortress Press, 1993) 28.

[15] Ibid. See *Luther's Works*, vol. 9, ed. Jaroslav Pelikan (St. Louis: Concordia Publishing House, 1955) 123.

[16] An early exponent of Calvinism in England, Perkins demonstrated a strong inclination toward pietism and wrote extensively on the inner devotional life of the Christian seeking spiritual perfection. Perkins's concern for holiness contributed to his interest in divine law as an ethical code for daily living. For a brief overview of Perkins and the Puritan Pietist tradition in England, see F. Ernest Stoeffler, *The Rise of Evangelical Pietism* (Leiden, The Netherlands: E. J. Brill, 1965) 49-58.

[17] Perkins, as quoted in Brown, 52. Perkins is noted for his advocacy of casuistry, a method of resolving conflicts between competing authorities—such as, for example, civil law and religious obligation—according to the circumstances of a given situation. Not surprisingly, conscience figured heavily in his reflections on casuistry. For the convenience of contemporary readers, the spelling variations in quotations from early English writers have been modernized.

[18] Abernethy, as quoted in Jonathan Wright, "The World's Worst Worm," *The Sixteenth Century Journal* 30 (1999): 121. Wright's article gives an excellent overview of what the idea of conscience meant in early seventeenth-century England and is highly recommended to readers who wish to explore the issue further.

properly operating conscience thus worked on two levels: warning against immoral behavior and, at the same time, confirming right choices or provoking repentance for wrong ones. Only among the elect, however, could conscience be counted upon to serve a redemptive purpose, leading the sinner to faith in Jesus Christ. For everyone else, "conscience was a tribunal, working just well enough to distinguish between just and unjust and to convict them on their own testimony, depriving them of all pretense for ignorance, but with no hope of preventing the inevitable decline to despair" as sinners realized their utter helplessness before the eternal judgment of God.[19]

As understood in early seventeenth-century England, conscience had little, if anything, to do with an individual's freedom of choice. It was, rather, a matter of judgment and responsibility. God, as the source of all truth and the architect of eternal law, ruled supreme in the realm of conscience and exercised absolute sovereignty over its activity. Likewise, the dictates of conscience carried a divine seal and so could not possibly be compromised by human interference. As Perkins observed, "conscience is appointed by God to declare and put in execution his just judgment against sinners, and as God cannot possibly be overcome by man, so neither can the judgment of conscience, being the judgment of God, be wholly extinguished."[20] The sanctity of conscience for early seventeenth-century Christians in England, therefore, had nothing to do with individual rights or freedoms and everything to do with God's sovereignty. Corrupted by sin and consequently fallible, an individual's conscience was not an absolute authority unto itself but, rather, it operated under the guidance of Scripture and the Holy Spirit.[21] Through the involuntary exercise of their God-given (and, under the guidance of Scripture and the Spirit, properly formed) consciences, individuals could distinguish between right and wrong, true and false, godly and ungodly.

---

[19] Wright, "The World's Worst Worm," 120.
[20] Perkins, as quoted in Wright, "The World's Worst Worm," 131.
[21] Thomas Morton, one of Perkins's contemporaries, wrote that "where the whole is corrupted, there every several part is corrupted...so that now the conscience is a false witness" although "there remain in it some relics of knowledge, truth, and light." See Wright, "The World's Worst Worm," 119-120.

Conscience was, in other words, a tool for discerning God's will, not an instrument for justifying personal opinions or beliefs.

John Smyth and Thomas Helwys did not live and write in a historical and theological vacuum. They were undoubtedly shaped by the ideas of their time, ideas that—in early seventeenth-century England—assumed a rather medieval concept of conscience and the Christian's relationship to God. Modern notions of natural rights or individual freedom simply were not part of the prevailing intellectual vernacular. These ideas would arrive soon enough with the dawning of the Enlightenment. They did not, however, provide the basis for Smyth and Helwys's arguments for religious freedom and the separation of church and state.

***

Ordained to the Anglican priesthood in 1595, John Smyth gradually drifted away from the established Church as his views became increasingly sympathetic to those of the Separatist movement.[22] After being ousted from his ministerial position in Lincoln, Smyth returned to his hometown of Gainesborough and soon became pastor of a Separatist congregation there. Near the end of 1607, Smyth's congregation relocated from England to Amsterdam. Within a year, and most likely under the influence of local Mennonites in Holland, Smyth became convinced that the practice of infant baptism lacked biblical warrant, so he baptized himself and forty other members of his fellowship, including Thomas Helwys, on the basis of their professed faith in Jesus Christ. Around this core of baptized believers, Smyth reorganized the congregation in keeping with what he understood to be the New Testament model. Soon, however, he began to question the validity of his baptism and, along with the majority of his fellow "baptists" in Amsterdam, sought membership in the Mennonite congregation—a move that coincided with Helwys's decision to part ways with Smyth and return to England with a like-minded portion of the Amsterdam

---

[22] John Smyth's life and ministry is a popular subject for Baptist historians. To list all of the relevant works on Smyth here would be unnecessary. James Coggin provides a good biographical account of Smyth in *John Smyth's Congregation: English Separatism, Mennonite Influences, and the Elect Nation* (Waterloo OT: Herald Press, 1991) 32ff. See also W. T. Whitley, *A History of British Baptists* (London: Charles Griffin & Company, 1923) 20ff.

congregation. Although Smyth died in August of 1612 before his lengthy petitions to the Mennonites could be answered, three years later the remaining members of his congregation were finally admitted to the Mennonite fellowship.[23]

As an early proponent and practitioner of believers' baptism, Smyth justifiably occupies a significant position in Baptist history. Although some scholars have cast doubt upon his theological originality, few question his importance.[24] To be sure, his rejection of infant baptism and his conception of the church as a gathered community of believers anticipated fundamental components of Baptist faith and practice even as they reflected his opposition to the Church of England. Perhaps Smyth's most quintessentially Baptist feature was his rigorous submission to the authority of Scripture. Indeed, in his written arguments against infant baptism and in defense of believers' baptism, Smyth articulated positions shaped decisively by the Bible. For him, the issue of baptism required fidelity to the Bible, regardless of the consequences. Questions of individual freedom or liberty of conscience, which in later years strongly influenced Baptist arguments against infant baptism, are not present in Smyth's writings.[25] Instead, his case both for believers' baptism and against infant baptism rested upon a quite literal interpretation of Scripture.

In his treatise, "The Character of the Beast, or the False Constitution of the Church" (1609), Smyth presented his arguments for believers' baptism and effectively responded to his critics on the other side of the issue. Addressing his work to nonconformist Puritans wishing to separate from the Church of England—a group whom Smyth, referring

---

[23] Torbet, *A History of Baptists*, 37.

[24] See James Coggins, "The Theological Positions of John Smyth," *The Baptist Quarterly* 30 (1984): 258ff. Smyth's originality, Coggins writes, "has been greatly overestimated." According to Coggins, Smyth's "radical" theology was largely derivative, shaped at first by Francis Johnson and the Ancient Church movement and, later, by the Dutch Anabaptists.

[25] In *The Axioms of Religion: A New Interpretation of the Baptist Faith* (Philadelphia: Judson Press, 1908) for example, E. Y. Mullins writes that the "cardinal evil" of infant baptism is that "the religious choice of the infant is forestalled by the parent. The religious destiny of the offspring is thus assumed by another without warrant from Scripture and without any rational justification from other sources. To baptize a child in infancy is to treat it not as a free moral personality, but as a thing" (157).

to their practice of infant baptism, labeled "Pedobaptists"—Smyth claimed that those who "defend the baptism of infants cannot with any truth or good conscience Separate from England as from a false Church though they may separate for corruptions."[26] A "pure" church that practiced infant baptism, in other words, was still a false church based on a biblically unsound foundation. "Considering what baptism is, an infant is no more capable of baptism than is any unreasonable or insensible creature," Smyth continued. "For baptism is not washing with water: but it is the baptism of the Spirit, the confession of the mouth, and the washing of water."[27] Referring to 1 Peter 3:21 and Hebrews 10:22, Smyth reasoned that infants could not possibly meet the first two conditions, for both of them "are proper to actual sinners," not infants who had neither the opportunity to sin nor the ability to repent. Without the first two components of true baptism, then, simply washing infants with water struck Smyth as mere "folly & nothing."[28]

The Pedobaptists' arguments "for the maintenance of their heresy," furthermore, reflected a "manifest perverting of the scriptures from their true sense."[29] Accordingly, the bulk of "The Character of the Beast" consisted of an extended conversation between Smyth and a proponent of infant baptism, identified only as Mr. Richard Clifton, in which Smyth carefully, and sometimes creatively, answered these "pedobaptist perversions" of Scripture. The exchange began with Smyth laying out his case against infant baptism. First, citing Mark 1:4-5 and Acts 8:37, he wrote that "there is neither precept nor example in the New Testament of any infants that were baptized, by John or Christ's Disciples: Only they that did confess their sins, and confess their Faith were baptized."

---

[26] John Smyth, "The Character of the Beast, or the False Constitution of the Church," 1609, in *The Complete Works of John Smyth*, vol. 2, ed. W. T. Whitley (Cambridge: Cambridge University Press, 1915): 567. The original spelling has been modernized for the convenience of the reader. Note Smyth's use here of "conscience" as related to the knowledge of truth; an appropriate synonym perhaps would be "integrity."

[27] Ibid.

[28] Ibid. "Baptism... now saves you, not as a removal of dirt but as an appeal to God for a clear conscience" (1 Pet. 3:21, RSV). "Let us draw near with a true heart in full assurance of faith, with our hearts sprinkled clean from an evil conscience and our bodies washed with pure water" (Heb. 10:22, RSV).

[29] Ibid., 568.

Second, in both Matthew 28:19 and John 4:1, "Christ commandeth to make Disciples by teaching them: and then to baptize them… but infants cannot by doctrine become Christ's Disciples: and so cannot by the rule of Christ be baptized." Finally, he declared, "if infants be baptized, the carnal seed is baptized: and so the seal of the covenant is administered to them to whom the covenant appertaineth not," which would contradict Romans 9:8.[30]

In the series of objections and rebuttals that followed, a great deal of attention, at least in the early stages of the debate, focused upon covenant theology, which emphasized not only the relationship that God established with Abraham but the terms of that relationship as well. "The covenant that we under the gospel do receive is the very same that was made to Abraham, etc.," wrote Clifton, citing Genesis 17:10. Therefore, just as God's covenant with Abraham included infants and was signified by their circumcision, those who participated in this covenant through Christ signify their membership through the baptism of infants. Though the outward ceremony had changed from circumcision to baptism, Clifton maintained, the covenant remained the same.[31] Smyth, however, dismissed Clifton's claim as suspect. God made two covenants with Abraham, he wrote, one carnal in nature and sealed by circumcision, the other spiritual in nature and sealed with the Holy Spirit. "That all these particulars are so," he continued, "I prove unto you plainly by these places of Scripture."[32]

Clifton and Smyth argued back and forth, with each one citing biblical texts where appropriate to support his position. Of particular interest here, however, is not necessarily the actual content of this debate. The crucial significance for contemporary Baptists looking to Smyth for theological insight lies in the fact that the men conducted their debate exclusively on the grounds of Scripture, with Smyth consistently taking a more narrow interpretation of the text against Clifton's expansive reading. "If you say that infants being under the covenant,

---

[30] Ibid., 574.
[31] Ibid., 578-579. "This is my covenant, which you shall keep, between me and you and your descendants after you: Every male among you shall be circumcised" (Gen. 17:10, RSV).
[32] Ibid., 580.

justified, & sanctified, therefore they have Faith and the graces of God in them," Smyth asserts, "I say that is contrary to the Scriptures which say faith cometh by hearing."[33] Infant baptism is wrong, Smyth steadfastly maintained, because it has no basis in Scripture.

Consider, for example, two dialogues between Clifton and Smyth. In one, Clifton cited Jesus' command in Mark 10:13-14 to let children come to him for the kingdom of heaven belonged to them. This passage, Clifton suggested, implied that Jesus approved of infant baptism. Smyth disagreed. If this reading was accurate, he asked, why did Jesus not instruct his disciples to baptize the children? "Surely, if they had been the infants of believers, or if the Apostles had known Christ's mind for baptism of infants he having so fit an opportunity would have put it in practice," Smyth observed. "But the deep silence of baptism in this place where there is so just an occasion doth instruct us evidently that Christ either did not deal faithfully which to say were blasphemy, or that he never purposed the baptism of infants."[34] In a later exchange, Clifton noted that in Acts 16:15-33, Paul and Silas baptized the families of Lydia and the Philippian jailer, thus lending apostolic approval to the practice of infant baptism. Smyth here again insisted that the text be read closely and at face value. "I say that though infants are a part of the family when the family hath infants in it, yet it doth not follow that wherever there is mention made of a Family, that therefore that Family had infants in it," he wrote. "Except therefore it be proved that the family of Lydia, and the Jailor had infants in it, this allegation is nothing."[35] Since the Bible said nothing about infants in either family, though, Clifton's "proof" can only be taken as mere speculation. At the same time, Smyth wrote, Acts 16:32 did present clear and convincing evidence in support of believers' baptism, for the apostles preached the gospel, and "only they that believed by the word preached were baptized."[36]

Smyth's assertion that the established Church of England was a false church followed directly from his argument against infant baptism. Since

---

[33] Ibid., 602.
[34] Ibid., 591-592.
[35] Ibid., 614.
[36] Ibid., 615.

the New Testament contained no references to infant baptism, any group that baptized infants operated outside the boundaries of authentic Christian practice. Such a church, Smyth believed, represented the instrument of the Antichrist and was established upon a false foundation—namely, the baptism of those whom "God never appointed to baptism: a subject that is as incapable of baptism as an infidel, a mad man, a natural fool, or any other subject that cannot confess their Faith or sins, or be made Disciples by instruction."[37] A Turk, for instance, could not be made a Christian simply by virtue of being "washed by water." The power of baptism resided not in water but in faith; belief must precede action. Likewise, a group of "washed" Turks could not in any reasonable sense be considered a Christian church. In accordance with Scripture, true baptism could only be administered to regenerate, confessing believers in Jesus Christ, and these baptized believers collectively formed the true church established by the command of Jesus himself.[38]

As with infant baptism, Smyth's problem with the Church of England did not turn on the question of "religious freedom" but on the question of biblical precedent. Indeed, for Smyth, true theology began and ended with Scripture, which, in turn, served as the only authoritative guide to Christian faith and practice. Ironically enough, then, Smyth's celebrated arguments in "The Character of the Beast" against infant baptism and the state Church of England were shaped not by radical notions of freedom, as many modern, moderate Baptists frequently claim, but by a rigorous, literal adherence to the biblical text and, implicitly, a submission to the lordship of Jesus Christ to which Scripture testified.

Likewise, Smyth's doctrinal statements offered no unqualified endorsement of individual freedom as a natural, human right. His "Short Confession" of 1609, while neatly summarizing his theological positions, did not once mention liberty of conscience.[39] The more extensive "Short

---

[37] Ibid., 645.
[38] Ibid., 654-655.
[39] "A Short Confession of Faith in XX Articles by John Smyth," in William L. Lumpkin, *Baptist Confessions of Faith* (Valley Forge PA: Judson Press, 1959) 100-101.

Confession of Faith" submitted to the Dutch Anabaptists in 1610 by Smyth and his followers also failed to include any reference to conscience.[40] Interestingly, Smyth did take up the issue of human free will and the image of God in his 1609 confession. In article two, he wrote that "God has created and redeemed the human race to his own image, and has ordained all men to life." Article three, in turn, stated that "God imposes no necessity of sinning on any one; but man freely, by Satanic instigation, departs from God." As a result, he observed in article five, "there is no original sin... but all sin is actual and voluntary."[41] Clearly, Smyth's understanding of sin is critical to his argument against infant baptism. It also bears a strong resemblance to the modern, moderate Baptist concept of individual free will: the idea that, as creatures made in the image of God, humans may freely make their own decisions about religious matters. After Smyth's death, his followers retained his interpretation of free will in their statement, "Propositions and Conclusions concerning True Christian Religion."[42]

As for the idea of conscience, Smyth's few writings on the subject were consistent with those of his early seventeenth-century contemporaries. In "A Letter written to Mr. A. S." (1606), Smyth described the evolution of his theological opinions as proof that God was at work in his conscience. "We call God to record to our souls," he wrote, "that the evidence of the truth *working upon our consciences through the Lord's unspeakable mercy*, even contrary to our rebellious nature, hath mightily convinced and violently carried us to this truth we profess and practice."[43] Clearly, Smyth understood that he had neither chosen nor discovered truth through the exercise of his own rational faculties. Instead, through the medium of conscience, God had carried him to the

---

[40] See "A Short Confession of Faith" in Lumpkin, *Baptist Confessions of Faith*, 102-113.

[41] "A Short Confession," in Lumpkin, *Baptist Confessions of Faith*, 100.

[42] "Propositions and Conclusions concerning True Christian Religion," in Lumpkin, *Baptist Confessions of Faith*, 124-142. Please see specifically articles 12, 14-21. This raises, however, an intriguing question: If the Dutch Anabaptists had indeed absorbed the remaining members of the Smyth group by 1615, can their ideas truly be considered reflective of early *Baptist* beliefs, or would they more accurately represent mainstream Mennonite beliefs at the time?

[43] "A Letter written to Mr. A. S. By John Smyth," in *The Complete Works of John Smyth*, vol. 2, 547, emphasis added.

point of persuasion. In "The Last Book of John Smyth, Called the Retraction of His Errors, and the Confirmation of Truth" (c.1612) Smyth acknowledged that he had been "somewhat lavish in censuring and Judging others" and formally retracted some of his more scathing remarks about his erstwhile theological opponents. In doing so, he also identified God as "the lord who is my Judge in my conscience" and the one to whom he was accountable for his words and actions.[44] Clearly, Smyth fit comfortably within the conventional thought of his day regarding conscience. Conscience for him did not serve as a tool for individual decision making; instead, it represented the means by which God both bent a person toward His will and rendered judgment upon a person's behavior.

Not surprisingly, when Smyth's followers invoked conscience in their consideration of the relationship between state authorities and religion, they did so in a similar manner. Article eighty-four of "Propositions and Conclusions" declared that "the magistrate is not by virtue of his office to meddle with religion, or matters of conscience, to force or compel men to this or that form of religion, or doctrine: but to leave the Christian religion free to every man's conscience.... for Christ only is the king, the lawgiver, of the church and conscience."[45] Christ's lordship over conscience, not a presumed autonomy of conscience or a claim of individual freedom, made magisterial interference in religious and ecclesial matters such as baptism nonsensical. The distinction is subtle, but important, especially in light of later Baptist interpretations of this idea. By its very nature, the exercise of conscience *had* to be free from human control, for conscience itself belonged exclusively to God. Liberty of conscience thus was a theological concept for John Smyth and his followers. It was not, as it would later become, an idea grounded in human nature and protected as a natural right.

***

Like Smyth, Thomas Helwys stands in the vanguard of the Baptist tradition of freedom as it is popularly understood. It is "beyond reason-

---

[44] John Smyth, "The Last Book of John Smyth, Called the Retraction of His Errors, and the Confirmation of the Truth," in *The Complete Works of John Smyth*, vol. 2, 753.

[45] "Propositions and Conclusions," in Lumpkin, *Baptist Confessions of Faith*, 140.

able contradiction that Thomas Helwys was, indeed, the bold architect of Baptist polity," declared historian William Estep. "It was he who incorporated the basic insights of his mentor, John Smyth, into what has rightly been termed the 'first Baptist confession of faith.'"[46] It is generally acknowledged that, with Helwys, the English Baptist tradition emerged as a distinctive theological movement apart from the Anabaptistic inclinations of Smyth and his followers. A leading figure in the small Baptist community in Amsterdam, Helwys parted ways with Smyth for reasons that remain at least partially shrouded in mystery. The primary issue, however, seems to have been Smyth's growing inclination toward the more radical positions of his Anabaptist friends in Amsterdam.[47] In late 1611 or early 1612, Helwys and twelve members of the Amsterdam congregation left Holland and returned to England, where they established the first Baptist church on English soil in Spittlefields, just outside London.

Helwys called for an unprecedented degree of religious toleration in England. That much is beyond dispute. He also, however, understood conscience as obligation, not choice, and, in stark contrast to Smyth, considered individual free will to be a "most damnable heresy." In the early 1900s, historian Champlain Burrage examined the four known works that Helwys wrote in 1611 and 1612.[48] From these documents, he

---

[46]William R. Estep, "Thomas Helwys: Bold Architect of Baptist Polity on Church-State Relations," *Baptist History and Heritage* 20 (July 1985): 32. The confession to which Estep refers here is "A Declaration of Faith of English People Remaining at Amsterdam in Holland" (1611).

[47]Whitley, *A History of British Baptists*, 30. Others have suggested alternative reasons for the split. Coggins believes that the Smyth group's decision to remain in Holland was interpreted by Helwys, who continued to identify strongly with his native land, as a refusal to try and convert England from its embrace of false doctrine. Helwys left Holland, Coggins writes, to pursue a missionary agenda in England. See Coggins, *John Smyth's Congregation*, 148ff. B. R. White cites theological disagreements over the meaning of baptism and the question of whether magistrates could belong to the church while serving the state as issues that contributed to the split. See White, *The English Baptists of the Seventeenth Century* (London: The Baptist Historical Society, 1983) 25-27.

[48]"A Declaration of Faith of English People Remaining at Amsterdam in Holland" (1611); "A Short and Plain Proof by the Word and Works of God that God's Decree is not the Cause of Any Man's Sin or Condemnation, and That all Men are Redeemed by Christ" (1611); "An Advertisement or Admonition, Unto the Congregation, Which Men Call the

distilled seven propositions as essential to Helwys' understanding of Christian faith and practice.[49] Individual freedom did not make the list. Nor should it have, in light of what Helwys actually wrote.

Consider the "Declaration of Faith of English People Remaining at Amsterdam in Holland," composed in 1611 by Helwys on behalf of his small congregation.[50] Designed to distinguish Helwys's church from the Smyth group, this confession affirmed that civil officials, as ministers of God ordained to keep the peace, may join and participate fully in the church, and that Christians may take public oaths "in a just cause for the deciding off strife."[51] Perhaps more significantly with regard to the question of human freedom, the declaration also departed from Smyth's position by denying free will as essential to human nature, though it did retain Smyth's belief in a general atonement. "Men are by nature the Children of wrath... borne in iniquity and in sin conceived... Wise to all evil but to good they have no knowledge," Helwys wrote. "And therefore man is not restored unto his former estate... having in himself all disposition unto good, and no disposition unto evil, yet being tempted might yield or might resist." Instead, Helwys continued, in his

---

New Fryelers, in the Low Countries" (1611); and "A Short Declaration of the Mystery of Iniquity" (1612).

[49] Champlain Burrage, *The Early English Dissenters, in the Light of Recent Research (1550-1641)* vol. 1, "History and Criticism" (Cambridge: Cambridge University Press, 1912) 253. The seven propositions are that baptism, not a church covenant, is the true basis of a church; each congregation may gather for worship and celebration of the ordinances, regardless of whether or not it has church officers; a church should not be so big that the members do not know each other; elders and deacons are the two church offices, responsible for tending to the spiritual and physical needs of the congregation respectively; these church offices should be filled by individuals who meet the relevant standards found in the New Testament; civil officials may be church members; a church member may take an oath. Futhermore, Burrage noted, Helwys considered believers' baptism an absolute necessity for salvation. It is worth noting that Helwys did not limit the office of deacon to men, describing those who could hold the office as "Men, and Women who by their office relieve the necessities of the poor." He offers no similar qualifier regarding the office of elder.

[50] Thomas Helwys, "A Declaration of Faith of English People Remaining at Amsterdam in Holland," 1611, in Lumpkin, *Baptist Confessions of Faith*, 116-123.

[51] Ibid., see articles 24 and 25, 122-123. Cf. articles 35 and 36 of "A Short Confession of Faith, 1610," in Lumpkin, *Baptist Confessions of Faith*, 111-112; also "Propositions and Conclusions," articles 85 and 86, in Lumpkin, 140.

fallen and sinful condition, man has "disposition unto evil, and no disposition or will unto any good, yet GOD giving grace, man may receive grace, or may reject grace."[52] "Choice," in other words, represented a human response to God's grace. Men and women did not take any initiative in making religious decisions; they simply reacted to God's movement in their lives.

Lest his rejection of individual free will be misunderstood, Helwys repeated and elaborated upon his position in *An Advertisement or Admonition, Unto the Congregations Which Men Call the New Freylers, in the Low Countries* (1611). In this document, Helwys sought to correct the apparently popular accusation that a belief in the general atonement of humanity through Christ's death on the cross necessarily required a belief in human free will. This, he wrote, was most certainly not the case:

> And whereas it is suspected that they which hold universal Redemption do, or must hold free will, we desire to testify unto all, for the clearing of ourselves from the suspect of that most damnable heresy, that God in mercy hath thus far given us grace to see that whosoever holds universal redemption by Christ, they cannot hold free will, if they have any understanding: for free will doth utterly abolish Christ, and destroy faith, and set up works: for free will is to have absolute power in a man's self to work righteousness and obey God in perfect obedience.[53]

Those who believed that humans enjoyed the exercise of free will, he continued, conveniently neglected the disastrous effects of the Fall and promoted a sin-free theology that did not hold true to Scripture. After the Fall, the image of God lingered only as a distant memory in the minds of sinful men and women. "The likeness or image of god, which is Perfection, righteousness, and true holiness," Helwys argued, "doth differ, and is cleanly contrary to the likeness and image of sinful Adam, who when he begat Seth his son was of himself an imperfect, unholy, unrighteous man." If those Christians who advocate free will "cannot see this, then they are void of all knowledge of God."[54] Helwys then advised

---

[52] Ibid., 117-118.
[53] Thomas Helwys, *An Advertisement or Admonition, Unto the Congregations Which Men Call the New Freylers, in the Low Countries* (n.p.p.: n.p., 1611) 91.
[54] Ibid., 92.

free will supporters to look at their genealogy. If their fathers begat them in the image of God, then they could legitimately claim to be "perfect, holy, and righteous, and so have free will." If, however, their fathers begat them in their own image, as Adam did Seth, then "let them with David cry out and confess: Behold, I was born in iniquity and in sin hath my mother conceived me. And if they confess that they were born in iniquity and conceived in sin... how doth the devil bewitch them to make them think that they are perfect and have free will."[55] Finally, Helwys punctuated his deconstruction of the free will argument with a final swipe at those who suggested that humans had any innate capacity to choose their own way in religious matters. "Let it here be observed," he declared, "that faith is a Created quality in man" and is ultimately the gift of God.[56]

By the time he wrote *A Short Declaration of the Mystery of Iniquity*, then, Helwys had explicitly and forcefully described the notion of individual free will as a devilish deception. Only God, through his abundant grace, could bring a person to the point of faith. Helwys built his argument for religious freedom in the *Mystery of Iniquity* upon this understanding of how God works in the human heart and mind. Like Smyth, Helwys understood conscience as the means by which God inclined stubborn and sinful men and women toward his will through the teachings of God's Word and the influence of God's Spirit. As such, only God could legitimately exercise any kind of claim upon a person's conscience. Herein lay Helwys's chief complaint against the English king: by insisting that his subjects be baptized into the Church of England in a manner contrary to the example of Scripture, the king had overstepped his authority in two significant ways. First, he had placed himself at the head of a falsely constituted church, and, second, by forcing individuals to act against their conscience, he had arrogantly usurped the sovereignty that *God alone* rightfully enjoyed over conscience.

Significantly, neither of these two complaints focused primarily upon the issue of individual freedom. The issue, instead, was theological.

---

[55] Ibid., 93.
[56] Ibid.

Book one of the *Mystery of Iniquity* compared the Roman Catholic Church and the Church of England with the first and second beasts, respectively, mentioned in the apocalyptic vision of Revelation. By formulating spiritual laws and doctrines apart from the plain teaching of Scripture, Helwys wrote, these false churches placed unnecessary and illegitimate burdens upon the consciences of their members. They trod where only God may go. In book two, Helwys took up in earnest the question of conscience. Citing Romans 13, he began by acknowledging that God had ordained the king to his position and given him absolute authority over his subjects in earthly matters. (In many ways, Helwys's "radical" treatise was quite conservative.) Earthly power, however, did not translate into spiritual authority; that belonged exclusively to God as a matter of conscience. "If our lord the king shall force and compel men to worship and eat the Lord's Supper against their consciences," Helwys argued, "he shall compel them to sin against God, and increase their own judgements."[57]

Indeed, as understood by Helwys and his contemporaries in the early seventeenth century, individuals would ultimately be held accountable to God for the degree to which they obeyed the dictates of conscience.[58] Accordingly, "is it not most equal that men should choose their religion themselves, seeing as how they only must stand before the judgement seat of God to answer for themselves, when it shall be of no excuse for them to say we were commanded or compelled to be of this religion by the king or by them that had authority from him?"[59] Given Helwys's well-documented rejection of free will, "choice" here must be understood, as it was in *An Advertisement or Admonition*, in the context of conscience and the obligation it placed upon individuals to respond obediently to God's guidance, or else suffer the painful consequences. In much the same manner, Helwys requested the king to allow his subjects to read the Bible "in their own language and to pray in their public worship in their own tongue" so that they "may enjoy this blessed

---

[57] Thomas Helwys, *A Short Declaration of the Mystery of Iniquity*, ed. Richard Groves (Macon GA: Mercer University Press, 1998) 37.
[58] Cf. Locke, "A Letter Concerning Toleration," 32.
[59] Ibid.

liberty to understand the scriptures with their own understanding and pray in their public worship in their own spirits?" In other words, Helwys asked, would the king allow his people's consciences to be formed rightly by God's Word and Spirit? "Then, if men err, their sin shall be upon their own heads" when they have to answer to God for their refusal to submit to God's will. Otherwise, Helwys warned, the guilt for such misshapen consciences will fall upon the king.[60]

Time and again throughout book two, Helwys stressed God's exclusive rule over the conscience. The king simply had no business interfering in religious matters, which, by their very nature, fell under the mandate of conscience. They were beyond his divinely ordained sphere of authority. "For our lord the king is but an earthly king, and he has no authority as a king but in earthly causes," maintained Helwys. "And if the king's people be obedient and true subjects, obeying all human laws made by the king, our lord the king can require no more." Helwys then offered what, for contemporary Baptists, has become the classic justification for absolute religious freedom:

> For men's religion to God is between God and themselves. The king shall not answer for it. Neither may the king be judge between God and man. Let them be heretics, Turks, Jews, or whatsoever, it appertains not to the earthly power to punish them in the least measure. This is made evident... by the scriptures.[61]

Helwys did not ground his argument for toleration upon a foundation of human rights or any "axiomatic" principle of individual freedom.[62] Instead, like Smyth before him, he cited Scripture as justification. His description of religion, furthermore, closely paralleled Perkins's definition of conscience as "placed in the midst between God and man." The king could not sanction religious faith because religion was a matter of conscience, and conscience belonged to God. Helwys's argument was not a treatise in support of individual freedom as an inalienable human right. It was, instead, a defense of divine prerogative

---

[60] Ibid., 44.
[61] Ibid., 53.
[62] See James Dunn, "Church, State, and Soul Competency," *Review and Expositor* 96 (1999): 66.

against royal presumption. As if to underscore this point, Helwys closed book two with a word of encouragement to those who might suffer persecution for their obedience to God's Word. In such circumstances, "they are not to resist, by any way or means although it were in their power, but rather submit to give their lives, as Christ and his disciples did, and yet *keep their consciences to God*."[63] Such was the obligation and mandate of conscience for Helwys.

Moreover, in urging believers to keep their consciences to God, Helwys also understood himself to be defending Christ's rightful prerogative as sole sovereign over the church. The Puritans, he argued in book three, claimed Christ as their king yet maintained the Anglican structure of church governance and submission to the King of England. "Can you divide Christ's government (as he is a king) from his power, or his power from his government? Will you make him a king without government?" he asked rhetorically. "If the lord bishops should compel you to deny Christ of the name of a king in or over his church, would you not then say they overthrow a fundamental point of faith?"[64] The dangerous consequences of submitting one's conscience to an authority other than Christ loomed large for Helwys. Scripture plainly taught that all who did not believe in Christ would be damned, he warned, "which you [Puritans] shall all be, every one of you that submit to any other government than that most holy and blessed government which Christ has established in the church, whereof he is head and king."[65] The integrity of conscience thus related directly to the integrity of the church.[66] Should the church fail "to keep its conscience to God," it could not stand as the true body of Christ, freed from the power of sin and bound in obedience to him only. Conscience, in other words, ultimately represented a matter of *corporate* concern to Helwys; thus the church (and its rightful king) stood at the center of his thought.

The early generations of English Baptists bore a distinct theological resemblance to Thomas Helwys. Indeed, like Helwys and, to a lesser

---

[63] Helwys, *A Short Declaration of the Mystery of Iniquity*, 62, emphasis added.
[64] Ibid., 79.
[65] Ibid., 84.
[66] Ibid., 84-85.

extent, Smyth, Baptists in the seventeenth century grounded their understanding of freedom not in "sacred individualism" but in divine grace. According to the Particular Baptists' "Second London Confession" (1677):

> The Liberty which *Christ* hath purchased for Believers under the Gospel, consists in their freedom from the guilt of Sin, the condemning wrath of God, the Rigor and Curse of the Law; and in their being delivered from this present evil World, bondage to Satan, and Dominion of Sin; from the Evil of Afflictions; the Fear, and Sting of Death, the Victory of the Grave, and Everlasting Damnation; as also in their free access to God; and their yielding obedience unto him not out of slavish fear, but a Child-like love and willing mind.[67]

For these Baptists, individuals did not enjoy liberty as a "natural right." In their "state of nature," so to speak, individuals lived in bondage to sin and death. Freedom came only as a gift of God, made possible by Christ's "purchase" realized on the cross and in the empty tomb, and even then, the proper object of a believer's freedom was obedience—not to personal preferences or individual opinions, but to God's will. The "Second London Confession" made this point absolutely clear: "God alone is Lord of the Conscience, and hath left it free from the Doctrines and Commandments of men which are in any thing contrary to his Word, or not contained in it."[68] Conscience was not absolute, but rather could be exercised only under the authority of God as revealed in Scripture. Such is the theological legacy of those first Baptists, John Smyth and Thomas Helwys.

Defined by Smyth, Helwys, and their fellow English Baptists in the early seventeenth century, then, Christian freedom and the liberty of conscience were, as theologian Curtis Freeman has argued, "rooted in the freedom conferred on believers by the gospel and through their participation in the new creation. The freedom of the church is

---

[67] "Second London Confession," in Lumpkin, *Baptist Confessions of Faith,* 279. The General Baptists' less Calvinistic confession, the Orthodox Creed (1678) contains similar affirmations of the church and the lordship of Jesus over human conscience. See, for example, Lumpkin, *Baptist Confessions of Faith,* 319, 331.

[68] Ibid., 280.

established only by the gospel of Jesus Christ, not by powers and authorities (including the state) from which believers are freed."[69] As modern notions of rights and individual freedom gained currency, however, cracks began to form in the bridge connecting seventeenth-century Baptist thought with the ideas of later Baptist generations. These cracks soon widened into significant gaps. "Although early Baptists seemed to find it unnecessary to provide any warrant other than the gospel for Christian liberty and liberty of conscience," writes Freeman, "subsequent generations increasingly turned to philosophical and political theories to justify these convictions."[70] Such a Christ-centered understanding of the source and nature of freedom contrasts sharply with the language of Baptists in the United States several generations later whose beliefs gradually conformed to the assumptions underlying the modern nation-state.[71] As Baptist theologians narrowed their focus from the church to the individual, the redemptive work of Jesus became increasingly less central to the Baptist understanding of religious freedom. Instead, in the rhetoric of Baptists such as John Leland, inspired by Thomas Jefferson and suffused with the enlightened language of natural rights and individual freedoms, the liberal democratic state became both the source and the security for religious liberty and rights of conscience.[72]

***

Even within the Baptist tradition as it developed in America, Leland's ideas about religious freedom and the separation of church and state represent a significant break with the past—this despite the fact that

---

[69] Curtis Freeman, "Can Baptist Theology Be Revisioned?" 280. See also McBeth, "English Baptist Literature on Religious Liberty to 1689," 278-283.
[70] Ibid.
[71] For a compelling argument regarding the quasi-theological assumptions of the modern liberal state, see William T. Cavanaugh, "The City: Beyond Secular Parodies," in *Radical Orthodoxy*, eds. John Milbank, Catherine Pickstock, and Graham Ward (New York: Routledge, 1999) 182-200. See also Cavanaugh, *Theopolitical Imagination: Discovering the Liturgy as a Political Act in an Age of Global Consumerism* (New York: T. & T. Clark, 2002).
[72] Thanks to Philip Thompson for articulating this idea nicely in "Religious Liberty, Sacraments, God's Image, and the State in Two Periods in Baptist Life and Thought," 21, unpublished paper presented at the Catholic Theological Society/National Association of Baptist Professors of Religion meeting at Villanova University, 4 June 2000.

Baptists in the United States tend to speak of Roger Williams (1603-1683), Isaac Backus (1724-1806), and Leland (1754-1841) in the same breath, assuming that their shared advocacy of religious freedom reflects a shared theological perspective and a common understanding of such ideas as liberty and conscience.[73] In reality, however, a great divide separated the ideas of Williams (who was only briefly affiliated with a Baptist congregation during his lifelong spiritual sojourn in search of the "true church") and Backus from those of Leland.[74] For Williams and

---

[73] J. M. Dawson's *Baptists and the American Republic* is a classic example of the tendency in Baptist thought to read the liberal democratic ideals of modern Baptists back into history. For Dawson, the careers of Williams, Backus, and Leland, simply represent different stages in the same fight, a struggle for the rights of individual conscience and religious freedom that ended triumphantly with the passage of the First Amendment. The possibility that the three men, whose careers in America together spanned almost two hundred years, could have entertained different ideas about religious freedom or been motivated by different factors does not seem to have concerned Dawson. Dawson, however, did not stand alone in this belief. Baptist historian Edwin Gaustad wrote in 1959 of a singular "Backus-Leland tradition" regarding matters of church and state. See Gaustad, "The Backus-Leland Tradition," *Foundations* 2 (1959): 131-152. Gaustad qualified his position somewhat in "Religious Liberty: Some Fine Distinctions," *American Baptist Quarterly* 6 (1987): 215-225, acknowledging that Backus and Leland were not of one mind regarding issues of church and state. James E. Wood, Jr., a prominent Baptist scholar of religious liberty issues, also made no discernable distinction among the various positions of Williams, Backus, and Leland. See James E. Wood, Jr., "Baptists and Religious Liberty," *Southwestern Journal of Theology* 6 (April 1964): 38-59. Numerous others have shared Dawson, Gaustad, and Wood's opinion over the years. James Dunn, for one, Wood's successor as executive director of the Baptist Joint Committee on Public Affairs, remains a prominent advocate of this position. See, for example, James Dunn, "The Baptist Vision of Religious Liberty," in *Proclaiming the Baptist Vision: Religious Liberty*, 34-35.

[74] William McLoughlin dissented from the consensus interpretation of Baptists and religious liberty in 1968, arguing that Backus, an evangelical pietist, resembled neither the more Puritan Williams nor the more rationalist Jefferson (one of Leland's heroes) in his understanding of the proper relationship between church and state. See McLoughlin, "Isaac Backus and the Separation of Church and State in America," *American Historical Review* 73 (1968): 1392-1413. Regarding Roger Williams, LeRoy Moore's historiographical essay on him may be of interest here, particularly concerning the "romantic" portrayals of the lifelong Seeker as an enlightened, secular democrat in a rather Jeffersonian mold. See Moore, "Roger Williams and the Historians," *Church History* 32 (1963): 432-451. A standard Baptist interpretation of Williams is Edwin Gaustad, *Liberty of Conscience: Roger Williams in America* (Grand Rapids MI: Eedrmans Publishing Company, 1991). A more nuanced perspective on Williams can be found in Timothy Hall's excellent *Separating Church and State: Roger Williams and Religious Liberty* (Urbana IL: University of Illinois Press, 1998).In

Backus, observes Freeman, liberty of conscience "derived from the Gospel and not from Enlightenment theories of natural rights."[75] Williams's complex theological treatises on religious freedom, most notably *The Bloudy Tenent of Persecution for the Sake of Conscience* (1644), had virtually no influence on the enlightened members of the Revolutionary generation who, as historian Perry Miller noted, drew their inspiration from very different sources.[76] Backus, too, belongs with Williams as an intellectually "pre-Lockean, theocentric, and typological" thinker, wrote William McLoughlin, for both men "limit civil

---

1972, McLoughlin distinguished Backus's willingness to endorse limited government support of religion from Leland's insistence upon a strict separation of the two. See McLoughlin, *New England Dissent, 1630-1833*, vol. 2, 928-935. There are two basic schools of interpretation regarding Backus. While McLoughlin has placed Backus squarely in the individualist, pietist strand of American Christianity, theologian Stanley Grenz has emphasized his more conservative Puritan nature. See Grenz, *Isaac Backus—Baptist and Puritan* (Macon GA: Mercer University Press, 1983). For more on Leland's understanding of church and state, as well as his affinity for Jeffersonian ideas, see J. Bradley Creed, "John Leland, American Prophet of Religious Individualism" (Ph.D. diss., Southwestern Baptist Theological Seminary, 1986).

Thanks in part to McLoughlin's heterodoxy, the allegedly monolithic Baptist tradition of religious liberty in America began to appear more diverse in the eyes of some historians. Indeed, since the 1980s, the question of whether *a* single tradition even exists has been a source of much debate among Baptist scholars, with a great deal of attention focused upon the similarities (or lack thereof) between the respective positions of Backus and Leland on matters of church and state. For an excellent historiographical account of this debate and its political implications for Southern Baptists, see Hankins, *Uneasy in Babylon*, 127-138.

[75] Freeman, "Can Baptist Theology Be Revisioned?" 280.

[76] Perry Miller, *Roger Williams: His Contribution to the American Tradition* (Indianapolis: The Bobbs-Merrill Company, 1953) 254. The most recent edition of Williams's seminal treatise is *The Bloudy Tenent of Persecution for the Sake of Conscience*, ed. Richard Groves (Macon GA: Mercer University Press, 2001). For an excellent presentation of Williams's theological understanding of liberty of conscience, see Hall, *Separating Church and State: Roger Williams and Religious Liberty*. Hall argues persuasively that the key to Williams's views about religious freedom lay in his dogmatic insistence on religious separatism, i.e. the need for true Christians to quarantine themselves against the spiritual corruption of unbelievers. A passion for theological purity, not individual freedom, motivated Williams in his quest for religious liberty. For a helpful historiographical survey of the literature on Williams, see William Lee Miller, *The First Liberty: Religion and the American Republic* (New York: Knopf, 1986) 166-171. Readers interested in Williams's thought and his significance in American history will find Miller's book helpful as well as Edmund S. Morgan, *Roger Williams: The Church and the State* (New York: Harcourt, Brace and World, Inc., 1967).

government to the function of maintaining civil peace until humanity is reconciled by the divine law."[77] Arguing their respective cases almost exclusively upon theological grounds, both men, and countless other Baptists whose names have largely been lost to history, spent many years, spilled much ink, and endured numerous hardships as dissenters in pursuit of religious liberty.

Leland certainly followed in the Baptist tradition of defending liberty of conscience and opposing state establishments of churches. "Yet to justify and display these convictions," writes Freeman, "he adopted Lockean and Madisonian language with its theories of natural rights and voluntary associations."[78] Moreover, adds church historian Brad Creed, "Leland, in his basic theological emphases, took individualism further than… his Baptist colleagues," this at a time when American culture was awash in the revolutionary rhetoric of freedom and democracy.[79] As Baptist convictions regarding church and state passed through Leland, liberal democratic political ideas of individual rights crept into the Baptist vocabulary and began to reshape Baptist theology. Indeed, Leland scarcely bothered to hide the philosophical and political influences of John Locke, Thomas Jefferson, and James Madison on his

---

[77] William G. McLoughlin, in *Isaac Backus and the American Pietistic Tradition* (Boston: Little, Brown, and Company, 1967) 98. In light of Backus's significance as an advocate of religious liberty, the fact that he has been the subject of only a handful of biographies—the last of them written in 1983—represents an obvious lacuna in Baptist scholarship. The earliest scholarly account of Backus's life was Alvah Hovey, *A Memoir of the Life and Times of the Rev. Isaac Backus, A.M.* (Boston: Gould and Lincoln, 1859). T. B. Maston, in *Isaac Backus: Pioneer of Religious Liberty* (London: James Clarke & Co., 1962) understood Backus as a "New Light" Baptist heavily influenced by John Locke's ideas about the proper relationship between church and state. Most of the scholarly debate about Backus, however, centers on two books that offer clearly contrasting portraits of the man. McLoughlin sees Backus as an early representative of the individualist, pietist strand of American Christianity. In *Isaac Backus—Baptist and Puritan*, Grenz argues that Backus can be better understood as part of the Puritan tradition of national covenants and corporate righteousness. Backus's basic argument for religious liberty began with the biblical truth that Christ's kingdom was not of this world. As the visible body of Christ on earth, Backus reasoned, the church should be supported solely by the voluntary gifts of those called out of the world and into the Kingdom of God. Compulsory taxation in support of established churches thus violated the essential nature of the church.

[78] Freeman, "Can Baptist Theology Be Revisioned?" 281.
[79] Creed, "John Leland, American Prophet of Religious Individualism," 1986, 71.

account of the Baptist faith.[80] As such, his career may well be understood as the cradle of Baptist democracy.

Perhaps Leland's dependence on Locke, Jefferson, and Madison should not be surprising, given the times in which he lived. Baptized in 1774 and established as a preacher in Virginia by 1776, Leland came of age as a Christian during the heady years preceding the American Revolution, a time in which the language of individualism dominated popular political and religious conversation.[81] Based upon the "fundamental presupposition of the free, uncoerced individual" created in the image of God, the belief that "to be true to God was to be true to the dictates of one's own conscience" thrived in this era of liberality.[82] Jefferson, particularly, made the political theories of Locke and others accessible to the American mind as he couched the rationale for American independence in terms of "the fundamental rights of the human and the unfettered liberty of the individual."[83] In this fertile soil of freedom and individualism, American democracy took root, and John Leland took notice.

A radical individualist (whether by nature or nurture is not known), Leland instinctively opposed hierarchies of any kind and favored limited government, both in political and religious matters. Accordingly, his views on church and state "were all of one piece" in a way they had not been for his predecessors.[84] As Creed explains, Leland's individualism shaped his view of society in a way that resembled the "social contract" ideas of Thomas Hobbes (1588-1679), John Locke (1632-1704), and Jean-

---

[80] Freeman, "Can Baptist Theology Be Revisioned?" 281. See also Gaustad, "Religious Liberty: Some Fine Distinctions," 219-220. Although Leland is often called a "Jeffersonian," his ideas about democracy owed as much to Madison as they did to Jefferson. Indeed, as Adriene Koch argued in *Jefferson and Madison: The Great Collaboration* (New York: Alfred A. Knopf, 1950) much of the political philosophy attributed typically to Jefferson alone was actually the product of his fruitful and friendly intellectual relationship with Madison.

[81] See Hatch, *The Democratization of American Christianity*, 6ff.

[82] Creed, 4-5.

[83] Ibid. Locke's influence upon Jefferson is well known, but Garrett Ward Sheldon provides a nice summary of this relationship in *The Political Philosophy of Thomas Jefferson* (Baltimore: The Johns Hopkins University Press, 1991).

[84] Ibid., 13.

Jacques Rousseau (1712-1778).[85] For Leland, writes Creed, "since the individual is the locus and authority, the fundamental unit, he alone can claim ontological status. [Leland] viewed social institutions and functions as nothing more than self-determining individuals who join together because they share a common existence."[86] Social bodies are necessary, Leland believed, but they exist only by the mutual consent of sovereign individuals who may freely dissolve the relationship at any time. Likewise, Leland understood human nature in competitive terms and "turned a quest for self-reliance into a godly crusade."[87] Speaking plainly and without theological flourish, writes historian Nathan Hatch, Leland "proclaimed a divine economy that was atomistic... rather than wholistic and hierarchical. This kind of liberal individualism could easily be embraced at the grass roots. Ordinary people gladly championed the promise of personal autonomy as a message they could understand and a cause to which they could subscribe—in God's name, no less."[88]

Leland, a tireless evangelist, enthusiastically preached to any who would listen. His message, however, seemed to reflect his view of human nature more than anything else. Religion, he wrote, was a matter between God and individuals. As such, the preservation of religious freedom was of the utmost importance. "Every man must give account of himself to God," he continued, "and therefore every man ought to be at liberty to serve God in a way that he can best reconcile to his conscience. If government can answer for individuals at the day of judgement, let men be controlled by it in religious matters; otherwise, let men be free."[89] Leland understood human freedom as coming from God, but he saw it as intrinsic to human nature, not a fruit of redemption. Liberty derives from God, he believed, "not as the lawgiver or the creator of a covenant, but as the giver and judge of individual

---

[85] See Thomas Hobbes, *Leviathan* (New York: The Liberal Arts Press, 1958); John Locke, *Second Treatise of Government*, ed. C. B. Macpherson (Indianapolis: Hackett Publishing Company, 1980); and Jean-Jacques Rousseau, *On the Social Contract*, ed. Roger D. Masters, trans. Judith R. Masters (New York: St. Martin's Press, 1978).

[86] Ibid., 117.

[87] Hatch, *The Democratization of American Christianity*, 101.

[88] Creed, "John Leland, American Baptist Prophet of Religious Individualism," 117.

[89] John Leland, "The Rights of Conscience Inalienable," 181.

conscience." Unlike the early Baptists who grounded liberty in the person and work of Christ, Leland claimed that "the locus of liberty is the God-given, truth-informed, individual conscience."[90] Born into a state of freedom, sovereign individuals were at liberty to submit their consciences to the will of God, should they so choose, and Leland insisted that this most private, most personal decision be kept beyond the influence of "external" forces.

These forces included the church, for in Leland's opinion, a church of Christ "is a congregation of faithful persons, called out of the world by divine grace, who mutually agree to live together, and execute gospel discipline among them."[91] While the idea that the salvation of individuals precedes the existence of the church meshed well with Leland's liberal notions of human nature, it bore little resemblance to the theology of Helwys and other early Baptists who understood the church to be the medium through which God brings people to salvation. Consider again the Second London Confession of 1677:

> The Grace of *Faith*, whereby the Elect are enabled to believe to the saving of their souls, is the work of the *Spirit of Christ* in their hearts; and is ordinarily wrought by the Ministry of the Word; by which also, and by the administration of *Baptism*, and the *Lord's Supper*, *Prayer*, and other *Means* appointed of God, it is increased and strengthened.[92]

The saving gift of faith, these early Baptists believed, began with the work of the Holy Spirit, received confirmation in the hearing of Scripture, and came to maturity through the concrete practices of the church. All three elements—the Spirit, the Word, and the church—thus worked together in enabling individuals "to believe to the saving of their souls."

Leland recognized no such role for the church in the salvation experience. "A connection to a visible, organized church was not a primary priority for Leland because he did not see the church as being essential to the work God had called him to do," notes Creed. "What was

---

[90] Michael J. Hostetler, "Liberty in Baptist Thought: Three Primary Texts, 1614-1856," *American Baptist Quarterly* 15 (1996): 251.
[91] John Leland, "The Virginia Chronicle," *The Writings of John Leland*, 108.
[92] "Second London Confession," in Lumpkin, *Baptist Confessions of Faith*, 268.

paramount for Leland was that the individual discover salvation. All other aspects of Christian discipleship, even one's involvement in the church, subsided in the face of that overwhelming urgency."[93] Leland considered the Bible alone to be the only authority a Christian needed, and thus he expressed great reservations about anything that might come between an individual and God. The ideal Baptist polity, Leland argued, reflected Jefferson's ideal government: the best church is the one which governs least, for "true Christianity took precedence over churches."[94]

Leland's intellectual debt to Jefferson (and, in fairness, Madison) extended far beyond this remark. During the early years of the American republic when the language of individual freedom took on decidedly religious connotations in evangelical circles, the political arguments for individual freedom flowed most prolifically from the pens of Jefferson and Madison. Historian Andrew Manis states that, in his theological formulations of religious freedom and church-state relations, Leland generally "began with the Enlightened ideas of Jefferson and Madison," sometimes even using their exact language, "but unpacked them in evangelical ways."[95] Citing the future president's "Bill for the Establishment of Religious Freedom in Virginia" (1786), Manis offers several examples of the ways in which Jefferson's political philosophy powerfully influenced Leland's theology.[96] Leland's view of temporal government, for instance, came almost verbatim from Locke, via

---

[93] Creed, "John Leland, American Prophet…" 155.

[94] Joe Coker, "Sweet Harmony vs. Strict Separation: Recognizing the Distinctions Between Isaac Backus and John Leland," *American Baptist Quarterly* 16 (1997): 245.

[95] Andrew Manis, "Regionalism and a Baptist Perspective on the Separation of Church and State," *American Baptist Quarterly* 2 (1983): 223. See also, among others, Albert Wardin, Jr., "Contrasting Views of Church and State: A Study of John Leland and Isaac Backus," *Baptist History and Heritage* 33 (1998): 14.

[96] Ibid., 220-221. Two examples of this obvious overlap should be sufficient to illustrate the point. "The holy author of religion chose not to propagate it by coercion," Jefferson wrote, a position echoed later by Leland, who asserted that "legal force is not the armor with which the Captain of our salvation clothes the soldiers of the cross." Civil rights, claimed Jefferson, "have no dependency on our religious opinions any more than on opinions in physics or geography"; Leland, meanwhile, argued that "government has no more to do with the religious opinions of men than it has to do with the principles of mathematics."

Jefferson: "Perhaps the legitimate designs of government cannot be better defined than by saying it is to preserve the lives, liberties, and property of the many units that form the whole body politic."[97] Acknowledging the role of the state in providing freedom for its citizens, Leland then added that "for these valuable purposes individuals have... to expose their lives in war to defend the state—to give up a little of their liberty to recompense those who should be employed to secure the rest."[98]

Not only did Leland accept without question the legitimacy of the state's claim of authority over its citizens' lives, but he also happily endorsed the privatization of religion, all in the name of religious liberty. Christ's government "is not of this world," he wrote, "and therefore the rulers of this world should have nothing to do with it."[99] The state, he believed, dealt with worldly things and thus it rightfully had power over the body. "But the divine government," Leland continued, alone was concerned with the soul and was "adapted to pardon the guilty, reform the heart, instruct the mind, and improve the morals of the wicked. The promotions and punishments of civil government are all on this side of the grave, but those of the divine government are in the succeeding world."[100] Body and soul, in other words, belonged to different kingdoms—one public, the other private—and it was the "glory of the United States that... equal rights are protected by law, and Christianity left in the hands of its author, and conscience free in the hearts of each possessor."[101] Ultimately, Leland believed religious liberty began and ended with the individual and "the inalienable right each individual has of worshipping his God according to the dictates of his conscience, without being prohibited, directed, or controlled therein by human law, either in time, place, or manner."[102]

---

[97] John Leland, "A Blow at the Root," in *The Writings of John Leland*, 238.
[98] Ibid.
[99] John Leland, "The Government of Christ a Christocracy," in *The Writings of John Leland*, 277.
[100] Ibid.
[101] John Leland, "Short Essays on Government," in *The Writings of John Leland*, 477.
[102] Leland, "A Blow at the Root," 239.

By translating Baptist theology into the increasingly familiar language of liberal democracy, Leland accomplished two things that his early Baptist (and frequently ostracized, if not persecuted) ancestors could have hardly imagined: he helped make Baptists both popular and patriotic. "While the older denominations had to make concessions to the popular mood" following the Revolution, writes Creed, "Baptists did not. They embodied it. They had a built-in appeal with their individualism and fierce devotion to liberty. The Baptist concern for individual rights, local church autonomy, and democratic ecclesiology paralleled the growth of democratic government. They communicated a sense of destiny during this era and identified their struggle with the aspirations of America."[103] Consequently, and ironically, given their professed aversion to any intersections between church and state, Baptists "emerged from the Revolution as more than protestors and dissenters. They took their place as standard bearers in the task of molding a social order and making a new nation."[104] Perhaps no Baptist relished this role of standard bearer more than Leland, who championed the young American state and its democratic ideals with religious fervor.

Leland actively participated in Virginia politics and, through his ongoing agitation for a political guarantee of religious freedom, became friends with both Jefferson and Madison. His alleged contribution to the passage of the First Amendment is the stuff of legend among Baptists in America. The story goes that Leland and Madison were running for the same seat at Virginia's convention to ratify the Constitution. The two candidates met and, in exchange for Madison's pledge to introduce an amendment to the Constitution in Congress guaranteeing religious freedom, Leland agreed to drop out of the race and swing his support, and that of the many Baptists in the district, to Madison. Madison won the race and later made good on his pledge, thus giving Baptists grounds to claim indirect responsibility for the First Amendment.[105]

---

[103] Creed, "John Leland, American Prophet…" 40.
[104] Ibid., 40-41.
[105] This tale, perhaps apocryphal, can be found in many places, but the most hagiographic account is in Dawson, *Baptists and the American Republic*, 108-112.

The First Amendment cemented Leland's loyalty to the new republic and convinced him its guarantee of religious freedom represented an answer to the prayers of Christians through the ages. "Nothing is more plain," he wrote, "than that the Almighty has set up the government of the United States in answer to the prayers of all the saints, down from the first proclamation of the gospel. Had such a government existed, from the beginning of the Christian era, what rivers of blood... would have been prevented." Leland warmly observed that the Constitution "has left religion *infallibly* where it should be left in all government, viz.: as a matter between God and individuals."[106]

In return for the state's generous gift of freedom and its acknowledgement that religion is a private affair, Leland offered his unwavering support to his country. During the War of 1812, for example, he lectured a gathering of young men soon to enlist in the American army about the necessity to risk their lives in defense of freedom. "It is expected that, while like Spartan youths you learn to know and plead for your rights, so also you will patiently bear that burden which is the price of your liberty," he preached. "Arise and avenge our wrongs, and never sheath your swords, or stack your arms, until the soil and shores of North America are freed from British cruelty."[107] Above all, though, Leland held Thomas Jefferson in especially high esteem. In his frequently-quoted public Fast Day sermon, "A Blow at the Root," Leland lavished praise on the newly elected third president. The "exertion of the American genius has brought forth the *Man of the People*, the defender of the rights of man and the rights of conscience to fill the chair of State," he declared. "Pardon me, my hearers, if I am over-warm," Leland continued. "I lived in Virginia fourteen years. The beneficent influence of my hero was too generally felt to leave me a stoic. What may be not expected, under the auspices of heaven, while JEFFERSON presides with Madison by his side.... Let us then adore that God has been so favorable

---

[106] John Leland, "Miscellaneous Essays," in *The Writings of John Leland*, 410, 428 (italics in the original).
[107] John Leland, "Address to the Association of the Sons of Liberty," in *The Writings of John Leland*, 374.

to our land, and nation."[108] Advancing age did not diminish Leland's vigorous support of individual rights and American democracy. "I have publicly pledged," he wrote, "that as long as I can speak with my tongue—wield a pen—or heave a cry to heaven, whenever the rights of men, liberty of conscience, or the good of my country were involved by fraud or by force, my feeble efforts would not rest dormant."[109]

To the end of his life, Leland remained passionately committed to natural rights, individual freedom, and the promise of American democracy. All three ideas were essential to his understanding of religious liberty and the separation of church and state. A man of his times, Leland absorbed the individualistic ideals that fueled the Revolutionary imagination of Americans like Thomas Jefferson. Not surprisingly, his theology reflected the times as well. As articulated by Leland, Baptist faith and practice began to resemble liberal democratic political theory. Baptist veneration of the First Amendment only underscored the confidence with which Leland and his theological heirs placed their faith in the American state, acknowledging the United States government as the guarantor of their religious freedom and, consequently, the legitimate object of patriotic devotion. Leland not only approved of this development, but proudly claimed his share of responsibility in making it possible. Jefferson's metaphorical wall of separation between church and state became a mirror: when Baptists like Leland looked at America, they saw themselves and were greatly pleased.

Leland thus charted a fateful course for subsequent generations of Baptists in America. His "voluntaristic notions of the self and the justifying language of natural rights continued to become more thoroughly individualistic in subsequent generations of Baptists," writes Freeman. "The historic Baptist conditions and practices persisted with Leland, but they were given new modern meanings and warrants in terms of liberal

---

[108] Leland, "A Blow at the Root," 255 (italics and capitals in the original). There is little doubt that Leland held Jefferson in the utmost esteem. He also regarded Andrew Jackson, another "man of the people," with great reverence. He closed one sermon, a political oration on the evils of secession, with the valediction, "Jackson, the Constitution, and the Union of the States forever!" See Leland, "Address," in *The Writings of John Leland*, 628-632.

[109] Dawson, *Baptists and the American Republic*, 136.

individualism. In time, the democratic language of rights became so identified with the religious convictions and practices that... Baptists failed to distinguish between the two."[110] As such, Leland contributed the raw material, the basic elements, essential to the grand synthesis of Baptist democracy.

***

As historian Nathan Hatch made clear in *The Democratization of American Christianity* (1989), Baptists were not the only religious group in post-Revolutionary America to experience the liberating effects of the new democratic ethos. The Second Great Awakening of the early 1800s, with its highly individualistic approach to conversion and religious experience, only furthered this sense of personal freedom in religion.[111] Baptists, though, took particular pleasure in highlighting the harmony between their understanding of the Christian faith and the ideals of the new Republic. During the colonial period, observed William McLoughlin, most Baptists had considered the state to be an oppressive corruptor of Christian truth. By the 1820s, however, "the Baptists saw the United States of America as their country and felt themselves wholly in harmony with its ideals and its future. Since they had this stake in society and felt that its values were their values, whatever hurt the nation hurt the Baptists and whatever was good for the Baptists was good for the nation."[112] Baptists had, in a sense, immersed their theology in the cultural waters of American democracy, absorbing both its ideals and its assumptions about freedom. In doing so, however, they charted a new course for themselves, leaving behind the original ideas of Smyth, Helwys, and their fellow English Baptists of the seventeenth century.

To be sure, throughout the nineteenth century, the principle of the separation of church and state remained a central feature of Baptist self-consciousness, but for reasons that often had more to do with preserving

---

[110] Freeman, "Can Baptist Theology Be Revisioned?" 283.

[111] See, for example, John B. Boles, *The Great Revival: Beginnings of the Bible Belt*, rev. ed. (Lexington KY: University Press of Kentucky, 1996).

[112] McLoughlin, *New England Dissent, 1630-1833*, vol. 2, 1274. See also Ammerman, *Baptist Battles*, 18. In her chapter "From English Dissent to Southern Establishment," pp. 18-43, Ammerman traces the process by which Baptists in the South moved from the culture's periphery to its center.

the integrity of the First Amendment than with defending distinctively theological convictions. While Southern Baptists in the years following the Civil War remained adamantly opposed to any kind of direct government aid to church institutions—such as, for example, Roman Catholic parochial schools—they nevertheless began to think of the state as a legitimate partner in the pursuit of religiously-inspired moral reform.[113] According to historian William Brackney, by the late 1800s the prevalent understanding of religious liberty among Baptists was less about the separation of church and state than it was about "the freedom to secure a Christian America, and other Christian nations as well, through the missionary enterprise."[114] The overlap that Baptists perceived between their religious doctrines and the principles of American democracy—that is, a shared commitment to freedom—made appeals to the state and a Christian nation not only possible but plausible. If church and state shared the same values and worked toward the same end, Baptists believed, then cooperation between the two seemed only natural. "To us has been given the responsibility of preserving our national identity," proclaimed the *Biblical Recorder*, North Carolina's Baptist newspaper, in 1895, "and with it comes also the duty of maintaining the strength and purity of our religion."[115] In other words, to be a good Baptist, one should be a good American.

---

[113] Spain, *At Ease in Zion*, 43. Martin McMahone has demonstrated that there was little consensus among nineteenth-century Baptists over just how to define the proper relationship between church and state. See Martin McMahone, "Liberty More Than Separation: The Multiple Streams of Baptist Thought on Church-State Issues" (Ph.D. diss., Baylor University, 2001).

[114] William H. Brackney, *The Baptists*, 101. In similar fashion, C. C. Goen, another Baptist historian, has commented upon the tendency of Baptists at the turn of the twentieth century to mix religion and politics in keeping with "the operating assumptions of the Protestant consensus. Thus they accepted without question devotional exercises in public schools, supported Sunday laws and prohibition, protested the teaching of evolutionary theory, and shared American nativist suspicions about Roman Catholicism as a 'foreign power.'" As Brackney did with Baptists in the 1800s, Goen found among Baptists of the early twentieth century strong evidence that suggested a desire "to shape a Christian nation even while [they] celebrated the virtues of voluntary religion." See C. C. Goen, "Baptists and Church-State Issues in the 20th Century," *American Baptist Quarterly* 6 (1987): 226ff.

[115] *Biblical Recorder*, 7 August 1895, 2.

In Leland, the notion of Baptist democracy in America gained its first great champion. What his ideas lacked in theological polish and sophistication, they more than made up for in popular resonance. As the nineteenth century turned into the twentieth, even this deficiency would be resolved with the emergence of articulate, educated, and influential Baptists like Walter Rauschenbusch, E. Y. Mullins, and George Truett, whose work in the first decades of the new century ultimately helped establish the assumptions of Baptist democracy securely within the Baptist mainstream.

2

Walter Rauschenbusch and the Democratic Kingdom of God

Two months before he died in July 1918, Walter Rauschenbusch wrote an anguished letter to Cornelius Woelfkin, his friend and former colleague at Rochester Theological Seminary. Since the beginning of the Great War in 1914, Rauschenbusch—the son of German immigrants who spoke German as his first language—had been the occasional subject of public speculation regarding his sympathies in the conflict. Did he favor the Germans or the Allies? Certainly his willingness to argue the case for Germany when few other Americans dared to do so suggested at least a measure of support for his ancestral homeland, though Rauschenbusch insisted it was more a matter of balancing what had become a one-sided conversation in the decidedly pro-British American press. If the United States was truly neutral, he reasoned, let both sides of the story be told. As his former student and biographer Dores Robinson Sharpe noted, Rauschenbusch "was not pro-German, [but] he was pro-Christian," and he adamantly refused to allow nationalist sentiment to compromise his sense of kinship with Christians living in Germany.[1]

---

[1] Dores Robinson Sharpe, *Walter Rauschenbusch* (New York: The MacMillan Company, 1942) 390. For years, Sharpe's biography was the only book-length account of Rauschenbusch's life in print. Though full of intimate details and enriched by virtually unlimited access to Rauschenbusch's papers, Sharpe's work has an unmistakable hagiographical quality about it that renders its conclusions somewhat qualified. The admiring tone of the book is understandable, in that Rauschenbusch's widow personally selected Sharpe, one of her husband's students and later his private secretary, to write an "official" biography. The Rauschenbusch family also helped Sharpe edit and revise his manuscript for publication. Incredibly, given the significance of Rauschenbusch in the history of American Christianity and social reform, more than forty years elapsed before another Rauschenbusch biography appeared, this one by Paul M. Minus, titled *Walter Rauschenbusch, American Reformer* (New York: The MacMillan Company, 1988). More critical than Sharpe's book, Minus's work placed Rauschenbusch within the long tradition of Christian social reformers in the United States. Winthrop Hudson, in his introduction to

Not long after the United States entered the war on the side of the Allies in April 1917, the rumors about Rauschenbusch's loyalties turned malicious and his patriotism began to be called into question. While he initially attempted to ignore these charges of disloyalty to the American cause, Rauschenbusch finally succumbed to the strong desire to defend himself and sent Woelfkin a private letter, with the implicit understanding that it would be later forwarded to the press. In the letter, dated 1 May 1918, Rauschenbusch described his strong commitment to the United States and its founding principles. Far from being anti-American or anti-democratic, he wrote, "the American ideals of democracy have dominated my intellectual life. My literary and professional work for years has been characterized by the consistent effort to work out democratic interpretations of history, religion, and social life."[2] Anyone familiar with his writings about social justice and the Kingdom of God, Rauschenbusch claimed, would immediately recognize the many ways in which American ideas of freedom, justice, and equality had shaped his perspective. "I am, therefore, not merely an American in sentiment," he wrote, "but have taken our democratic principles very seriously and used my life to inculcate them here and

---

Walter Rauschenbusch: Selected Writings (New York: Paulist Press, 1984) 3-41, stressed that, despite his reputation as a social reformer, Rauschenbusch always understood himself primarily as an evangelist concerned with saving souls. Mennonite scholar Donovan E. Smucker has also done a good deal of work on Rauschenbusch through the years, most notably in *The Origins of Walter Rauschenbusch's Social Ethics* (Montreal: McGill-Queen's University Press, 1994). Because of the influence of his thought on Martin Luther King, Jr., Rauschenbusch received a fair measure of attention in scholarly journals during the 1950s and 1960s, and he remains a favorite subject for writers seeking to explore the social aspects of Christianity. See, for example, Harlan Beckley, *Passion for Justice: Retrieving the Legacies of Walter Rauschenbusch, John A. Ryan, and Reinhold Neibuhr* (Louisville KY: Westminster/John Knox Press, 1992) and William Ramsay, *Four Modern Prophets: Walter Rauschenbusch, Martin Luther King, Jr., Gustavo Gutierrez, and Rosemary Radford Reuther* (Atlanta: John Knox Press, 1986). Of the handful of dissertations dealing with Rauschenbusch, David Alan McClintock's "Walter Rauschenbusch: The Kingdom of God and the American Experience" (Ph.D. diss., Case Western Reserve University, 1976) deserves attention for its perceptive account of how the cultural assumptions of Christendom informed Rauschenbusch's theological approach to social reform.

[2] Sharpe, *Walter Rauschenbusch*, 386, quoting Rauschenbusch's letter to Cornelius Woelfkin.

abroad."[3] While obviously written in the spirit of patriotic self-defense, Rauschenbusch's comments to Woelfkin nonetheless suggested that he perceived a certain harmony between his understanding of Christian theology and the ideals of American democracy. The similarities indeed ran deep.

Rauschenbusch's self-conscious commitment to spreading the ideals of American democracy through his work should not be surprising, given the optimistic times in which he lived and wrote. In keeping with the progressive spirit of the early twentieth century, Rauschenbusch believed that God was not only moving history toward its consummation in a divine kingdom of freedom, justice, and equality, but that democracy represented God's chosen instrument for bringing about this new order of humanity. As the foremost democracy in the world, an idealized America offered a glimpse of what the future kingdom might look like.

While others shared his optimistic assessment of the United States, democracy, and the progressive trend of civilization, Rauschenbusch understood better than many of his contemporaries that this idealized America bore scant resemblance to the dreary reality of life in the nation's many urban tenement districts and working class neighborhoods, where the relentless pressures of poverty crushed dreams of better lives and slowly squeezed the hope out of defeated men and women. As a pastor in one of the poorest areas of New York City, he had witnessed the high toll that a capitalist economy extracted from those who labored under its disciplines of daily wages, uncertain employment, and unsafe work conditions. While the idle prospered, the exhausted often went hungry. When spent laborers had outlived their usefulness, their employers simply swept them aside and replaced them with younger, stronger workers.

The church, Rauschenbusch concluded, contributed to this problem, its individualistic interpretation of the gospel and its preoccupation with personal sin tending to stifle—if not completely suppress—any sense of Christian social responsibility. He set out, therefore, to awaken the collective conscience of America's churches not only to the problems of

---

[3]Ibid.

the poor but, more importantly, to the promise of God's Kingdom as well. Through his numerous books, countless articles in popular magazines and newspapers, and almost constant speaking engagements, in addition to his teaching responsibilities at Rochester Theological Seminary, Rauschenbusch became one of the most visible and respected proponents of the Christian "social gospel" during the first two decades of the twentieth century.

Rauschenbusch was also a Baptist. From a young age, he had absorbed the democratic ethos of Baptist theology and its emphasis on freedom and the equality of all people before God.[4] As Rauschenbusch grew older, these fundamental convictions gradually worked their way into his understanding of the New Testament and its relevance to the social crisis of the early 1900s. Expressed most persuasively in his final book, *A Theology for the Social Gospel* (1917), Rauschenbusch's conception of the Kingdom of God—the biblical image he used to describe God's ongoing, redemptive work in history—vividly illustrated his optimistic Baptist faith in democracy. The Kingdom, he declared, represented "the only true Democracy."[5] As democratic ideas and practices increasingly defined the world's political, economic, and social realities, Rauschenbusch confidently predicted, so the Kingdom of God would expand its borders and extend its influence over humanity.

Rauschenbusch's strong faith in democracy did not make him unique among the Baptists of his day. Neither did his commitment to the mission of America in the world. His compelling vision of the Kingdom of God as a blend of theological doctrine and American democratic ideals, however, catapulted him to national prominence during the first two decades of the twentieth century. "Our Baptist faith, like our

---

[4] In a series of five articles titled "Why I Am a Baptist" that appeared in the *Rochester Baptist Monthly* between November 1905 and March 1906, Rauschenbusch outlined his reasons for becoming (and remaining) Baptist. A recurrent theme in the articles is Rauschenbusch's appreciation of the spiritual freedom Baptist theology afforded the individual Christian and the democratic nature of Baptist congregational life. See Walter Rauschenbusch, "Why I Am a Baptist," *Rochester Baptist Monthly*, November 1905, 203; December 1905, 85-88; January 1906, 106-108; February 1906, 134-136; March 1906, 156-159.
[5] Walter Rauschenbusch, *A Theology for the Social Gospel* (New York: The MacMillan Company, 1917) 180.

American political constitution, is founded on great principles," he wrote in 1905, weaving the ideals of church and state together in a seamless garment of democracy.[6] Perhaps more than any other Baptist between 1900 and 1925, then, Rauschenbusch carried the assumptions of Baptist democracy beyond the confines of the Baptist world and into the greater American conversation.

***

Born in 1861, Walter Rauschenbusch was the first of August and Caroline Rauschenbusch's sons (and, overall, one of three Rauschenbusch children) to survive infancy. Following Walter's healthy arrival, August wrote to his brother in Germany to inform him of the good news and to share his hope that "God will make a Christian and a preacher out of [Walter], a Rauschenbusch and a man of deeds."[7] August himself provided a model for his son to follow.[8] Although raised as a Lutheran in Germany, August immigrated to the United States in 1846 and soon thereafter became convinced that believers' baptism represented the only truly biblical form of the practice. In May 1850 he was baptized as an adult in the Mississippi River and began serving as a Baptist missionary to German immigrants along the Missouri frontier.[9] Eventually, August

---

[6] Walter Rauschenbusch, "Why I Am a Baptist," *The Rochester Baptist Monthly*, December 1905, 88.

[7] Minus, *Walter Rauschenbusch*, 2.

[8] Several scholars have looked to Rauschenbusch's childhood and his understanding of family dynamics for insight into his theological approach to social issues. One of them, Steven Sundquist, argues that Rauschenbusch's turbulent family life created a formative lens that decisively shaped his theology and compelled him to try and bring peace and community out of turmoil and conflict. See Sundquist, "The Kingdom of God and the Theological Ethics of Walter Rauschenbusch," *American Baptist Quarterly* 22 (March 2003): 77-98. Another, Susan Curtis, examines the ways in which Rauschenbusch's idea of God as a loving Father affected (or, perhaps, reflected) his own conception of what a good father should be like. Rauchenbusch, Curtis writes, "tried to become the ideal father about which he had written in his theology—an indulgent, loving companion rather than a wrathful judge" (112). See Curtis, *A Consuming Faith: The Social Gospel and Modern American Culture* (Baltimore: The Johns Hopkins University Press, 1991) 101-114. A third study dealing, in part, with Rauschenbusch and his conceptions of the ideal family is Janet Fishburn, *The Fatherhood of God and the Victorian Family* (Philadelphia: Fortress Press, 1981).

[9] Carl Schneider considers August Rauschenbusch's conversion to the Baptist faith to be evidence of his increasing Americanization. It was culture and not theology, Schneider argues, that inspired Rauschenbusch to abandon his Lutheran heritage. Aside from his

settled in Rochester, New York, where he taught German at the Rochester Theological Seminary.

Walter Rauschenbusch spent four years in Germany as a child and later returned after high school for a year of study at a private secondary academy in Westphalia noted for its rigorous humanities program and conservative religious atmosphere.[10] Upon completion of his course of study in Germany, Rauschenbusch enrolled at the University of Rochester in July 1883, while at the same time taking classes at the neighboring Rochester Theological Seminary. In 1884, he received his bachelor's degree from the university. A year later, he graduated from the seminary's German Department, and in 1886, he finished his theological training in the English Department of the seminary. Upon graduation, Rauschenbusch had planned for a career as a missionary in India for the American Baptist Missionary Society, but one of his Old Testament professors at the Rochester seminary expressed his concern over Rauschenbusch's liberal interpretations of Scripture and effectively derailed his appointment.[11]

---

adherence to the practice of believers' baptism, Rauschenbusch's basic theological outlook remained consistent with the Augsburg Confession after his conversion. The Baptist interpretation of the Christian faith, however, seemed to him more consistent with the promises of freedom and emancipation embodied in the American democratic system. Rauschenbusch became Baptist, in other words, because Baptists were more "American" than Lutherans. See Schneider, "The Americanization of Karl August Rauschenbusch, 1816-1899," *Church History* 24 (1955): 3-14. Ramsay, for one, traces Walter Rauschenbusch's lifelong concern for the plight of immigrants to his close identification with them through his father's experience. See Ramsay, 10-11.

[10] Minus, *Walter Rauschenbusch*, 19-22. While in Germany, the multi-lingual Rauschenbusch often wrote letters home to his family in various languages, sometimes using several in the course of a single correspondence. He was fluent in English, German, and French and could read and write proficiently in Greek and Hebrew. Rauschenbusch's several years in Germany, first as a child and later as a teen, not only exposed him to a world beyond the United States, but also nurtured in him a genuine love for the cultural and intellectual heritage of his parents' homeland. Years later, the outbreak of World War I would test Rauschenbusch's divided loyalties in an agonizing fashion.

[11] G. Bromley Oxnam, *Personalities in Social Reform* (New York: Abingdon-Cokesbury Press, 1950) 58. See also Sharpe, *Walter Rauschenbusch*, 58. Referring to the work of German theologian Albrecht Ritschl in the nineteenth century, Williston Walker gave a helpful definition of Protestant liberalism as "a new apologetic synthesis between Christian faith and the new knowledge contributed by scientific and historical scholarship." See Walker, *A*

While in seminary planning for a career in missions, Rauschenbusch had also begun to explore the call of pastoral ministry. He spent the summers of 1884 and 1885 in Louisville, Kentucky, as the supply preacher for a small German Baptist church. The experience, he wrote to friends at the time, deeply impressed him. Rauschenbusch's seminary studies exposed him to such liberal Protestant thinkers as Horace Bushnell and Albrecht Ritschl, who nicely complemented his limited pastoral training in Kentucky by emphasizing to him the priority of "right living" over "right thinking" for those who would be disciples of Jesus.[12] These ethical considerations helped determine Rauschenbusch's decision to enter the ministry. "Very soon the idea came to me that I ought to be a preacher, and help save souls," he told an audience at the Cleveland Y.M.C.A. in 1913. "I wanted to go out as a foreign missionary—I wanted to do hard work for God. Indeed, one of the great thoughts that came upon me was that I ought to follow Jesus Christ in my personal life, and live over again his life, and die over again his death. I felt that every Christian ought in some way or other participate in the dying of the Lord Jesus Christ, and in that way help to redeem humanity."[13] This understanding of Christian discipleship, Rauschenbusch said, became the guiding vision for his subsequent life and ministry. His first pastorate served as the proving grounds for that vision.

In June 1886, the Second German Baptist Church in New York City called Rauschenbusch as its pastor. The position offered a distinct challenge for the recent seminary graduate. Located on the border of the rough Hell's Kitchen neighborhood, notorious for both its crime and poverty, the Second German Baptist Church was a congregation of 125 members, most of whom were German-speaking immigrants who lived

---

History of the Christian Church, 4th ed. (New York: Charles Scribner's Sons, 1985) 637. Theologian H. Richard Niebuhr offered a more caustic assessment of theological liberalism's central message: "A God without wrath brought men without sin into a kingdom without judgment through the ministrations of Christ without a cross." See Niebuhr, *The Kingdom of God in America* (Chicago: Willett, Clark, and Company, 1937) 193.

[12] For a detailed account of Rauschenbusch's seminary experience, see Minus, 35-48.

[13] Walter Rauschenbusch, "The Kingdom of God," in *The Social Gospel in America*, ed. Robert T. Handy (New York: Oxford University Press, 1966) 265.

in the crowded tenement districts nearby.[14] Ministering among this industrious, but nevertheless poor, congregation, Rauschenbusch encountered for the first time the dismal, draconian aspects of working class life in America. He did not come to the Second German Baptist Church as a social radical in any sense of the word, but his pastoral ministry with decent, hard working men and women trapped by forces beyond their control in the miserable slums of New York proved to be transformative.[15]

The harsh reality of urban life—indeed, the very fact of urban life itself—was still a relatively new phenomenon in the United States during these turn-of-the-century years. Simply put, the country was in the midst of a seismic demographic shift, with Americans moving in droves from the farms to the cities while enormous waves of immigrants—18.5 million of them between 1900 and 1930, more than the total for the previous eighty years combined—added even more pressure to these already swollen metropolitan areas.[16] In the first three decades of the twentieth century, the number of Americans living in cities more than doubled; the number of rural residents, meanwhile, grew only 17 percent during that same time span. The 1920 census reported that, for the first time in the country's history, more Americans lived in cities than in small towns and on farms.[17]

---

[14] Paul L. Higgins, *Preachers of Power: Henry Ward Beecher, Phillips Brooks, and Walter Rauschenbusch* (New York: Vantage Press, 1950) 61. See also Minus, *Walter Rauschenbusch*, 49ff. Rauschenbusch was ordained to the ministry several months after the Second German Baptist Church called him to be its pastor. Minus recalls the grave reservations both of Rauschenbusch's parents expressed about their son's ordination, fearing that he was already too much of a theological liberal to make a responsible Baptist preacher. Both parents eventually supported their son's ordination. See Minus, *Walter Rauschenbusch*, 53.

[15] Max L. Stackhouse, "The Formation of a Prophet: Reflections on the Early Sermons of Walter Rauschenbusch," *Andover Newton Quarterly* 9 (January 1969): 159. See also Winthrop S. Hudson, "Walter Rauschenbusch and the New Evangelism," *Religion in Life* 30 (1961): 414; and Sharpe, *Walter Rauschenbusch*, 195ff.

[16] Ahlstrom, *A Religious History of the American People*, 749-750.

[17] U. S. Bureau of the Census, *Historical Statistics of the United States: Colonial Times to 1970*, pt. 1 (Washington, D.C., 1975) 11. According to the 1900 United States census, there were 30,160,000 Americans living in urban areas (defined as cities with 2,500 or more residents) compared with 45,835,000 living in rural areas. By the 1930 census, those

The pronounced effect of this demographic development upon the national character cannot be understated. "One of the keys to the American mind at the end of the old century and the beginning of the new was that American cities were filling up in very considerable part with small-town or rural people," wrote historian Richard Hofstadter. "The whole cast of American thinking in this period was deeply affected by the ... phenomenon of urban life, its crowding, poverty, crime, corruption; impersonality and ethnic chaos." To those Americans whose memories stretched back to the (real or imagined) days of small-town decency and simplicity, the bustling cities represented a strange threat to civilization itself.[18] Adding to this strangeness was the sheer diversity of languages, cultures, and religious practices sprinkled throughout America's cities as the new immigrants (who tended to be Roman Catholic, Orthodox, or Jewish) found jobs and established their own ethnic residential enclaves. Basic cultural assumptions from America's past—the experience of belonging to a local community, the emotional and economic security of extended family networks, the implicit understandings that facilitated personal and business relationships, the shared sense of moral decency—quickly evaporated in the heat generated by urban factories and teeming tenement apartment buildings. With this move to the cities came countless new problems and the need for creative new solutions.

As Rauschenbusch discovered soon enough, the churches were not immune from these new realities, and he frequently recalled how his encounters with the raw injustices and the uniformly miserable living conditions in the city determined the trajectory of his ministry. Referring to his burgeoning social conscience as a young pastor, Rauschenbusch remembered that "it came through personal contact with poverty, and when I saw how men toiled all their life long, hard, toilsome lives, and how at the end had almost nothing to show for it; how strong men begged for work and could not get it in hard times; how little children

---

numbers had grown to 68,955,000 and 53,820,000, respectively. The 1920 census showed 54,158,000 Americans living in urban environments and 51,553,000 in rural areas.

[18] Richard Hofstadter, *The Age of Reform: From Bryan to FDR* (New York: Vintage Books, 1955) 176. For a similar account of the rise of the city from the perspective of American religion, see Ahlstrom, *A Religious History of the American People*, 735ff.

died—oh, the children's funerals! They gripped my heart—that was one of the things I always went away thinking about: Why did the children have to die?"[19]

The church's apparent indifference to the suffering multitudes of the city particularly distressed Rauschenbusch.[20] In 1892, as a step toward making their churches more responsive to the obvious needs surrounding them, Rauschenbusch and a handful of other likeminded Baptist ministers formed the Brotherhood of the Kingdom, a fellowship for discussing the day's social issues in a theological context. The Brotherhood also published a short-lived newspaper, *For the Right*, to serve as a voice for the working class and a forum for their ideas.[21] Helping the church realize its responsibility for the most vulnerable members of society soon became the dominant theme of Rauschenbusch's ministry. At the same time, however, a gradual loss of hearing made it increaseingly difficult for him to continue serving as pastor to his own church. No longer able to hear his parishioners, Rauschenbusch left the Second German Baptist Church in 1897 and accepted a position in the German Department at Rochester Theological Seminary, with additional teaching duties in the areas of New Testament and politics.[22] Five years later, he

---

[19] Rauschenbusch, "The Kingdom of God," 265-266. In addition to his pastoral experiences, Rauschenbusch also attributed his social awakening to the agitation of Henry George, who ran for mayor of New York in 1886 on the issues of a redistributive "single tax" and public programs for care of the needy. See, for example, his tribute to George in *Christianizing the Social Order* (New York: MacMillan and Company, 1915) 394. Klaus Juergen Jaehn provides a very thorough study of Rauschenbusch between 1886 and 1891, the period in which his social thought crystallized. See Jaehn, "Formation of Walter Rauschenbusch's Social Conscience as Reflected in His Early Life and Writings," *Foundations* 16 (1973): 294-326; 17 (1974): 68-85.

[20] Ramsay, *Four Modern Prophets*, 12-13.

[21] For a good history of the Brotherhood and its influence upon Rauschenbusch, see Minus, *Walter Rauschenbusch*, 83ff.

[22] Ibid., 141ff. As a lecturer, Rauschenbusch's deafness was much less of a factor than it had been in the church. Gradually he became proficient at reading lips and was able to communicate effectively with students and colleagues. Minus notes that Rauschenbusch's social activism was already a concern to the trustees of the seminary, who hesitated to approve his appointment. Only after Rauschenbusch supplied them with an article in which he had compared the pros and cons of socialism (presumably emphasizing the latter) did the board deem him a satisfactory candidate. See Minus, 100. Throughout his career, Rauschenbusch nimbly walked the line separating "radical" politics from

became the seminary's professor of church history, a post he held until his death.

Rauschenbusch's understanding of history profoundly influenced his approach to theology and social reform. According to the German theologian Albrecht Ritschl, Christianity represented "the perfected spiritual and moral religion," whose ultimate end rested in the establishment of the Kingdom of God, which Ritschl defined as "the moral unification of the human race, through action prompted by universal love to our neighbor."[23] History, in other words, served as the gradual process by which God educated humanity in the ways of the Kingdom, always progressing toward the Christian ideal of morality.[24] Along with other Baptist intellectuals of his day, such as Shailer Mathews and Gerald Birney Smith of the University of Chicago, Rauschenbusch endorsed this progressive understanding of history and believed himself to be living at a decisive time in the development of humanity toward the Kingdom ideal.

At Rochester, removed from the immediate problems of the city, Rauschenbusch the church historian began to make theological sense out of his passion for social justice, building upon the ideas he had first shared with the Brotherhood years earlier and placing them in the context of the Kingdom of God ideal. His first book, *Christianity and the Social Crisis*, created a sensation upon its publication in 1907 and catapulted Rauschenbusch to national prominence as an advocate of what was increasingly known in the United States as the "social gospel."[25] In *Christianity and the Social Crisis*, Rauschenbusch argued that

---

mainstream ideas. He could openly proclaim himself a socialist in *For the Right*, yet several years later also appear on the speaker's platform at the 1900 Republican National Convention. See McClintock, 57-58.

[23] Albrecht Ritschl, *The Christian Doctrine of Justification and Reconciliation*, ed. H. R. Mackintosh and A. B. Macauley (Edinburgh: T. & T. Clark, 1900) 10, 280. William Hutchinson provides a good summary of Ritschl's influence on Protestant liberalism in the United States in *The Modernist Impulse in American Protestantism* (Durham NC: Duke University Press, 1992) 122-132.

[24] Ibid., 304ff.

[25] Rauschenbusch knew that his book had very radical implications, which he feared could end up costing him his job. See Minus, 158. The book, despite its popular success, received mixed reviews from conservative Baptists and academic proponents of the Social

a complete understanding of the Christian faith must contain a social dimension that anticipated the redemption of all human relationships and institutions. The gospel of Jesus Christ, he maintained, included more than just the message and the means of individual salvation. Instead, it announced the Kingdom of God, an entirely new social order foretold by the Old Testament prophets, embodied in the life and ministry of Jesus, and characterized by peace, justice, and equality for all humanity. The Kingdom, he declared, "is not a matter of getting individuals into heaven, but of transforming the life on earth into the harmony of heaven."[26] In the preface to the book, Rauchenbusch acknowledged his debt to his former congregation in New York City for their influence in shaping his social conscience. "If this book in some far off way helps to ease the pressure that bears down on them and increases the forces that bear them up," he wrote, "I shall meet the Master of my life with better confidence."[27] Following upon the great success of *Christianity and the Social Crisis*, Rauschenbusch continued to articulate his vision of the Kingdom of God through a steady stream of books and articles over the next ten years, most notably *Christianizing the Social Order* (1912) and *A Theology for the Social Gospel*, calling America's

---

Gospel. A Cincinnati Baptist newspaper called Rauschenbusch "a socialist of the German school," while a prominent New York Baptist published a forty-two page pamphlet refuting the book's arguments and imploring believers to reject it as false doctrine. See Minus, 162-163. One reviewer in the Baptist *Standard*, which faithfully reflected the views of Baptists at the University of Chicago, called Rauschenbusch's work "rhetorical," and lacking in "scientific" substance. See the *Standard*, 18 May 1907, 15. It should be noted, however, that the dean of Chicago's divinity school was Shailer Mathews, whose understanding of social Christianity diverged from that of Rauschenbusch. For two interesting comparisons between the respective approaches of Rauschenbusch and Mathews to the Social Gospel, see Roger Haight, "The Mission of the Church in the Theology of the Social Gospel," *Theological Studies* 49 (1988): 477-497; and Winthrop S. Hudson, "Walter Rauschenbusch and the New Evangelism," *Religion in Life* 30 (1961): 412-430.

[26] Walter Rauschenbusch, *Christianity and the Social Crisis* (New York: MacMillan and Company, 1907) 65.

[27] Ibid., xxxviii.

Christian community to a deeper understanding of evangelism, one that ministered to the physical, as well as the spiritual, needs of the world.[28]

After nearly two decades as a scholar, Rauschenbusch's health had begun to fail by the end of 1917. He managed to finish *A Theology for the Social Gospel*, based on the prestigious Taylor Lectures he delivered at Yale in 1916, but he was largely a spent man. The ongoing war in Europe continued to weigh heavily upon his soul, a burden that only grew heavier as the United States entered the conflict in April. Rauschenbusch's German heritage, especially when combined with his reputation as both a socialist reformer and theological liberal, made him a tempting target for the criticism of political and religious conservatives.[29] While steadfastly maintaining both his loyalty to the United States and his lifelong support of democracy, Rauschenbusch's growing opposition to the war on the grounds of Christian pacifism further alienated him from his fellow Americans consumed with patriotic fervor.[30] "It was hard enough to combine Christianity and

---

[28] In "Walter Rauschenbusch and the New Evangelism," Winthrop Hudson reminds readers that, despite his well-deserved reputation as a social prophet and advocate of reform, Rauschenbusch understood himself primarily as a preacher called by God to save souls. Rauschenbusch, writes Hudson, "was an evangelist in the tradition of the great revivalists, seeking to win men to Christ and to put them to work in the interests of his kingdom" (412). See also Smucker, 23. For a good examination of Rauschenbusch's philosophical approach to social reform, see Gary Scott Smith, "To Reconstruct the World: Walter Rauschenbusch and Social Change," *Fides et Historia* 23 (1991): 40-63.

[29] Minus, 189-190. At the same time, as George Marsden observes, theological liberals roundly condemned conservative premillennialists of disloyalty for their refusal to support the American war effort. Liberals such as Shailer Mathews and Shirley Case Jackson of the University of Chicago understood the war as part of a larger struggle for the survival of democratic civilization. Before World War I, many premillennialists advocated an anti-political position that placed little confidence in the human ability to solve intractable problems of the world. After the war, their attitude would change dramatically. See Marsden, *Fundamentalism and American Culture: The Shaping of Twentieth Century Evangelicalism, 1870-1925* (New York: Oxford University Press, 1980) 143ff.

[30] Ibid., 177-184; also Sharpe, 382. Rauschenbusch, writes Minus, urged American Christians to resist efforts to enlist their religion in support of the war. Even so, insists Sharpe, Rauschenbusch never did become an absolute pacifist. Rauschenbusch's Baptist contemporaries E. Y. Mullins and George Truett took a very different approach to the war, both of them justifying it as a regrettable, but ultimately necessary, step toward accomplishing God's will that autocracy should be defeated.

capitalistic business," he lamented in *May 1917*. "Now we are asked to combine Christianity and war."[31] Once confident about the progressive unfolding of the divine will for humanity through the establishment of the Kingdom of God on earth, the ailing Rauschenbusch could only watch and despair as the belligerent—and, for the most part, self-consciously Christian—kingdoms of the world blasted away at one another on the devastated plains of Europe. On 25 July 1918, Rauschenbusch died in Rochester after a long, torturous battle with stomach cancer.

***

The melancholy that surrounded Rauschenbusch's final days provided an ill-fitting coda to a life and ministry largely driven by an inspired optimism. It was an optimism grounded in his strong faith that God was active in the world, accomplishing his will, and gradually establishing His kingdom of righteousness in the midst of a redeemed humanity. It was an optimism predicated on the belief that, as Christianity's influence spread beyond the exclusively "religious" sphere of life, Jesus' teachings of justice and equality for all people would transform the values of American society accordingly. It was, finally, an optimism fueled by the conviction that America's churches collectively represented a tremendous, untapped resource for effecting positive social change. If faithful Christians sitting in the pews on Sunday morning could be inspired to translate their pious sentiments into bold programs of action, Rauschenbusch believed, then the chronic problems of the city—poverty, crime, vice, disease, and more—could be eliminated. In the first decades of the twentieth century, many American Christians shared Rauschensbusch's optimism. Indeed, while he was perhaps the greatest proponent of a socially oriented Christianity, Rauschenbusch was certainly not alone in his advocacy. He represented, rather, one voice among many proclaiming the social gospel.

As a movement—or, rather, a surging wave of religious idealism—the social gospel flourished roughly between 1880 and 1920 during the

---

[31] Minus, *Walter Rauschenbusch*, 182.

"Progressive Era" of great reforming enthusiasm in the United States.[32] The spirit of the times, wrote historian Arthur Link, "manifested itself in an organized way mainly in the cities—in efforts to make the churches more responsive to social and economic needs, in campaigns to clean up the slums and protect the weak and helpless, and in spasmodic drives to wrest control of city governments from grafters often allied with vested economic interests."[33] For journalist Mark Sullivan, writing in the ebb tide of Progressive enthusiasm, the reform efforts of the day were "characterized by concern for the fortunes of fellowmen, a desire to make the world better, an awakening to the possibility of a finer way of life, a fervor of many souls to bring in a juster, more lovely era."[34] Advocates of the social gospel were sympathetic to the work of Progressive reformers—they shared many of the same passions and concerns—but they were parallel, not concerted, movements.

The Progressives, who tended to come from the bourgeois business and professional classes of the large cities, believed fervently in the right of individuals to chart their own courses in life, free from the political and economic machinations of corrupt leaders who would exploit for profit the relatively weak positions of those under their influence. They

---

[32] The standard scholarly account of the social gospel is still Charles Howard Hopkins, *The Rise of the Social Gospel in American Protestantism, 1865-1915* (New Haven CT: Yale University Press, 1940). There are also several excellent, concise overviews of the Social Gospel movement. Among these are Robert Handy's introduction to his *The Social Gospel in America, 1870-1920*, 3-16; and Ahlstrom, 785-809. Handy also effectively places the social gospel movement in the context of evangelical Protestant triumphalism in *Christian America: Protestant Hopes and Historical Realities* (New York: Oxford University Press, 1984) 134-146.

[33] Arthur S. Link, *Woodrow Wilson and the Progressive Era, 1900-1917* (New York: Harper, 1954) 1-2. The two traditional scholarly positions on the Progressives have been best articulated by Richard Hofstadter and Robert Wiebe. In *The Age of Reform*, Hofstadter argues that the Progressive movement was led by established bourgeois professionals and businessmen trying to retain their elevated status in society while acting as advocates for "the people" out of a sense of *noblesse oblige*. Wiebe disagrees, claiming in *The Search for Order, 1877-1920* (New York: Hill and Wang, 1967) that the Progressives were, in fact, representatives of a "new middle class" of forward-looking pragmatists seeking structure in the midst of the chaos caused by industrialization. For a brief, but helpful, scholarly treatment of the Progressive Era, see Arthur Link and Richard McCormick, *Progressivism* (Wheeling IL: Harlan Davidson, Inc., 1983).

[34] Mark Sullivan, *Our Times*, 122.

intuitively sensed that the interests of money, big business, and the intellectual elite had somehow conspired to keep real power away from the average American.[35] Accordingly, then, it was their duty to right these wrongs by exposing corruption and alleviating the unfairly harsh conditions of modern life. The Progressive Era indeed witnessed a number of significant reforms: the Hepburn Act (1906) giving the International Commerce Commission the power to set maximum railroad shipping rates, the Meat Inspection Act (1906), the Pure Food and Drug Act (1906), and many other pieces of legislation aimed at addressing fair labor and business practices, housing issues, and political corruption. Perhaps most importantly in terms of its effect on the American mindset, however, was the Progressive belief in democracy itself. As one historian noted, during the Progressive Era, "the very principles of democratic government became almost ends in themselves."[36]

The social gospel movement—with its emphasis on the fair distribution of wealth, decent housing, and the eradication of ignorance, all in the name of Jesus Christ—articulated this secular Progressive spirit in a distinctively Christian fashion. According to historian Charles Howard Hopkins, the primary assumption of the social gospel—indeed the very intellectual soul of the movement—was "a belief in an indwelling God, [who was] working out his purposes in the world" through the gradual establishment of His kingdom.[37] Along these lines, then, proponents of the social gospel anticipated that, through the reform efforts of Christians working together for the common good, the Kingdom of God would soon become a reality, bringing with it social harmony and the elimination of the worst of social injustices.[38] This fervent optimism cast a decidedly utopian light upon the movement, infusing it with an electric

---

[35] George E. Mowry, *The Era of Theodore Roosevelt, 1900-1912* (New York: Harper, 1958) 52.

[36] Ibid.

[37] Hopkins, 320. Ahlstrom notes that, while the social gospel held some ideas in common with liberal Protestant theology, the two must not be confused. Liberalism flourished in socially conservative classes where the goals of the social gospel were anathema. Social gospelers were usually theological liberals, writes Ahlstrom, but the statement cannot be reversed. See Ahlstrom, 788.

[38] Handy, *The Social Gospel in America*, 10.

sense of urgency and spiritual crisis. The problems of the city demanded immediate action and could no longer be ignored by those who claimed to be disciples of Jesus. Implicit in the coming of God's Kingdom was an ongoing imperative to decide between the privileged or the poor, between the status quo or reform, between evil or good—or, in the provocative spirit of so much social gospel preaching, between Pontius Pilate or Jesus Christ. Social gospelers constantly reminded those who would listen that lives, both temporal and eternal, hung in the balance of each decision.

In an important way, the social gospel movement also drew inspiration from one of the most fundamental of all American assumptions: the idea that the United States had a unique mission to serve as a model of the "Christian nation." Social gospel advocates were "in many respects representative of their time and operated largely within the patterns of the quest for a Protestant America," historian Robert Handy has noted. "The new social Christianity had a vision of a vastly better human society, but it was essentially the old vision of a religious nation socialized."[39] By deliberately applying the moral teachings of Jesus beyond the churches to all areas of society, champions of the social gospel thought of themselves as participants in the great struggle to preserve Christian civilization in the United States from the corrosive influence of sin at work in the nation's economic, political, and legal institutions. In their efforts to save American Christendom, the social gospelers rejected the idea that the state should, in any formal or legal sense, become an official arm of the church (or vice versa). They did, however, consider Christianity to be indispensible to the successful development of democracy—so much so that they tended to describe the spread of democratic ways as 'Christianization.'"[40] For apostles of the social gospel, the establishment of the Kingdom of God, when it finally

---

[39] Handy, *Christian America*, 139-140.
[40] Ibid., 144. According to theologian H. Richard Niebuhr, to be reconciled to God in the early 1900s "meant to be reconciled to the established customs of a more or less christianized society. As the Christian church became the protector of the social mores, so its revivals tended to become instruments for enforcing the prevailing standards." See *The Kingdom of God in America*, 181.

arrived in full, would truly represent a glorious triumph of democracy, with America leading the way for the rest of the world.

***

The tendency to conflate the values of democracy with those of Christianity, an inclination that reflected the social gospel movement's vision of America as a Christian nation, exerted a pronounced influence upon Walter Rauschenbusch, the movement's most visible champion.[41] "Perhaps these nineteen centuries of Christian influence have been a long preliminary stage of growth, and now the flower and the fruit are almost here," he mused near the end of *Christianity and the Social Crisis*. "If at this juncture we can rally sufficient religious faith and moral strength to snap the bonds of evil and turn the present unparalleled resources of humanity to the harmonious development of a true social life, the generations yet unborn will mark this as that great day of the Lord for which the ages waited."[42] A truly Christian society, however, could only take shape around democratic principles. "Christianizing the social order," Rauschenbusch argued in *Christianizing the Social Order*, "means bringing it into harmony with the ethical convictions which we identify with Christ," or, in other words, democracy in its various

---

[41] At stake in the present contest between concentrated wealth on the one hand and common good on the other, he warned in *Christianity and the Social Crisis*, was the future of Christian civilization itself. History demonstrated that great injustice, not great wealth, caused empires to collapse, and Rauschenbusch believed that the economic inequalities of American society had now brought the United States to the brink of disaster. The continued survival of Christendom, he counseled, "will depend almost wholly on the moral forces which the Christian nations can bring to the fighting line against wrong, and the fighting energy of those moral forces will depend on the degree to which they are inspired by religious faith and enthusiasm. It is either a revival of social religion or the deluge" (286). See McClintock for an excellent study of Rauschenbusch's commitment to the preservation and advancement of Christendom. For another example of a prominent Baptist who preached the social gospel's vision of a "Christian civilization," see Samuel Zane Batten, *The Christian State: The State, Democracy, and Christianity* (Philadelphia: The Griffith and Rowland Press, 1909).

[42] Rauschenbusch, *Christianity and the Social Crisis*, 422. Max Stackhouse explores the dichotomy between the "already" and "not yet" aspects of the Kingdom as described by Rauschenbusch in "The Continuing Importance of Walter Rauschenbusch," in *The Righteousness of the Kingdom*, ed. Max L. Stackhouse (Nashville TN: Abingdon Press, 1968) 13-59.

forms.[43] Time and again throughout his career, he returned to this theme in his work.

Rauschenbusch was not alone among Baptist intellectuals of his day in making this connection between democracy and Christianity. Just as Ritschl had described Christianity as the latest stage of religious development toward the Kingdom of God, the University of Chicago's Gerald Birney Smith considered democracy to be the latest stage in humanity's progressive advancement away from submissive obedience to authority and toward individual freedom and self-determination.[44] Christian faith and the democratic spirit, he believed, thus complemented and mutually reinforced one another; where one flourished, so did the other. Shailer Mathews, one of Smith's colleagues at Chicago, agreed. "In the struggle for democracy in which we are now involved," wrote Mathews in 1917 during World War I, "we are not combating but cooperating with the prevailing tendency of social evolution."[45] Moreover, he continued, the call of democracy must ultimately be understood as "an echo of the louder call to loyalty to the fundamental principles of life embodied in the religion of Jesus."[46]

For Rauschenbusch, the intimate relationship between democracy and Christianity reached back to the earliest recorded experiences of Israel in the Old Testament. He began his seminal work, *Christianity and the Social Crisis*, with a lengthy description of what he saw as a parallel between the political life of the twelve tribes of Israel and that of the early American republic. Both Israel and the United States, he claimed, were founded as democratic societies with a basic sense of social equality and fairness. Furthermore, both the Israelite and American peoples were "equipped with a kind of ingrained, constitutional taste for democracy which dies hard."[47] In time, however, Israel drifted away from its old egalitarian practices, thus prompting the Old Testament prophets and,

---

[43] Rauschenbusch, *Christianizing the Social Order*, 125.
[44] See Gerald Birney Smith, *Social Idealism and the Changing Theology* (New York: The Macmillan Company, 1913) 205ff.
[45] Shailer Mathews, *The Spiritual Interpretation of History* (Cambridge MA: Harvard University Press, 1917) 208.
[46] Ibid.
[47] Rauschenbusch, *Christianity and the Social Crisis*, 15.

later, Jesus to call Israel back to its original, democratic ways of fraternal love and ethical conduct.[48] Likewise, the church, after a promising beginning as a democratic community rooted in mutual goodwill and service, had become hierarchical and exclusive in nature.[49] Rauschenbusch perceived the same drift away from pure democracy happening in the United States, and he called upon the nation to consider the continued relevance of Jesus' democratic teachings in modern America.

The tragic social consequences of this drift away from egalitarian democracy—along with the promise of its impending restoration, as described in Jesus' teachings about the Kingdom of God—served as the driving force behind both *Christianity and the Social Crisis* and *Christianizing the Social Order*, in which Rauschenbusch further developed his ideas about democracy and the Kingdom. He fervently believed that finally, after centuries of domination by the priestly and aristocratic classes, the church was beginning to recover its original democratic voice at a critical juncture in history. "We are standing at the turning of the ways. We are actors in a great historical drama," Rauschenbusch wrote in Christianity and the Social Crisis. "It rests upon us to decide if a new era is to dawn in the transformation of the world into the kingdom of God, or if the Western civilization is to descend to the graveyard of dead civilizations and God will have to try once more."[50]

In 1907, the year *Christianity and the Social Crisis* was published, Rauschenbusch explored the organic connection between the future of Western civilization and the promise of the Kingdom of God in an article titled, appropriately enough, "What is a Christian Nation?" As an extended answer to that question, Rauschenbusch suggested six characteristics that distinguished a nation as "Christian." A Christian nation, he wrote, is one that: showed mercy in helping the weak; dealt with lawbreakers redemptively, not punitively; exerted "an educational and bracing influence on the individual by its common industrial and

---

[48] Ibid., 53.
[49] Ibid., 143ff.
[50] Ibid., 210.

political life"; valued people above property and placed a premium on spiritual pursuits; based its community life on "the principle of love and solidarity, equality and service"; and was thoroughly saturated with "a consciousness of God in its national outlook on past, present, and future.[51]

Specific truth claims about the divinity, or even the person, of Jesus Christ did not factor into Rauschenbusch's definition of a Christian nation. Instead, as he later noted in *Christianizing the Social Order*, many of the most basic social organizations in American life had already been "christianized" through the adoption of more democratic practices and attitudes. The family had become christianized as fathers acted less despotically and more lovingly toward their wives and children. "Based on equal rights, bound together by love and respect for individuality, governed under the law of mutual helpfulness," he wrote, "the family today furnishes the natural habitation for a Christian life and fellowship."[52] Likewise, the church had become more Christian as it had become more democratic in organization and temperament.[53] Thanks to the public schools, education, once reserved only for the wealthy classes, had "passed through a regenerating process. As with the family and the Church, the line of progress ran from tyranny to freedom, from aristocratic privilege to democracy of opportunity, from self-seeking to the enthusiasm of service."[54] Referring specifically to the Christian character of the American political system, meanwhile, Rauschenbusch conceded that "democracy is not equivalent to Christianity, *but in politics democracy is the expression and method of the Christian spirit*. It has made the most permanent achievements in the younger communities of the Anglo-Saxon group, but it is making headway throughout the world, and is the conquering tendency in modern life."[55] Democracy's belief in human dignity and worth, its commitment to the rights of the poor and helpless, and its "fighting courage bred by bold religion" all represented essential

---

[51] Walter Rauschenbusch, "What is a Christian Nation?" *The Standard*, 23 February 1907, 6.
[52] Rauschenbusch, *Christianizing the Social Order*, 133.
[53] Ibid., 141-142.
[54] Ibid., 147.
[55] Ibid., 153. Emphasis added.

elements in the struggle to Christianize American life, claimed Rauschenbusch.[56]

The only aspect of American society that remained to be christianized, he believed, was the economic realm of life.[57] Accomplishing this task, however, would prove a daunting challenge. Rauschenbusch knew this to be the case and directed his most blistering criticism toward the deeply entrenched powers that governed the nation's business interests. In his *Prayers of the Social Awakening* (1910), for example, he offered scathing prayers for judgment "Against the Servants of Mammon" who "grind down the strength of the workers by merciless toil and fling them aside when they are mangled and worn; who rackrent the poor and make dear the space and air which thou hast made free; who paralyze the hand of justice by corruption and blind the eyes of the people by lies."[58] Much more pastoral, however, were his prayers "For Men in Business" who daily faced the temptations of unearned wealth and excessive self-interest. "Grant them far-sighted patriotism to subordinate their profits to the public weal," Rauschenbusch wrote, "and a steadfast determination to transform the disorder of the present into the nobler and freer harmony of the future."[59]

To this end, Rauschenbusch devoted most of *Christianizing the Social Order* to exploring what a christianized economic life in the United States might look like. It would be, a society he maintained "in which all unearned incomes were stopped, in which men had the right to a living as they now have the right to life, and in which the chances of prosperity and distinction were open to all on fairly equal terms."[60] A christianized economic life, in other words, would be "an order in which justice and economic democracy prevailed."[61] Again, for Rauschenbusch, the promise of a truly Christian society depended upon the successful spread of democracy, which he described as "a spiritual hope and a

---

[56] Ibid., 154-155.
[57] Ibid., 156.
[58] Walter Rauschenbusch, *Prayers of the Social Awakening* (Boston: Pilgrim Press, 1910) 101-102.
[59] Ibid., 63-64.
[60] Rauschenbusch, *Christianizing the Social Order*, 365.
[61] Ibid.

religious force. It stands for the sanitation of our moral relationships and for the development of the human soul in freedom and self-control."[62] Where the democratic spirit reigned, Rauschenbusch fervently believed, Christianity would triumph, for "Democracy is the archangel whom God has sent to set his blazing foot on these icebergs of human pride and melt them down."[63]

Consider Rauschenbusch's prayer for public officials in *Prayers of the Social Awakening*. "We bless thee [God] that the new spirit of democracy has touched even the kings of the earth. We rejoice that by the free institutions of our country the tyrannous instincts of the strong may be curbed and turned to the patriotic service of the commonwealth," he wrote. "Give our leaders a new vision of the possible future of our country and set their hearts on fire with large resolves. Raise up a new generation of public men, who will have the faith and daring of the Kingdom of God in their hearts, *and who will enlist for life in a holy warfare for the freedom and rights of the people*."[64] The struggle to keep democracy pure and dedicated to the common good did not, for Rauschenbusch, simply represent a matter of good government. It was, rather, a kind of holy warfare waged in defense of the Kingdom of God and its ideals of freedom and individual rights.

In similar fashion, Rauschenbusch wrote approvingly in 1913 of what he called the "True American Church," consisting of the Baptists and five other Christian denominations that had "all thoroughly assimilated the principle of democracy" and thus represented the "fullest expression of our native American religious life."[65] Profoundly shaped by cultural forces of American history, he observed, the democratic denominations "in turn have formed the moral and spiritual life of our nation. Our literature, our national aspirations and convictions, the moral ideas which are axiomatic with the average American bear the

---

[62] Ibid., 363.
[63] Ibid., 364.
[64] Rauschenbusch, *Prayers of the Social Awakening*, 75-76. Emphasis added.
[65] Walter Rauschenbusch, "The True American Church," *The Congregationalist*, 23 October 1913, 562. The other denominations that Rauschenbusch considered part of the True American Church along with the Baptists were the Methodists, Presbyterians, Congregationalists, Disciples, and Reformed Christians.

impress of that religious genius which characterizes these churches collectively and distinguishes them from other types."[66] By glossing over the various denominations' doctrinal differences and focusing instead on their shared commitment to "democracy," Rauschenbusch sought to define the True American Church in terms broad enough to include most, if not all, of his fellow citizens in the process of "Christianization." If membership in the True American Church simply required a profession of faith in democracy and the American way of life, then even non-believers could conceivably participate in the redemption of the nation.[67]

While his audience and reputation extended far beyond the boundaries of Baptist life in the United States, Rauschenbusch always considered himself to be thoroughly Baptist in both belief and practice. Indeed, despite all of his radical social ideas and scathing critiques of American society and America's churches, he stood chest-deep in the waters of the mainstream North American Baptist thought of his day. Certainly his identification of the Kingdom of God with the ideals of democracy suggested a theological perspective shaped profoundly by the Baptist world in which he lived. For Rauschenbusch, local Baptist churches offered fleeting, yet faithful, glimpses of the pure democracy that the Kingdom of God promised.

In a series of articles for the *Rochester Baptist Monthly* titled "Why I Am a Baptist" and published in 1905 and 1906, Rauschenbusch repeatedly expressed an admiration for his denomination's democratic orientation. The Baptists' commitment to democracy, he pointed out, only confirmed their status as the most faithful expression of authentic Christianity. "Our churches are Christian democracies," he wrote, and

---

[66] Ibid.
[67] See Handy, *Christian America,* 142. Stanley Hauerwas, among others, has noted the ambiguity in Rauschenbusch's use of the word "democracy." Rauschenbusch, he writes, "was as enthusiastic about democracy as he was unclear about its nature" See Hauerwas, "The Democratic Policing of Christianity," *Pro Ecclesia* 3 (1994): 219ff. Interestingly, Rauschenbusch's idea of a True American Church, reflecting the ideals and values of American culture more than those of any specific religious group, almost exactly anticipated the argument that Will Herberg made more than forty years later in *Protestant-Catholic-Jew: An Essay in American Religious Sociology* (Garden City NY: Doubleday, 1955).

"that democracy of the Baptist churches is something to be proud of. One of the noblest elements in the life of our Teutonic ancestors was that their village communities governed themselves in the town meeting. That has been called the mark of the Aryan race. It was the germ of all popular liberties. A Baptist church meeting is exactly that sort of self-governing assembly of the people."[68] Moreover, Baptist church polity corresponded "more completely to primitive Christianity," he noted. "The farther we get back to apostolic Christianity the completer the democracy we encounter."[69]

Rauschenbusch's formulation of the relationship between Christianity and democracy freely mixed cultural and religious imagery together, with Teutonic (or, as Rauschenbusch's Baptist contemporaries more often put it, Anglo-Saxon) ancestors mingling with early Christian apostles around the legendary wellspring of participatory democracy. The impulse toward self-government, it seemed, remained essentially the same in either setting, be it a pagan town meeting or a Christian congregational gathering. Baptist faith and practice thus served as a kind of figurative link between the cultural and religious dimensions of democracy, following closely the noble traditions of both and creating a template for what a truly Christian civilization—or, in terms more appropriate to Rauschenbusch's work, a truly Christian social order—might look like: an egalitarian community formed around biblical principles, open to all on the basis of genuine religious experience, and freely entrusted to the leadership of ordinary men and women.

Two other public addresses by Rauschenbusch further reflected his understanding of Baptists, democracy, and the Kingdom of God. Largely because of the Baptist example, he told the gathered messengers at the Northern Baptist Convention in May 1910, the "right of private judgment in religious matters has become an axiom of American thought. Most of our denominations have accepted the Christian principle of democracy for their church organizations." As a result, he concluded, "the essential

---

[68]Walter Rauschenbusch, "Why I Am a Baptist," *The Rochester Baptist Monthly*, January 1906, 107.
[69]Ibid.

principles of Baptist life and thought are triumphant" in American religious life.[70]

Slightly more than a year later, he spoke at the Baptist World Alliance meeting in Philadelphia on the familiar subject of "The Church and Social Crises." Because of their commitment to democracy in all its forms, Rauschenbusch claimed, Baptists should be in the vanguard of the movement to reorganize American society according to Kingdom principles. "We have embodied the principles of democracy in the congregational organization of our churches," he said. "We have exalted individual liberty in making religion the free act of the soul, and repudiating coercion in religion. We have always multiplied most among the common people, because we have a natural affinity for their convictions and spirit."[71] Baptists, he continued, "are the predestined friends of the young democracy in all nations" and our churches "should incarnate a type of religion that is not the foe of liberty, but the inspiring soul of it, and thus fill the working people with religious faith in their cause, and religious patience and courage in their battles."[72] The Baptists' contribution to the imminent Kingdom of God, in other words, depended upon their continued fidelity to democratic ideals. As the Baptist spirit of democracy spread, so would popular enthusiasm for the Christian principles of justice and equality for all people that defined the new social order in God's Kingdom.

***

---

[70] Quoted in Minus, 154. Rauschenbusch's use of the word "axiom" to describe "the right of private judgment in religious matters" suggests the influence of Mullins. As a well-read Baptist scholar, Rauschenbusch in 1910 would surely have had at least a passing familiarity with Mullins' *The Axioms of Religion*. Nowhere, though, does he specifically refer to Mullins as either an inspiration or a resource. The two Baptist leaders were at least acquaintances, insofar as they served together for several years in the early 1900s on the General Board of the Baptist Congress, a scholarly organization of Baptist intellectuals, and delivered prominent addresses at the Baptist World Alliance meeting in 1911. The nature of any further relationship between the two men is purely a matter of speculation.

[71] Walter Rauschenbusch, "The Church and Social Crises," address to the Baptist World Alliance, 24 June 1911, in *The Baptist World Alliance: Second Congress Record of Proceedings* (Philadelphia: Harper and Brother, 1911) 376.

[72] Ibid.

Nowhere did Rauschenbusch the Baptist more boldly identify the ideals of democracy with those of Christianity than in his final book, *A Theology for the Social Gospel*. "We have a social gospel," he declared in the book's opening sentence. "We need a systematic theology large enough to match it and vital enough to back it."[73] With *A Theology for the Social Gospel*, Rauschenbusch attempted to fill this gap and provide social Christianity with a solid theological rationale. He approached the task, appropriately enough, in a systematic fashion, justifying in his first three chapters the need for such a theology and then, over the course of the next fifteen chapters, explaining how individual Christian doctrines may be understood afresh in light of the new imperatives of the social gospel. Providing the theological center of gravity for the book was Rauschenbusch's concept of the Kingdom of God: everything both flowed from it and, ultimately, returned to it. Indeed, as Rauschenbusch realized, the Kingdom of God was the social gospel itself.[74] In keeping with his Baptist roots, however, Rauschenbusch understood the Kingdom as thoroughly democratic in nature.

From the very beginning of *A Theology for the Social Gospel*, Rauschenbusch emphasized the close, almost symbiotic, relationship between social Christianity and the ideals of democracy. The social gospel, he claimed in the book's first chapter, supplied "the religious reaction to the historic advent of democracy. It seeks to put the democratic spirit, which the Church inherited from Jesus and the prophets, once more in control of the institutions and teachings of the Church."[75] Note this initial assumption upon which Rauschenbusch's

---

[73] Rauschenbusch, *A Theology for the Social Gospel*, 1.

[74] Ibid., 131. In "The Legacy of Walter Rauschenbusch," *Religion in Life* 37 (1968): 382-400, Henry William Eberts makes the ironic observation that a kingdom seems like a strange political model for a committed democrat like Rauschenbusch to place at the center of his theology. Given the prominence of Ritschl in Rauschenbusch's thought, however, the association makes sense.

[75] Ibid., 5. In pointed contrast to Rauschenbusch, Shailer Mathews in *The Social Gospel* (Philadelphia: Griffith and Rowland Press, 1910) insisted that Jesus never specifically advocated democracy, "nor is it possible to find in the New Testament any teaching which commits the gospel to any particular theory of government" (56). A government, he argued, "is not Christian because it is of this or that form" (60-61). Mathews did concede,

theology rested: the democratic enthusiasm that animated the Social Gospel represented a kind of spiritual legacy passed down directly from Jesus and the prophets to their modern-day heirs. In order to stay vital and relevant, Rauschensbusch insisted, theology must always grow and adapt to new realities as they emerge.[76] In a modern, democratic age, then, the success or failure of a theology for the social gospel would be measured by the extent to which it both reflected the ideals of democracy, as taught by Jesus, and enabled those ideals to transform the church in America.

To that end, Rauschenbusch called upon Christians to rediscover the authentic principles and practices of their faith, beginning with an understanding of sin as primarily a corporate phenomenon. For far too long, he wrote, the church had been obsessed with issues of individual morality and salvation, while neglecting the more profound matter of collective sin. Christian theology had thus suffered accordingly. In the new, social gospel-inspired commitment to Christian solidarity lay hope. "There is nothing else in sight today which has power to rejuvenate theology," Rauschenbusch maintained, "except the consciousness of vast sins and sufferings, and the longing for righteousness and the new life, which are expressed in the social gospel."[77] The Old Testament prophets and, later, Jesus provided a guiding precedent for this way of approaching sin and redemption. Their abiding concern, Rauschenbusch noted, "was not for [themselves] alone but for [their] nation. This form of religious experience is more distinctively Christian than any form which is caused by fear and which thinks only of self."[78] With its roots deeply embedded in the biblical tradition, social Christianity claimed all of creation—not merely the individual soul, but all aspects of a nation's social, political, religious, and economic life—as the legitimate arena for God's redemptive work. Just as the prophets and Jesus focused their reforming energies on the biblical nation of Israel, the apostles of the

---

however, that political democracy tended to prevail in places where the gospel had taken hold.
[76] Ibid., 1.
[77] Ibid., 14.
[78] Ibid., 20.

Social Gospel understood their mission as nothing less than the transformation of America.

Rauschenbusch claimed that a social understanding of the Christian faith must decisively transform the respective definitions of sin and salvation. Sin, he wrote, "is essentially selfishness" and a refusal to subordinate private interests to the common good.[79] Individual sins had definite and immediate consequences upon the lives of others. The social impact of a person's sinfulness "stands out in its true proportion, not when he is tripped up by ill-temper **or** side-steps into shame," Rauschenbusch argued, but rather "when he seeks to establish a private kingdom of self-service and is ready to thwart and defeat the progress of mankind toward peace, toward justice, or toward a fraternal organization of economic life, because that would diminish his political privileges, his unearned income, and his power over the working classes."[80] True original sin, according to Rauschenbusch, manifested itself socially: by exerting its demonic power through the pressures of enforced cultural habits, customs, and prejudices, an evil society corrupted individuals and schooled them in the practices of sin.[81]

Against this reality of sin as "organized wrong," Rauschenbusch placed the biblical concept of the Kingdom of God as "organized good." The Kingdom, he explained, was the "realm of love" where individuals cooperated in mutual service and common endeavor according to the "spirit of the prophets and the teaching of Jesus."[82] If selfishness defined the nature of sin, Rauschenbusch reasoned, then salvation must come through service to others. Herein lay the key to the social gospel's understanding of the Kingdom of God. "When we submit to God, we submit to the supremacy of the common good," asserted Rauschenbusch. "Salvation is the voluntary socializing of the soul," the transformation from selfishness to service.[83] The reach of this salvation extended far beyond the individual soul. Certainly men and women, as

---

[79] Ibid., 50.
[80] Ibid., 52.
[81] Ibid., 60ff. For a more thorough discussion of Rauschenbusch's understanding of the Kingdom of Evil, see 77-94.
[82] Ibid., 54-56.
[83] Ibid., 97.

individuals, could claim salvation through faith "as an energetic act of the will, affirming [their] fellowship with God and man, declaring [their] solidarity with the Kingdom of God, and repudiating selfish isolation."[84] More significantly, however, the Kingdom of God had the power to bring salvation to what Rauschenbusch called the "super-personal forces" of the world, such as economic systems, political states, or any other entity that coercively assimilated individuals "to its moral standards, and enforce[ed] them by the social sanctions of approval or disapproval."[85]

As with individuals, Rauschenbusch claimed that the salvation of these super-personal forces consisted in their submission to the law of Christ.[86] This submission took different forms depending upon the nature of the unsaved organization. For economic powers, submission to the law of Christ required them to "give up monopoly power and the incomes derived from legalized extortion, and to come under the law of service, content with a fair income for honest work." For nation-states, the corresponding step in coming under the law of Christ "is to submit to real democracy. Therewith they step out of the Kingdom of Evil and into the Kingdom of God."[87] Democracy, in other words, expressed the law of Christ in the political realm and defined the boundary that separated those nations living in harmony with God's Kingdom from those living in defiance of it.

Rauschenbusch believed that the life and ministry of Jesus announced the dawning of the Kingdom of God as the creation of a new humanity aligned with the divine will for righteousness and love. The first generations of Christians had lived in hopeful expectation that the Kingdom of which Jesus spoke would soon be realized in its fullness but, with the passing of generations, the Kingdom of God as an ethical ideal gradually faded into theological obscurity. In its place arose the institutional church, with its own selfish interests and priorities that

---

[84] Ibid., 102.
[85] Ibid., 110.
[86] Ibid., 111.
[87] Ibid., 117.

rarely intersected with those of God's Kingdom.[88] This development, Rauschenbusch claimed, brought disastrous consequences upon Christendom. Not only did theology and Christian ethics lose their vital connection with the teachings of Jesus and salvation become an individual concern, but Christianity lost its power as a revolutionary force for change in the world.[89] Without the Kingdom of God as a living and guiding inspiration, popular movements for democracy and social justice either stalled or shriveled up altogether.[90]

Rauschenbusch intended to reverse these unfortunate developments by proclaiming anew the Kingdom of God as "the end to which God is lifting the [human] race. It is realized not only by redemption, but also by the education of mankind and the revelation of [God's] life within it."[91] The Kingdom, Rauschenbusch continued, embodied "humanity organized according to the will of God" and, as such, tended toward the social order that guaranteed the freest development for all people.[92] Inevitably, this social order was a democracy. More to the point, Rauschenbusch believed that popular democracy represented a crucial link in a progressive chain reaction sparked by the spiritual realization of God's Kingdom in the world. The Kingdom's "capacity to save the social order depends on its pervasive presence within the social organism," he explained. "Every institutional foothold gained gives a purchase for attacking the next vantage-point. Where a really Christian type of religious life is created, the intellect and education are set free, and this in turn aids religion to emancipate itself from superstition and dogmatism. Where religion and intellect combine, the foundation is laid for political democracy. Where the people have the outfit and the spirit

---

[88] Ibid., 131-132. Like many, if not most, of his fellow Baptists, Rauschenbusch considered the "institutional" (that is, the Roman Catholic) church to be the primary antagonist to the pure religion established by Jesus and practiced by the New Testament church. See, for example, the work of Chicago's Gerald Birney Smith in *Social Idealism and the Changing Theology*, 1-46. As will be noted in later chapters, Mullins and Truett joined Rauschenbusch in this understanding of church history.

[89] Ibid., 133-137.
[90] Ibid., 136.
[91] Ibid., 140.
[92] Ibid., 142.

of democracy, they can curb economic exploitation."[93] Economic justice led to a sense of social unity and, finally, to relationships of love and service among individuals. Where men and women live in this manner, Rauschenbusch concluded, "they are not far away from the Kingdom of God."[94]

Between the present age and the fulfillment of the Kingdom, however, stood a world unable to conceive of God in a positive manner and reluctant to embrace God's Kingdom. Rauschenbusch maintained that society shaped popular conceptions of God, and that "under tyrannous conditions the idea of God was necessarily tainted with the cruel hardness of society. This spiritual influence of despotism even made the face of Christ seem hard and stern."[95] Religion thus overlapped considerably with politics and economics: freedom in the latter areas of life made freedom in the spiritual realm possible. At this juncture, he wrote, "we see one of the highest redemptive services of Jesus to the human race. When he took God by the hand and called him 'our Father,' he democratized the conception of God."[96]

Suddenly, the possibility arose that God was, indeed, for humanity and not in league with the powerful political and economic forces of society arrayed against it. The social gospel served as God's agent for extending to all areas of life the democratization that Jesus brought to the concept of God. "This reformatory and democratizing influence of the social gospel is not against religion but for it," claimed Rauschenbusch. "The worst thing that could happen to God would be to remain an autocrat while the rest of the world is moving toward democracy," he continued. In such an event, Rauschenbusch not only insisted that God

---

[93] Ibid., 165. Rauschenbusch here echoes the thought of Richard T. Ely, who understood economic justice as the ultimate end of social progress. As Christian ethics infiltrates the practice of economics, he wrote in *Social Aspects of Christianity* (New York: Thomas Y. Crowell and Company, 1889), "political economy is thus brought into harmony with the great religious, political, and social movements which characterize this age; for the essence of them all is the belief that there ought to be no contradiction between our actual economic life and the postulates of [Christian] ethics and a determination that there shall be an abolition of such things as will not stand the tests of this rule" (128).
[94] Ibid., 166.
[95] Ibid., 174.
[96] Ibid., 175.

"would be dethroned with the rest," but that, in some sense, the dethroning had already begun—hastened, he added, by the perception that Christianity was anti-democratic and opposed to the freedom and equality of all people. "This feeling will deepen as democracy takes hold and becomes more than just a theory of government," he wrote. "We have heard only the political overture of democracy, played by fifes; the economic numbers of the program are yet to come, and they will be performed with trumpets and trombones."[97]

In refashioning God as a democrat, the social gospel sought to ensure Christianity's continued relevance in the modern world. The old faith, Rauschenbusch insisted, still retained its power to inspire new hopes for freedom and social equality, but it needed a contemporary platform upon which to take its stand against injustice. Furthermore, a democratic understanding of God fueled the social gospel's vision of a world transformed in the name and spirit of Jesus. "If [God] lives and moves in the life of mankind," wrote Rauschenbusch, "he can act directly on the masses of men. A God who strives within our striving, who kindles his flame in our intellect, sends the impact of his energy to make our will restless for righteousness, floods our sub-conscious mind with dreams and longings, and always urges the race on toward a higher combination of freedom and solidarity—that would be a God with whom democratic and religious men could hold converse as their chief fellow-worker."[98] While political democracy represented only a first step in the progressive realization of the Kingdom of God in the world, it nonetheless served as the essential template for what must follow in the economic, social, and spiritual orders of human existence. Indeed, as Rauschenbusch described it, very little distinguished the social gospel's concept of the Kingdom of God from the ideals of democracy for, ultimately, the Kingdom of God was "the only true Democracy."[99]

***

Walter Rauschenbusch's vision of the Kingdom of God as a democracy reflected both the optimism and the prejudices of his time,

---

[97] Ibid., 178.
[98] Ibid., 179.
[99] Ibid., 180.

resembling nothing so much as an idealized version of late nineteenth-century American democracy.[100] His vision, however optimistic it might have been, did contain sharp edges. Prophetically, he understood American democracy in terms of both crisis and opportunity. The systemic greed, corruption, and injustice that defined life for the working classes in Rauschenbusch's America gave him ample reason for despair. Democracy, it seemed, had defaulted on its promise of equal opportunity: the labor of many created wealth for a few, the deliberations of the powerful ignored the cries of the weak, and the avenues for self-improvement and advancement opened only for those already privileged by education, birth, or income. Therein lay the crisis of democracy as Rauschenbusch saw it.

Against this bleak reality, Rauschenbusch held up the Kingdom of God as the ideal democracy, the goal toward which he believed America (and, ultimately, the world) must continue to move. Wherever the Kingdom of God reigned, he proclaimed, the Christian principles of mutual love and selfless service, the hallmarks of true democracy, served as the basis for all social relationships. Therein lay the opportunity of democracy, the chance to transform imperfect reality into an ideal social order. For Rauschenbusch, "christianization" was synonymous with democratization insofar as the truly Christian society would also be a truly democratic one.

This fusion of democracy and Christianity reflected the ongoing theological influence of Albrecht Ritschl on Rauschenbusch's thought: as history gradually progressed toward fulfillment of the Kingdom of God, the ideals of democracy would increasingly define all forms of human interaction. It also reflected the prevailing Baptist understanding of the proper relationship between church and state at the turn of the twentieth century. Like his Baptist contemporaries Mullins and Truett, Rauschenbusch assumed that an essential moral harmony existed between church and state in America even as he insisted that they be separate.[101]

---

[100] McClintock, "Walter Rauschenbusch," 448.
[101] According to James Dunn, "many of the most dedicated advocates of church-state separation have been at the same time prophets to the powers that be, serious social critics, champions of peace and justice." Rauschenbusch, he points out, was not only the "father of the social gospel," but professed "a Baptist appreciation for the separation of church and

"Historical experience has compelled us to separate Church and State because each can accomplish its special task best without the influence of the other," he wrote in *Christianity and the Social Crisis*. But, he continued, church and state "are not unrelated. Our life is not a mechanical duality, built in two air-tight compartments. Church and State both minister to something greater and larger than either, and they find their true relation in this unity of aim and service."[102] Rauschenbusch believed that this "something greater and larger," ultimately, was the Kingdom of God. "The machinery of Church and State must be kept separate," he wrote, "but the output of each must mingle with the other to make social life increasingly wholesome and normal. *Church and State are alike but partial organizations of humanity for special ends. Together they serve what is greater than either: humanity. Their common aim is to transform humanity into the kingdom of God.*"[103]

For conclusive evidence of this moral identification between church and state, Rauschenbusch looked no further than his own denomination. The Baptist spirit of democracy as expressed in the multitudes of self-governing congregations across the nation, he believed, provided a ready glimpse of the Kingdom of God in which justice, equality, and mutual love prevailed. Likewise, these democratic Baptist religious ideals had also found political resonance in the American system of government, despite its obvious imperfections and limitations. As one historian has observed, Rauschenbusch "was surprisingly optimistic about the state's ability to pursue the same social and spiritual goals as the church. Following his logic, Baptists (and American Christians generally) could insist on strict separation... while at the same time rejoicing in every activity of government that advanced the purposes of the churches."[104]

In his longing for such a "christianized" social order, Rauschenbusch, like most other advocates of the social gospel, demonstrated a

---

state." See Dunn, "Religious Liberty and Church/State Separation Go Hand in Hand," in *Defining Baptist Convictions: Guidelines for the Twenty-first Century*, ed. Charles B. DeWeese (Franklin TN: Providence House Publishers, 1996) 72.
[102] Rauschenbusch, *Christianity and the Social Crisis*, 380.
[103] Ibid, emphasis added.
[104] Goen, "Baptists and Church-State Issues in the 20th Century," 227.

remarkably ecumenical spirit. "I am a Baptist, but I am more than a Baptist," he wrote in 1906. "All things are mine; whether Francis of Assisi, or Luther, or Knox, or Wesley; all are mine because I am Christ's."[105] Rauschenbusch did not discriminate among those willing to join in the struggle for freedom, equality, and social justice in America, encouraging Christians of all persuasions and non-Christians alike to heed the call of the Kingdom of God (though he did retain a nagging suspicion of Catholics). Nevertheless, his fundamental theological orientation always reflected the Baptist perspective he learned first from his immigrant father, to whom Baptist doctrine seemed inseparable from American identity. When Rauschenbusch described the Kingdom of God as a democracy, he did so as a Baptist prophet who had taken American democratic principles seriously and, in his words, had spent a lifetime trying "to inculcate them here and abroad." What made such a happy convergence possible, finally, was Rauschenbusch's confidence that church and state in America traveled in the same direction, moving progressively together toward a realization of the Kingdom of God, the one true democracy.

---

[105] Walter Rauschenbusch, "Why I Am a Baptist," *The Rochester Baptist Monthly*, March 1906, 159.

3

E. Y. Mullins and the
"Baptist Empire" of American Democracy

While greatly influential in the North, Walter Rauschenbusch and his ideas about the Kingdom of God received little notice in the South. In large part this lack of attention was due to the fact that, despite significant industrial growth in the years following Reconstruction, the old Confederacy remained a predominantly agricultural society in the early 1900s. Problems associated with industrial capitalism and the working classes simply did not resonate among the farmers and small-town merchants of the South. One of the few Southern Baptists who did formally address the social gospel's challenge was Edgar Young Mullins, president of the Southern Baptist Theological Seminary in Louisville, Kentucky. Some Christians, he wrote in 1908, "are asserting that individualism is a false teaching and that the gospel aims primarily at social results."[1] While he understood the motivations behind this perspective, Mullins nevertheless considered it misguided. "To regenerate the individual," he concluded, "is the sole condition of permanent moral progress" and, as such, represents the true mission of Christianity.[2] Indeed, for E. Y. Mullins, the priority of the individual in spiritual matters represented the starting point for all religious reflection, and over the course of a long and fruitful career, he constructed an enduring theological legacy—some would even say the *definitive* theological legacy for Baptists—around this conviction.[3]

---

[1] Mullins, *The Axioms of Religion*, 201.
[2] Ibid., 204.
[3] James Dunn has lauded Mullins as the singular Baptist theologian whose work provided the sturdy conceptual foundation for the traditional Baptist understanding of religious liberty and the separation of church and state. "A common sense faith that is accessible to every soul is ever eagerly sought," he wrote. "It may well be that the time has come for Mullins' message of soul competency and religious liberty." See James Dunn, "Church, State, and Soul Competency," 71.

When Mullins assumed the top position at Southern Seminary in 1899, the school was in an undeniably difficult situation. Its previous head, William Whitsitt, had resigned under pressure and numerous local churches, upon whose support Southern depended, were threatening to curtail their financial contributions to the seminary.[4] By 1924, Southern's fortunes had dramatically improved, thanks largely to Mullins's stewardship. The campus had moved from downtown Louisville to a large suburban tract of land; new, state-of-the-art classroom and administrative buildings had appeared; the faculty had expanded; the curriculum, already strong, had become more rigorous; student enrollment had returned to levels not seen since before the Whitsitt controversy; and the school's endowment had grown substantially. Furthermore, the prolific Mullins, with numerous books and articles to his credit, was widely considered to be the most influential theologian in Southern Baptist life; his very presence at Southern significantly elevated the academic reputation of the denomination's flagship institution.

In recognition of—and gratitude for—Mullins's years of service, the seminary marked his silver anniversary as president in September 1924 with two days of special services and tributes from his colleagues and other prominent Southern Baptists.[5] Among the guests was George Truett, the well-known pastor of the First Baptist Church of Dallas, Texas. While not close friends, the theologian and the pastor regarded one another warmly and had worked together on a number of occasions. (Several years later, Truett would preach at Mullins's funeral.) Speaking on the second afternoon of the celebration, Truett joined his fellow

---

[4] Whitsitt, a church historian by training, had angered the Landmarkers by suggesting in *A Question in Baptist History: Whether the Anabaptists in England Practiced Immersion Before the Year 1641?* (Louisville KY: Chas. T. Dearing, 1896; reprint ed., New York: Arno Press, 1986) that Baptists had "invented" the practice of baptism by immersion in 1641. To the Landmarkers, who believed there existed an unbroken lineage of Baptist churches stretching from John the Baptist to the present, Whitsitt's claim amounted to a scandalous heresy. The trustees of Southern saw no way to settle the controversy short of Whitsitt's resignation, which he tendered in 1899. For a concise account of the controversy, see W. R. Estep's article on Whitsitt in *Dictionary of Baptists in America*, ed. Bill J. Leonard (Downer's Grove IL: Intervarsity Press, 1994) 287.

[5] The schedule for the Mullins anniversary celebration may be found in *Review and Expositor* 22 (1925): 6.

orators in praising "one of [God's] chiefest gifts to His people in modern times, the humble and noble President of this great institution."[6] He proceeded to describe world events that had transpired since Mullins took the helm at Southern. Of these events, Truett concentrated his remarks primarily upon the Great War and its effects on civilization. "I believe here at this critical time in the world's life, with autocracy terribly stricken by the recent war, our belief is that the Day of Days has come for our Baptist peoples of Europe," said Truett. "Autocracy and democracy are utterly irreconcilable. Autocracy must pass, is passing; and with it will go sacramentalism and sacerdotalism, the grave clothes of a moribund and decadent faith." E. Y. Mullins, declared Truett, is a brave champion of this new Baptist vision of democracy for the world.[7]

Others at the anniversary celebration recognized this quality in Mullins as well. Henry Alford Porter, the pastor of St. Louis's Third Baptist Church and Truett's immediate predecessor on the afternoon program, observed that "this is a Baptist age because we are living in a world of expanding democracy." By re-interpreting Baptist principles in keeping with this new world order, Mullins had greatly advanced the Baptist cause.[8] "If Baptists are to do their part in the coming reconstruction of the world, now is the time for them to re-examine and restate their historic position," said Porter. "This Dr. Mullins has done with firm-footed thinking and surpassing clarity."[9]

Mullins's enthusiasm for democracy as a fundamental aspect of Baptist faith and practice flowed easily from his conviction that Christianity could be made intelligible for thinking people in a scientific age. This latter achievement, many of his peers believed at the time, represented his most enduring contribution to contemporary theology. Modern Christians, claimed Porter in his address, "are desperately afraid that nothing has been left unchanged, and that science has undermined Christianity. And some are being swept helplessly downstream clinging

---

[6] George Truett, "A Quarter Century of World History," *Review and Expositor* 22 (1925): 50.
[7] Ibid, 58.
[8] Henry Alfred Porter, "An Interpretation, One Among a Thousand," *Review and Expositor* 22 (1925): 22.
[9] Ibid., 23.

helplessly to the floating wreckage of their faith."[10] By "showing how the old faith can live with the new knowledge," Porter asserted, Mullins "has not only conserved the central certainties of the faith, but has conserved to the faith many thinking men and women who would otherwise be lost to it."[11] In short, exclaimed another anniversary speaker in September of 1924, Mullins had "come to be the outstanding Baptist leader and statesman and theologian" of his generation.[12]

Almost eighty years after his death, Mullins remains one of the outstanding figures in Southern Baptist life, one with whom all contemporary Baptist theologians in America must come to terms, regardless of whether they agree with him.[13] According to theologian Fisher Humphries, Mullins's best-known work, *The Axioms of Religion: A New Interpretation of the Baptist Faith* (1908), "has done more than any other single volume to define Baptist identity," especially in the South.[14] Simply put, Mullins was a towering figure in Southern Baptist life who cast a very long theological shadow. He was, writes literary critic Harold Bloom, the "true and belated father" of Southern Baptists, the Baptist equivalent of Luther, Wesley, or Calvin.[15] For most of the twentieth

---

[10] Ibid., 19.

[11] Ibid., 20.

[12] A. T. Robertson, "A Sketch of the Life of President Mullins," *Review and Expositor* 22 (1925): 9.

[13] Baptists in the South from all over the theological spectrum—not just those on the moderate-to-liberal side—acknowledge Mullins's influence. According to Albert Mohler, the conservative president of the Southern Baptist Theological Seminary, Mullins "shaped the denominational consensus that, in turn, shaped Southern Baptist life and thought well into the twentieth century." Mohler's primary criticism of Mullins revolves around the hyper-individualism associated with the doctrine of soul competency, upon which Mullins based his understanding of the Baptist faith. Soul competency, writes Mohler, "serves as an acid dissolving religious authority, congregationalism, and mutual theological accountability." See Albert Mohler, Jr., "Baptist Theology at the Crossroads: The Legacy of E. Y. Mullins," *The Southern Baptist Journal of Theology* 3 (Winter 1999): 4, 19. While critical of Mullins, Mohler's essay nevertheless provides a very solid overview of Mullins's career as a theologian and educator.

[14] Fisher Humphries, "E. Y. Mullins," in *Baptist Theologians*, eds. Timothy George and David Dockery (Nashville TN: Broadman Press, 1990) 335. See also E. Glenn Hinson, "E. Y. Mullins as Interpreter of the Baptist Tradition," *Review and Expositor* 96 (1999): 117.

[15] Harold Bloom, *The American Religion: The Emergence of the Post-Christian Nation* (New York: Simon and Schuster, 1992) 46, 199. Bloom, however, does not see Mullins's

century it would have been virtually impossible for a Southern Baptist seminarian to escape a significant, if not formative, intellectual encounter with Mullins. Likewise, it would be difficult for anyone exposed to Mullins's work, particularly *The Axioms of Religion*, to miss the manner in which his fervent devotion to the ideals of American democracy mixed freely with his conception of Baptist identity.

At the center of both Mullins's embrace of democracy and his understanding of Christian faith in a modern context—the two aspects of his work emphasized by Truett and Porter at his silver anniversary celebration—lay an abiding commitment to individual freedom. For Mullins, writes Baptist historian Bill Leonard, "freedom was at the heart of the Baptist legacy," and his efforts to shape Southern Baptist theology in the twentieth century reflected this belief.[16] This legacy of freedom, though, is mixed at best. Mullins's theology of personal freedom, articulated most famously in his doctrine of "soul competency," served as a powerful apologetic weapon in his struggle to preserve the integrity of Christianity against the skepticism of a scientific age. At the same time, however, his celebration of individual freedom also led him to blur the distinctions between Baptist beliefs and the ideals of American democracy, even as he consistently (and without irony) championed the separation of church and state. Indeed, as Mullins wrote on more than one occasion, the American form of government represented nothing less than the political expression of Baptist religious principles. The idea of freedom, for Mullins, provided the essential conceptual link between Baptist theology and American democracy. It also made him the most effective theological exponent of "Baptist democracy" between 1900 and 1925.

---

theological contributions in a positive light. Rather, he believes, Mullins's intensely individualistic understanding of religion is characteristic of the modern-day Gnosticism beneath the surface of American Christianity. For an extended critique of Mullins along these lines, see Bloom, *The American Religion*, 200ff.

[16]Leonard, *God's Last and Only Hope*, 51. Leonard claims that, for most of their history, Southern Baptists have been at least as "Southern" as they have been "Baptist." Southern culture, in other words, has been both reflected in and shaped by the theology and polity of Baptists in the South. Leonard identifies the Mullins-inspired strain of radical individualism as one of the primary factors in this symbiotic relationship.

***

By his own account, E. Y. Mullins entered a world strongly shaped by the Baptist tradition. "My father was a Baptist minister," Mullins once wrote, "and his father was also a Baptist minister. The families on the sides of both my father and mother have been Baptists through several generations. It was, of course, not likely that I would escape being a Baptist, if I became anything religiously."[17] For Mullins, though, the process of becoming something "religiously" unfolded gradually over the course of twenty years, as faith and reason wrestled for control of his soul. Born in Mississippi in 1860, he spent most of his childhood in Texas, where his family moved when he was eight.[18] Not long after reaching the Lone Star State, Mullins's father organized the First Baptist Church of Corsicana, Texas, as well as a small school in the town. "I was taught in the principles of right living by my parents," wrote Mullins. "They sought to win me to the Christian life. But there was not the slightest effort on their part to coerce my action or influence me to a premature decision."[19] As a youth, Mullins worked at the local newspaper as a newsboy and a typesetter. Later, he learned Morse code, and, by the age of fifteen, he had risen to the position of head operator at

---

[17] E. Y. Mullins, "Why I Am a Baptist," *Forum* 75 (1926): 725.

[18] Except where noted, information about Mullins's early years (i.e. before becoming president of Southern Seminary) comes primarily from the first ten chapters (pages 9-103) of Isla May Mullins, *E. Y. Mullins: An Intimate Biography* (Nashville TN: The Sunday School Board of the Southern Baptist Convention, 1929). For years, this volume, written by Mullins's widow, was the only book-length biography of E. Y. Mullins available. Considering Mullins's significance for Southern Baptist life and thought, this lack of academic attention to his life is quite remarkable. Mrs. Mullins's book is certainly informative, but it neither aspires to nor pretends to be a scholarly examination of E. Y. Mullins and his life's work. Though Mullins has been the subject of numerous unpublished dissertations, only one book has taken a serious look at his career, William E. Ellis's *A Man of Books and a Man of the People: E. Y. Mullins and the Crisis of Moderate Southern Baptist Leadership* (Macon GA: Mercer University Press, 1985). As the title suggests, Ellis focuses primarily on Mullins's role as a moderate Baptist leader during the fundamentalist-modernist controversy of the 1920s and his (ultimately unsuccessful) attempts to find a middle ground between the two sides upon which a stable evangelical consensus could be constructed. The most significant unpublished study of Mullins is Russell H. Dilday, Jr., "The Apologetic Method of E. Y. Mullins" (Th.D. diss., Southwestern Baptist Theological Seminary, 1960).

[19] Mullins, "Why I Am a Baptist," 725.

the local telegraph office.[20] A good student, Mullins entered the Agricultural and Mechanical College of Texas (now Texas A&M) in 1876 as a member of the school's inaugural class and performed well there. After graduation, he accepted a job in a Galveston, Texas, telegraph office, where he also studied law in his spare time.[21]

During and immediately following his college years, Mullins "became skeptical on several points of Christian teaching," he later recalled. "All along, however, there was a conflict between my intellectual questionings and my religious yearnings. My conscience was keenly alive and the fundamental need and demand for religion was always present. Strange as it may seem, it was in the period of intellectual doubt that I was converted."[22] Despite his upbringing, the twenty-year-old Mullins had heretofore experienced neither a personal spiritual awakening nor a strong conviction of religious belief. Indeed, his persistent skepticism kept faith at bay. That changed one night in Dallas, when he attended a revival service at the First Baptist Church. The preacher, Mullins remembered, "made a powerful appeal to the religious side of my nature. Without any emotional cataclysm of any kind I yielded my will to Christ."[23] Soon thereafter, on 7 November 1880, Mullins was baptized by his father in Corsicana.

Immediately, his life took a new direction. "The moral and spiritual reenforcement [sic] which followed this act," he reflected years later, "completely transformed my purposes and plans."[24] Mullins quit his telegraph job, abandoned the idea of practicing law, and, in 1881, he set off for the Southern Baptist Theological Seminary in Kentucky. At Southern, Mullins completed the "full curriculum" of studies, which included extra courses in Greek, Hebrew, and German.[25] He also studied

---

[20] Ellis, *A Man of Books and a Man of the People*, 6.
[21] Ibid., 9.
[22] Mullins, "Why I Am a Baptist," 725.
[23] Ibid.
[24] Ibid.
[25] Ellis, *A Man of Books and a Man of the People*, 12-13. A less rigorous course of study was available for students who were not able to meet the foreign language requirements of the full curriculum. These "English graduates" did not take the extra courses in Greek, German, and Hebrew.

theology under James Pettigru Boyce, one of the founders of the seminary and a moderate Calvinist. Throughout his career, Mullins maintained a deep admiration and profound respect for Boyce, to whom, as Boyce's "grateful pupil and successor in office," he affectionately dedicated his systematic theology text, *The Christian Religion in Its Doctrinal Expression,* in 1917. Capping a successful four-year stint for Mullins in Louisville, his seminary classmates honored him as one of five students chosen to speak at their 1885 graduation.

Mullins intended to serve as a missionary to Brazil after finishing seminary, and probably would have done so had health problems not prevented his overseas appointment. Instead, he became the pastor of the First Baptist Church of Harrodsburg, Kentucky, where he had often filled the pulpit as a supply preacher while a student at Southern. In 1888, the Lee Street Baptist Church in Baltimore called Mullins as pastor. Accepting the attractive offer of a larger congregation and a higher salary, Mullins and his new wife, the former Isla May Hawley, moved north. They stayed in Baltimore for seven years. In 1895, Mullins was named associate secretary of the Southern Baptist Foreign Missions Board in Richmond, Virginia, but left that post after less than nine months to become the pastor of the First Baptist Church of Newton Center, outside of Boston, his last position before returning to Louisville as president of Southern in 1899.

As president of the Southern Baptist Theological Seminary, Mullins earned the respect of Baptists on both sides of the Mason-Dixon Line. His pastoral experience in Baltimore and Boston not only gave him credibility with Northern Baptists, who tended (not unjustly) to think of their counterparts in the south as narrowly conservative, but also exposed him to the modernist theology gaining currency in the north. The University of Chicago and Colgate University both offered Mullins teaching positions during his first few years at Southern, and he enjoyed a good relationship with leading modernists such as Shailer Mathews, the dean of Chicago's divinity school.[26] Once he began publishing widely, Mullins's books and articles placed him in conversation with Baptists across the country and in the midst of ongoing arguments over

---

[26] Ellis, *A Man of Books and a Man of the People,* 60.

such issues as higher criticism of the Bible and evolution.[27] While conversant in the language of modern theology, Mullins could also, in good conscience, contribute an essay to *The Fundamentals* in which he defended the deity of Christ and the validity of Christian experience.[28] Comfortable with both the intellectual rhetoric of Chicago and the evangelical devotion of Louisville, Mullins served as a kind of theological bridge between Northern and Southern Baptists during the early years of the twentieth century.

Though familiar with the ongoing conversations in more liberal academic circles of his day—the pragmatism of William James, the experientialism of Friedrich Schleiermacher, the personalism of Borden Parker—Mullins himself was no liberal.[29] If anything, Mullins can best be described as a well-read theological centrist with evangelical sympathies, a committed Baptist who tried to make his faith convictions intellectually respectable in the modern academic climate of the early twentieth century.[30] Consensus and moderation defined the Mullins style, both personally and theologically. In his position on social issues, for example, Mullins managed to remain generally supportive of reform efforts while at the same time keeping a comfortable distance from any actual reform advocacy. Society, he wrote in 1905, "owes each man an opportunity. Equality of individual worth carries with it the necessary implication that no man should be crowded to the wall from lack of opportunity. The powerful should be restrained and held within proper limits. Men differ in natural ability, of course, and individuality should be respected. But the cunning or wise or mighty individual shall not

---

[27] Ibid., 74.

[28] See E. Y. Mullins, "The Test of Christian Experience," in *The Fundamentals: A Testimony to the Truth* (Chicago: Testimony Publishing Company, 1917) 3: 76-85.

[29] Ellis, *A Man of Books and a Man of the People*, 77. An excellent example of this tendency is Mullins's encounter with Harvard psychologist and philosopher William James, whose view of religious experience as set forth in *The Varieties of Religious Experience* (1903) Mullins critiqued as incomplete. With James' definition as a foundation upon which to build, Mullins offered his own, "complete" account of religious experience as a valid "scientific" phenomenon. See "Is Jesus Christ the Author of Religious Experience?" *The Baptist Review and Expositor* 1 (1904): 55-70.

[30] Ibid.

ruthlessly crush his feebler brother."[31] Few, if any, of Mullins's readers would disagree with these mild sentiments, regardless of where they might stand on particular social reform questions. This talent for locating and claiming the inoffensively common ground, in many ways, represented the crux of Mullins's effectiveness as a leader and a theologian.[32]

By the end of his first decade at Southern, Mullins had emerged as leading religious voice in the South, if not nationally.[33] He published his second book, *The Axioms of Religion*, in 1908 and basked in the praise it quickly received from Baptists in all sections of the United States, as well as in Great Britain. By virtue of his position at Southern, Mullins naturally enjoyed an audience as a denominational spokesperson, but as his influence as a theologian spread, his visibility as a Baptist leader rose commensurately. In 1921, the Southern Baptist Convention elected him president, a post he held until 1924. As president of the convention, Mullins played a major role in crafting the document that became the Baptist Faith and Message statement of 1925, a comprehensive account of what Southern Baptists generally believed about certain basic tenets of the Christian faith.[34] From 1923 through 1928, Mullins also served as the

---

[31] E. Y. Mullins, *Why Is Christianity True?* (Philadelphia: American Baptist Publication Society, 1905) 352-353.

[32] For an excellent assessment of Mullins as a denominational compromise figure, particularly between the fundamentalist and liberal factions, see Curtis W. Freeman, "E. Y. Mullins and the Siren Songs of Modernity," *Review and Expositor* 96 (1999): 23-42. Some contemporary Southern Baptist scholars argue that Mullins's moderation was precisely what made him a weak leader and, ultimately, responsible for the denomination's decades-long drift toward liberalism that was finally corrected in the last twenty years of the twentieth century. See, for example, Mohler, "Baptist Theology at the Crossroads"; Russell Moore and Gregory Thornberry, "The Mystery of E. Y. Mullins in Contemporary Baptist Historiography," *The Southern Baptist Journal of Theology* 3 (Winter 1999): 44-57; and Thomas J. Nettles, "E. Y. Mullins—Reluctant Evangelical," *The Southern Baptist Journal of Theology* 3 (Winter 1999): 24-42.

[33] Ellis, *A Man of Books and a Man of the People*, 81-82.

[34] It may be instructive here to point out Mullins's understanding of religious creeds and their proper place in Baptist life, particularly in light of the fact that so many of his spiritual descendents among moderate Baptists are so fiercely opposed to them (and frequently invoke Mullins to bolster their position). "I think creeds perform a useful function in educating us as to unity of faith and practice," wrote Mullins in 1912, "so long as they are not worn as death masks for defunct religions, or employed as lashes to chastise others, so long as they do not arrest life and growth—in short creeds help rather than

president of the Baptist World Alliance, a position that gave him an opportunity to share his theological views about Baptists and democracy with an international audience.[35]

Mullins was, in short, the man who ushered Baptists and their theology through the bewildering maze of modern thought and into the twentieth century. "Right here is where Dr. Mullins is rendering a service of untellable worth," exclaimed Henry Alford Porter, referring to Mullins's effectiveness in interpreting modernity for his fellow Baptists. "Right here is where he becomes preeminently the man of the hour. Right here is where he is seen to be a man from God for such a period as theological transition and adjustment as this."[36] It was, to be sure, a confusing time to be a Christian.

***

Mullins's celebrated efforts to justify the intellectual legitimacy of religious faith in a scientific age reflect the dramatic shift that occurred in American thought during the latter half of the nineteenth century as "science" seemed to replace "religion" as Western culture's final authority in determining truth.[37] Beginning in the late nineteenth

---

hinder." See E. Y. Mullins, *Baptist Beliefs* (Philadelphia: American Baptist Publication Society, 1912) 9-10.

[35] As president of the Baptist World Alliance, Mullins was chiefly responsible for crafting the official statement issued by the participants in the organization's 1924 meeting in Stockholm, Sweden. The document bore the unmistakable stamp of Mullins's influence and was later seen by many to be a kind of test run for the 1925 Southern Baptist Faith and Message statement. For the complete text of the statement, see "A Message of the Baptist World Alliance to the Baptist Brotherhood, to Other Christian Brethren, and to the World," *Review and Expositor* 21 (1924): 19-30.

[36] Porter, "An Interpretation," 19.

[37] For a thorough account of the ways in which this intellectual shift affected Baptist thought, see Curtis Freeman, "E. Y. Mullins and the Siren Songs of Modernity," especially pp. 24-30. Up until the closing decades of the nineteenth century, Freeman writes, Baptists in the United States had operated largely under the "grand American synthesis" of evangelical Christianity and Enlightenment rationalism, with Francis Wayland (1796-1865) being perhaps the foremost exponent of "reason" among Baptists. Later theologians, such as James Pettigru Boyce (1827-1888) followed Wayland in asserting that theology represented a rational, scientific enterprise in which one collected facts about God that, when interpreted according to common sense reason, yielded a coherent understanding of divine truth. By the late 1800s, however, other Baptists no longer felt secure in this "Bible as a collection of facts" perspective. Rejecting a purely rational approach to religion, they took

century, advances in biology and biblical studies began to challenge the assumptions of orthodox Protestantism in America. Charles Darwin published *On the Origin of the Species* (1859), which argued that existing forms of life had gradually evolved in complexity through a process of "natural selection." This evolutionary process, Darwin provocatively suggested several years later in *The Descent of Man* (1871), also accounted for the present state of humanity. The biblical story of a loving God's creation of the universe bore little relevance to Darwin's theories, which seemed to argue that the natural world was the product of random chance and not deliberate design.[38]

Nonetheless, despite their initial concerns about the impact of Darwinism on orthodox Christian thought, many leading theologians in the North soon managed to reconcile Darwinian ideas with biblical accounts of God and creation.[39] Without a doubt, the evolution question subtly influenced nearly all major religious conversations during the first years of the twentieth century, but the real furor over evolution in the

---

their search for truth beyond objective "fact" and into the realm of subjective "experience." William Newton Clarke (1841-1912) for one, suggested that religious experience provided a more appropriate starting point for theological reflection than did common sense reason. Other influential Baptists such as Shailer Mathews and Harry Emerson Fosdick echoed Clarke's celebration of experience. These two streams of thought, Freeman argues, created the treacherous theological currents of the early 1900s—namely the conflict between fundamentalism and modernism—which Mullins tried to navigate.

[38] Ferenc Morton Szasz, *The Divided Mind of Protestant America, 1880-1930* (Tuscaloosa AL: University of Alabama Press, 1982) 3. Contrary to popular belief, Szasz writes, the conflict between Darwin and Christianity was fairly muted before 1914. *The Fundamentals* (1910) for example, contained very little material explicitly addressing the issue (9). George Marsden chronicles the Christian evangelical encounter with, and response to, Darwinism in *Fundamentalism and American Culture*. Both Marsden and Szasz offer excellent resources for understanding the conflict between modernists and fundamentalists as well as the personalities involved in the struggle.

[39] Very early in the debate, Darwinism was regarded as clearly heretical in the South. Many (though by no means all) Northern theologians and ministers, however, continued to regard evolution as an open question. See Marsden, *Fundamentalism and American Culture*, 104. In these more liberal theological circles, the concept of "theistic evolution"—a purposeful development of the universe guided by the hand of a loving God—eventually gained currency. Advocates of theistic evolution tended to cite the optimistic and progressive evolutionary theories of Herbert Spencer in preference to the gloomy, atheistic ideas of Darwin, which allowed no discernable pattern or purpose in the evolutionary process. See Szasz, *The Divided Mind*, 9.

United States did not erupt until after World War I, when conservative evangelical concerns about the health of Western culture brought the issue once again to the forefront of public consciousness. The war, these evangelicals argued, demonstrated the decadence of a Western civilization enchanted with atheistic theories and the lure of sophisticated modernity. Evolution, historian George Marsden has written, "became a symbol [of civilization's decline]. Without the new cultural dimension it is unlikely that the debate over Darwinism could have been revived in the spectacular way it was."[40] Popular interest in the issue crested in 1925 with the sensational trial of John Scopes, a high school teacher in Dayton, Tennessee, charged with teaching evolution in defiance of state law.[41]

Despite the intense amount of heat generated by the evolution question, the most troubling issues for Christians in America around the turn of the century dealt with the origins and interpretation of the Bible itself. The late-nineteenth-century advent of "higher criticism" in biblical scholarship presented as much, if not more, of a challenge to the Protestant Christian worldview as had Darwin's biological theories.

Originating in a handful of German universities, higher criticism subjected the Bible to rigorous analysis and deconstruction in hopes of uncovering the "authentic" message of the text from beneath accumulated layers of tradition, myth, and misguided interpretation. According to both Jewish and Christian tradition, for example, Moses wrote the first five books of the Bible, or the Pentateuch. The new breed

---

[40] Marsden, *Fundamentalism and American Culture*, 149.

[41] The essential account of the Scopes trial and the events surrounding it is Edward J. Larson's *Summer For the Gods: The Scopes Trial and America's Continuing Debate Over Science and Religion* (New York: Basic Books, 1997). Scopes was convicted of teaching evolution in Tennessee, but his conviction was later overturned on a technicality. Although both sides claimed a measure of victory in the case, the opponents of evolution suffered a great deal of abuse in the popular press of the day, which portrayed them as intellectually backwards and culturally unsophisticated. The Scopes trial, many scholars have assumed, represented the high-water mark of fundamentalism in America, after which their fortunes as a serious religious movement declined precipitously. As Larson argues, however, fundamentalists did not completely disappear from public life, but instead created alternative private institutions, such as Bryan College, where their doctrines (including creationism) could be safely taught without ridicule. For a fascinating study of "scientific creationism" and other fundamentalist alternatives to evolutionary theory, see Ronald L. Numbers, *The Creationists* (New York: A. A. Knopf, 1992).

of biblical critics, however, suggested that multiple authors, none of whom were Moses, writing in different places at different times produced fragments of Scripture that were later woven together by redactors to produce what tradition called the Pentateuch. While perhaps unintended by its practitioners, the effect of higher criticism on Christians outside of the academy was to call into question both the reliability of the Bible and its accessibility to readers who were not university-trained biblical scholars.[42]

In the United States, many of the same Christians who had made peace with evolution also embraced higher criticism as a positive application of the scientific method to biblical scholarship. Heralding the advances of science as further evidence of God expanding the range of possibilities open to humanity, advocates of what became known as the "new theology" worked diligently to conform their religious convictions to modern realities—otherwise, they feared, enlightened culture would soon discard the Christian faith as hopelessly irrelevant. This new liberal Protestant theology, wrote historian Martin Marty, "was intended to be an inclusive and universal Christianization of the world view, a philosophy that could be accepted by all or that would provide synthesis and meaning to all who bothered with it."[43] Humanity, liberal Protestants proclaimed, had come of age, so to speak, and now worked in partnership with God to build His kingdom on earth."[44] Sin, for instance, was no longer seen by liberal Protestants as a theological problem; it was, rather, a sociological dysfunction to be cured through education and opportunity.

Not all Protestants in the United States agreed with the new theology's grand claims. Indeed, many were fiercely determined to resist them. In the latter years of the nineteenth century, Charles Hodge and B.

---

[42] Szasz, *The Divided Mind*, 42.
[43] Marty, *Righteous Empire*, 190. William Hutchinson offers an excellent account of the "New Theology" and its cultural implications in *The Modernist Impulse in American Protestantism*, 76-144. See also Ahlstrom's account of "the golden age of liberal theology," 763-789. To appreciate just how much of a departure this new theology was from standard evangelical Christian thought about science, God, and the universe, see Mark Noll, *The Scandal of the Evangelical Mind*, particularly 83-107.
[44] Marty, *Righteous Empire*, 194-195.

B. Warfield of Princeton Theological Seminary championed a militantly conservative doctrine, popularly known as the Princeton Theology, which remained true to eighteenth-century Common Sense philosophy. Based on the principles of biblical inerrancy and Reformed theology, the Princeton theologians and their sympathizers met the rising tide of modernism head on, refuting liberal attempts to relegate such fundamental Christian doctrines as the virgin birth of Jesus, the resurrection, and the miracles to the status of myth.[45] In 1910, two wealthy California businessmen pledged $250,000 to facilitate the publication and distribution of a series of pamphlets clearly stating the orthodox Christian positions on a host of doctrinal issues. The twelve-volume set contained essays by well-respected theologians from across the denominational spectrum and was named, simply, *The Fundamentals*. Those who endorsed the conclusions of *The Fundamentals* became known as "fundamentalists," and they insisted, not without reason, that the "modernists" and "liberals" had sapped Christian faith of its meaning by interpreting its historical truth claims as pure symbolism. Indeed, the essential question for fundamentalists, observed one historian in 1937, was not so much theological as historical: "whether the scriptural records of the Old and New Testaments were to be taken as an unquestionable record of fact or as a body of ancient literature which had in it an element of legend."[46] The fundamentalist reaction to modernism had a polarizing effect on nearly every Protestant organization in the United States, creating deep fissures and, in some cases, outright schism in the churches and dominating intra-denominational politics for most of the 1920s.[47]

***

---

[45] See Ahlstrom, 812ff. For a representative collection of primary texts written by the Princeton theologians, see Mark Noll, ed., *The Princeton Theology, 1812-1921: Scripture, Science, and Theological Method from Archibald Alexander to Benjamin Breckinridge Warfield* (Grand Rapids MI: Baker Book House, 1983).

[46] Preston William Slosson, *The Great Crusade and After, 1914-1928* (New York: The MacMillan Company, 1937) 430. See also Mark Noll, introduction to *The Princeton Theologians*, 11-48.

[47] For a good, concise overview of the fundamentalist controversy, see Alhstrom, 909-915. Marsden's *Fundamentalism and American Culture* remains the standard scholarly interpretation of the movement.

As president of Southern Seminary, Mullins was well aware of the new theology and readily identified its dangers for Baptist Christians. "Doctrinally, there is a peril which needs to be addressed by Baptists," he wrote in 1911. "We live in a scientific age. The supreme criterion of truth is that of causation, and this principle is taken from the sphere of physical science. The whole intellectual movement of modern times has been in the direction of reconstructing all doctrines and all systems of truth in obedience to this principle." Such an exclusively quantitative understanding of truth, Mullins noted, ignored "the personal and voluntary principles in the conception of truth itself."[48] Intellect alone did not make a complete person. As Mullins saw it, then, the challenge for Baptists in this scientific age lay in widening the definition of truth to allow for such factors as personality and individual will, while not surrendering any ground to scientifically minded religious skeptics.

The modernist way, Mullins argued, did not represent a valid option for orthodox Christians. "Modernism soft pedals or denies the resurrection," he wrote, and, in an effort to be "relevant" to the scientific mind, it reduced Jesus to a great ethical teacher. "You cannot leave out the supernatural and keep the Christian religion," he maintained.[49] Mullins acknowledged that such an insistence on preserving the miraculous content of Christian doctrine left Christians open to ridicule, if not outright derision, by practitioners of the "hard sciences." This kind

---

[48] E. Y. Mullins, "Baptists in the Modern World," *Review and Expositor* 8 (1911): 351. In an 1894 letter to the American Historical Association, Henry Adams captures the spirit of this scientific age, expressing his confidence that the methods of modern science will soon spill over into the humanities and reshape historical study in accordance with scientific discipline. See Adams, *The Degradation of Democracy* (New York: Peter Smith, Inc., 1949) 125-133. For an interesting account of the relationship between Mullins and J. Gresham Machen, a leading fundamentalist and defender of the "common sense" school of reason, see Sean Michael Lucas, "Christianity at the Crossroads: E. Y. Mullins, J. Gresham Machen, and the Challenge of Modernity." *The Southern Baptist Journal of Theology* 3 (1999): 58-78. In 1926, the two men wrote a series of articles debating such issues as the proper response of Christianity to modernism, the priority of Christian experience, and the relationship between science and religion. Another good resource on this subject is William Brackney's *The Baptists*, which provides a nice overview of the ways in which Baptists dealt with modernism and its effects on denominational unity. See *The Baptists*, 28-34.

[49] E. Y. Mullins, *Faith in the Modern World* (Nashville TN: The Sunday School Board of the Southern Baptist Convention, 1930) 30-31.

of scientific antagonism toward religion, he believed, betrayed a double standard. "It is amazing with what vehemence the modern scientist can preach modesty to his theological opponent, and practice dogmatism and arrogance in the realm of theological opinion," he wrote. "Nine-tenths of present-day conflicts... between science and religion probably result from failure to recognize the separateness of the two." Mullins offered a simple solution: "Religion must be judged as religion, not as biology or sociology or anything else, if it is to be appreciated and understood."[50]

Seen in this light, Mullins observed, the conflict between religion and science did not seem quite so irreconcilable after all. In fact, he wrote, "Christianity joins hands with science in respect for facts and hatred and repudiation of sham and make-believes. The common ground of science and the Christian religion is *loyalty to fact*."[51] Science and religion, Mullins continued, fully share the same "basic attitudes and instincts. Both work by faith. Both have a large capacity for belief. Both learn by experience that doubt paralyzes while faith stimulates."[52] Just as the hypotheses of chemists, physicists, and biologists must be tested in the crucible of laboratory experience before they can be accepted as valid by the scientific community, Mullins argued that a personal experience with Jesus made the Christian faith real in the lives of its adherents. The essential role of experience, in other words, made religion worthy of respect as a scientifically legitimate pursuit. Religion, Mullins maintained, "is a living experience of a very definite kind. In this respect it is like every other sphere of experience. It can be reduced to intelligible and systematic expression for the intellect. Hence it is properly a field in which a scientific expression of meaning is possible."[53]

Upon the foundation of Christian experience, Mullins thus sought to construct a theology capable of withstanding the challenge of modernity. This task was essential in order for the preacher's message to be relevant

---

[50] E. Y. Mullins, *Christianity at the Crossroads* (Nashville TN: The Sunday School Board of the Southern Baptist Convention, 1924) 59.
[51] Mullins, *Faith in the Modern World*, 26. Italics in original.
[52] Ibid., 36-37.
[53] E. Y. Mullins, *The Christian Religion in its Doctrinal Expression* (Philadelphia: Roger Williams Press, 1917) 25.

to an audience steeped in scientific skepticism. "Experimental knowledge of the truth as revealed to the heart of the individual directly by the Father," he insisted, "is the only possible key to the Kingdom of God." Focusing theology on individual experience, however, did not mean adopting it as the sole criterion of truth. Christian doctrine could not be derived from "subjective personal experience."[54] Any attempt to do so misrepresented the faith, for Christianity was not a set of ideals or a mystical collection of spiritual insights. It was, rather, a "historical religion" grounded in the person of Jesus Christ as the "sole founder and supreme authority" and the Bible as "our only source of authoritative information about Christ and his earthly career."[55] Mullins understood these two factors, the person of Jesus and the Bible, as objective anchors preventing Christian experience from drifting into the realm of private piety, for genuine personal experience "under the guidance of God's Holy Spirit" would always be consistent with the experiences recorded in Scripture.[56]

Within the framework provided by the historical reality of Jesus and the authority of the Bible, an experience-based approach to Christian theology gave individual believers a great deal of freedom. No person or church could legitimately define or interpret Christian experience for another. Certainly, Mullins acknowledged, there were elements common to all Christian experience: the person of Jesus Christ as revealed in Scripture and mediated by the Holy Spirit, for example, was the same for everyone. Jesus did not change. Individual experiences of him, however, could vary. Some may be more intellectual and others more emotional, but all were equally valid as expressions of the living, risen Christ at work in the lives of his people.[57] Personal communion between the believer and God made the experience of faith real, and such a genuine religious encounter could only occur through the unmediated communication of the soul with God, acting through the power of the Holy Spirit. External influences only contaminated the purity of the

---

[54] Ibid., 3.
[55] Ibid.
[56] Ibid.
[57] Ibid., 87.

individual experience. This freedom of the human soul, in Mullins's view, was the one given, the one absolute, which even God could not limit.

Because of their consuming passion for freedom, observed Mullins, Baptists captured the modern spirit better than any other religious denomination. "The Baptist type of religion is most fundamentally in accord with the ongoing of the world toward democracy," he wrote in 1911. Baptists, it seemed, professed a religious faith that reflected the prevailing attitude of the day. They offered an echo, not an alternative—and this, Mullins argued, happily worked to their advantage.

Freedom, he stressed, was the key. "It would be calamitous to the social and political development of the world, as well as to Baptists as a people," wrote Mullins, "should [Baptists] in this age of the triumph of the principles of democracy, abandon their own ideals of individualism and independency."[58] This overarching commitment to freedom enabled reasonable people to agree with the Baptist faith as articulated by Mullins and still maintain their intellectual respectability and credibility in a modern scientific age. After all, what did Baptists believe in the realm of religion that was not taken for granted in scientific, philosophical, or political circles? Scientific principles set the standard for any truth claim, personal experience represented a valid form of knowledge, and individual freedom was the highest good. Christianity, in other words, simply made sense in the modern world.

***

During his twenty-five years as the president of Southern Seminary and an apologist for the Christian faith, Mullins's scholarly and popular works displayed a remarkable degree of consistency, with his ideas about Baptists, theology, freedom, and democracy changing little over time. The Mullins of 1924 sounds very much like the Mullins of 1904. His first book, for example, *Why Is Christianity True?* (1905), provided an apology for orthodox Christianity against modern religious skeptics; his last book, *Christianity at the Crossroads* (1924), argued in a similar vein that modern science had failed in its attempt to replace religion as the answer for humanity's problems. Both the dominant questions and their

---

[58]Mullins, "Baptists in the Modern World," 348.

respective answers remained constant despite the nearly twenty years separating the two volumes. While fragments of Mullins's favorite themes appear in all his books, *The Axioms of Religion: A New Interpretation of the Baptist Faith* (1908) provides the single best account of his interpretation of Christianity. Written by Mullins at roughly a third of the way through his academic career, Axioms formally introduced the concept of "soul competency" in the United States and made the crucial connection between Baptist ideas about freedom and American democracy that became a centerpiece of Mullins's thought for the rest of his career. As such, *The Axioms of Religion* stands as an extraordinary distillation of "Baptist democracy" in the first quarter of the twentieth century by the leading Southern Baptist theologian of the day.

The book began with Mullins presenting his familiar argument that changing times require ongoing adjustments and reinterpretations of Christian doctrine. The challenges of modern, scientific thought demand an adequate response from religion, he insisted, lest the latter pass into irrelevance. "The time has come for the various Christian bodies to give a fresh account of themselves to the world, and in an entirely new way. The questions should not be one of past service merely, but of fitness for present service," Mullins wrote. "The aim of this book is to make this statement from the point of view of the Baptists."[59] Appropriately, Mullins noted, the foundation for this fresh account of the Baptist faith is none other than the Kingdom of God. As Mullins saw it, the "spiritual laws" of the Kingdom reflected the values of freedom, personal relationships, individual experience, and autonomy of the soul.[60] Churches can either reproduce these Kingdom principles or obscure them by their polity, Mullins asserted, hinting at his fundamental argument. "Sacerdotalism dims the truth of God's direct relations with men," he wrote. "Episcopies and hierarchies obscure the truth that all men are free and individually responsible to God."[61] The religious landscape, it seems, abounds with churches that, by their repressive polities, obscure the Kingdom's ideal of freedom. Is there a church, Mullins asked

---

[59] E. Y. Mullins, *The Axioms of Religion*, 25-26.
[60] Ibid., 38-41.
[61] Ibid., 43.

rhetorically, formed in accordance with Kingdom principles, a church that proclaims freedom and cherishes the autonomy of the individual soul?

Mullins believed that such a church did indeed exist. The Baptists, he wrote, "certainly have a consistent record. In their advocacy of soul freedom in its completest measure, and of the principle of the separation of church and state, in their insistence upon believers' baptism and a regenerate church membership, there is not a fleck or stain upon the fair page of their history."[62] As evidence for this claim, Mullins cited the record of Baptists in America.

Both before and after the American Revolution, Baptists in New England and Virginia persistently fought for liberty and equality, Mullins wrote, and their cause attracted the support of such great American statesmen as George Washington, Thomas Jefferson, and James Madison.[63] "There is no evidence that Baptists came to their view of soul freedom and separation of church and state gradually," he continued. "There is nowhere a wavering note on this great theme. It seems to have been a divinely given prophetic insight into the meaning of the gospel and the implicit teaching of Scripture."[64] Though self-evident to Baptists, Mullins noted, the idea that church and state should be separate did not strike their fellow Americans as readily apparent, for "it was not until after the promulgation of the federal constitution that Congress was awakened to the danger of perpetuating the un-American theory of the union of church and state."[65] True to their nature, Baptists took the lead in remedying the problem by pressing for a constitutional amendment guaranteeing religious liberty for all Americans.

Less than three chapters into *Axioms*, Mullins had already nestled Baptist principles snugly into the story of American origin. George Washington supported the Baptist cause of liberty. The separation of church and state, a prophetic insight given by God with particular clarity to the Baptists, became a foundational principle for the new republic.

---

[62] Ibid., 44.
[63] Ibid., 46.
[64] Ibid., 47.
[65] Ibid., 49.

Perhaps most remarkably of all, Baptists, because of their prophetic insight, intuitively perceived the true values of America more accurately than did the framers of the Constitution, who had failed to exclude the "un-American theory of the union of church and state" from their finished product. From Mullins's perspective, history clearly demonstrated that the Baptist principles of freedom and equality lay at the very foundation of American democracy.

The apparent relationship between Baptists and democracy went even deeper than mere historical coincidence. Near the end of chapter three, Mullins attempted to sum up in a single principle the Baptist contribution to religious thought. Introducing what was to become his most significant theological legacy, he identified this distinguishing principle as "the competency of the soul in religion." Simply put, Mullins explained, "the idea of the competency of the soul in religion excludes at once all human interference, such as episcopacy and infant baptism, and every form of religion by proxy. Religion is a personal matter between the soul and God."[66] In soul competency, Mullins saw a perfect balance of responsibility and freedom: the responsibility of individuals to determine their own spiritual destinies coupled with the complete freedom to do so in the manner, and at the time, of their own choosing. The doctrine, wrote Mullins, "is, of course, a New Testament principle and carries at its heart the very essence of that conception of man's relationship to God which we find in the teaching of Christ."[67] The inevitable corollary of soul competency in religion, Mullins continued, was democracy in church government. "The independence and autonomy of the local church," he concluded, "is not merely an inference from a verse of Scripture here and there. It inheres in the whole

---

[66] Ibid., 54

[67] Ibid. As Bloom observes, however, Mullins conceded the point that soul competency and its derivative principle of church-state separation could not be derived from any specific biblical text. See Bloom, 206. According to Mullins, "Scripture nowhere enjoins in so many words separation of Church and State." Instead, the New Testament text taken as a whole testifies to the principle of soul competency and religious liberty. See *The Axioms of Religion*, 47.

philosophy of Christianity."[68] If the doctrine of soul competency distinguished Baptists from other Christians, then its derivative principle of democracy represented the distinctively Baptist form of governance.

The fact that soul competency was, first and foremost, a Baptist principle was of enormous importance for Mullins, as it placed Baptists in the vanguard of modern thought. In Mullins's view, just as experiential theology made Christianity legitimate in a scientific age, the experientially grounded principle of soul competency made Baptists the standard-bearers of this legitimacy. "Properly understood, the doctrine of the soul's competency in religion," as advanced by Baptists, "is the summary of our progressive life and civilization. The competency of man in religion is the competency of man everywhere."[69] Freedom gave rise to progress, and Mullins effectively positioned Baptists as freedom's champions. America, meanwhile, was "the arena which God has supplied for the free and full play of the principle [of soul competency], and from here it is destined to spread until it covers the earth."[70]

From the principle of soul competency, and in the interest of advancing human progress, Mullins derived six "self-evident" axioms of religion that "will not be denied so far as they are general principles by any evangelical Christian or intelligent unbeliever. They are the alphabet of the Christian religion." Mullins's strategy of stating Baptist beliefs in axiomatic fashion reflected his ongoing desire to establish a "scientific" foundation for Christianity—that is, one that "reasonable" people could not dismiss as mere superstition. "What we wish the world to see," he wrote, "is that [the Baptist] conception of the church and Christianity rests upon an impregnable foundation."[71] The axioms themselves were straightforward and each related to a different sphere of human existence:

---

[68] Ibid., 55. Mullins seems to have been the first Baptist theologian to use the phrase "autonomy of the local church," which implied a lack of accountability to Scripture or the Holy Spirit that earlier Baptists would have found troubling.
[69] Ibid., 65-67.
[70] Ibid., 68.
[71] Mullins, *The Axioms of Religion*, 74.

The theological axiom: the holy and loving God has a right to be sovereign.
The religious axiom: all souls have an equal right to direct access to God.
The ecclesiastical axiom: all believers have a right to equal privileges in the church.
The moral axiom: the responsible man must be free.
The religio-civic axiom: a free church in a free state.
The social axiom: love your neighbor as yourself.[72]

These six axioms, "taken in communion with the fundamental general principle out of which they spring—the competency of the soul in religion under God—may be regarded as the platform of human rights in religion," declared Mullins. "All the axiomatic truths announced are in complete harmony with the ideals of the Kingdom of God," which, as Mullins previously noted, were grounded in freedom and individual autonomy.[73]

Explaining his first axiom, Mullins carefully stated that while the theological axiom "respects human freedom," it nonetheless maintained that God is sovereign over all creation.[74] This delicate balance of human freedom and divine authority depended upon God's character as a holy and loving Father. "Assume that God is holy and that he is also loving," Mullins wrote, "and the human heart rests in the idea of his sovereignty, indeed demands it as the only possible ground for security and peace and the ultimate triumph of holiness and love among men."[75] Having thus asserted God's "right to be sovereign," Mullins, in the remaining five axioms, turned his attention to the possibilities this sovereignty opened up for humanity.

The religious axiom "simply asserts the inalienable right of every soul to deal with God for itself. It implies, of course, man's capacity to commune with God" on an individual, personal level.[76] It also assumed

---

[72] Ibid., 73-74.
[73] Ibid., 77.
[74] Ibid., 90-91.
[75] Ibid., 89.
[76] Ibid., 92.

an essential equality among all believers in the eyes of God, granting "equal access to the Father's table, the Father's ear, and the Father's heart."[77] Religion, insisted Mullins, must be understood as a relationship "between God and the individual man. Religious privilege and religious duty subsist between man and God in the first instance in their capacity as individuals and only secondarily in their social relations."[78] According to the clear teaching of the New Testament, Jesus alone served as mediator between God and the individual. Due to the pernicious practice of infant baptism, however, Christian tradition had abandoned this biblical truth and illegitimately placed priests and parents in positions of spiritual authority.[79]

Just as the religious axiom proclaimed the right of all individuals to enjoy equal access to God, the ecclesiastical axiom maintained that all believers have a right to equal privileges in the church. "The first and finest expression of Christ's lordship over the individual believer is the gift of autonomy to him," Mullins wrote. "Christ discovers each man to himself and starts him on an autonomous career, but never for a moment does he relax his grasp upon that man's conscience and life. Yet nothing thrills men into such a sense of freedom and power."[80] Believers thus become members of the church based purely on their own free will; though joined in close spiritual communion with their fellow Christians,

---

[77] Ibid.

[78] Ibid., 92-93. Charles Marsh, in his portrait of Douglas Hudgins, a Southern Baptist pastor in Jackson, Mississippi, during the civil rights era, dramatically illustrates the practical effects of such an individualistic theology. By limiting the scope of the church's authority to "spiritual" matters and moral issues such as drinking, dancing, and gambling, Hudgins abdicated his prophetic responsibility to the community. Mullins's way of being Baptist, Marsh suggests, simply endorses the status quo of the world and leaves the church captive to the surrounding culture. See Marsh, *God's Long Summer*, 82-115. For another examination of the dangers a "spiritual" understanding of Christianity poses to the integrity of the church's witness, see William Cavanaugh, *Torture and Eucharist: Theology, Politics, and the Body of Christ* (Malden MA: Blackwell Publishers, 1998) and its account of the Roman Catholic Church's response to the Pinochet regime in Chile.

[79] Ibid., 100ff. Chapter seven concludes with an extended critique of infant baptism in light of the religious axiom.

[80] Ibid., 128.

they lose none of their Christ-given autonomy.[81] Accordingly, then, democracy represented the only proper institutional expression of the religious and ecclesiastical axioms. The model churches depicted in the New Testament, after all, were themselves pure democracies. Mullins considered this point absolutely crucial to his argument. "What I am in particular concerned to show," he wrote, "is that democracy alone accords with the nature of the Kingdom of God; that the direct relations of men to God and their equality as brethren require a democratic church polity. No other polity leaves the soul free."[82]

As the early church drifted away from "the simple democratic polity of the New Testament" and became an establishment supported by the state, Mullins noted, Christianity "ceased to be a leaven of spirituality and righteousness permeating society everywhere, and became instead a political force operating after the manners and with the ends of such a force."[83] Mullins believed that the influence of an autocratic state tended to corrupt the witness of the church, and he warned here of the dangers posed by too comfortable a relationship between the two. Democracy, though, seemed congenial to the mission of the church. "It can be maintained that as Baptists hold it, this [democratic] form of polity is eminently suited for the work which Christianity is to perform in the world," observed Mullins.[84] In the context of the ecclesiastical axiom, of course, Mullins's comments about democracy must be understood as referring only to church governance. As his earlier observations about Baptists and American history suggested, however, a situation could conceivably emerge in which the state did not threaten the Baptist mission to the world but, rather, complemented it.

Further explorations of that possibility would have to wait for later chapters, though, as Mullins turned his attention to his fourth axiom,

---

[81] The parallels here between Mullins and John Locke are unmistakable. Locke understands the church as a voluntary association, into which people may enter and exit according to the dictates of their individual consciences. At no time does the individual surrender any of his or her essential freedom to the authority of the church. See Locke, "A Letter Concerning Toleration," 20ff.
[82] Mullins, *The Axioms of Religion*, 134.
[83] Ibid., 144-145.
[84] Ibid., 146.

which he considered to be the basis of all ethics. According to this moral axiom, Mullins claimed, the soul must be free in order to be responsible, for "the Gospel message is never forced upon the will. Indeed the will cannot be 'forced.' The ideas of the will and of force are incompatible and incommensurable."[85] The absolute freedom of conscience of which Mullins wrote did not, he believed, need any justification. Simply stating it as a fact sufficiently established its validity, for though he readily acknowledged that good defenses of freedom existed on theological, metaphysical, and psychological grounds, Mullins breezily asserted that "our purpose here does not require that we present them even in outline. We are dealing with an axiom."[86] No less an authority than Jesus himself recognized this axiom as self-evident truth. "Jesus taught the moral freedom of man. Not only so, he asserted it for himself," Mullins noted, citing the story recorded in Luke 2:41-52 of the twelve-year-old Jesus teaching in the temple as an example of his "self-assertion." Throughout Jesus' relationship with God, Mullins continued, "there is never on the Father's part the slightest movement or impulse to override the voluntary choice of Jesus."[87]

For Mullins, the moral axiom of freedom could be reduced to the principle of self-determination. Freedom "means that when a man acts he acts for himself," he wrote. "The choice is his own. He is not compelled but impelled. He is self-determined. This is the core of manhood and personality. This is the inner glory of our being. It is the one spark of fire which kindles about our humanity its unique splendor."[88] In all aspects of life, Mullins explained, freedom means self-determination. "In civic life," for example, "political freedom is self-government. A government of the people by the people for the people is

---

[85] Ibid., 150. Again, note the similarities here between Mullins's position and Locke's ideas about the will and coercion. See Locke, "A Letter Concerning Toleration," 18-19.
[86] Ibid., 151.
[87] Ibid., 152. Significantly, Mullins did not cite the story of Jesus in the garden of Gethsemene, in which he prayed fervently that God would deliver him from the ordeal of crucifixion before eventually submitting to God, saying "Yet not as I will, but as you will" (Matt. 26:36-39). Obedience, not self-assertion, seems to be the dominant characteristic of Jesus as he heads to the cross.
[88] Ibid., 153.

a free government."[89] The same applied to freedom in religion, which rejected all forms of compulsion. Positively stated, religious freedom "is God appealing to the soul through the truth and calling forth the soul's intellectual and obedient response. It is the soul's approach to God through faith and prayer and fellowship and obtaining grace to help in time of need."[90]

Having thus made his case for freedom as self-determination, Mullins next made a crucial move, explicitly connecting the freedom of Christ with the ideals of political freedom. "The Anglo-Saxons made one chief contribution to the civilization of the world. This was the love of individual freedom," he wrote, referring to a traditional belief that an ancient, unwritten "Anglo-Saxon constitution"[91] contained the foundations of modern liberal democracy. "But it is exactly this gift which Christ bestows. The same love of freedom and sense of personality, the same self-assertion and love of adventure, the same response to the challenge of danger and of great undertaking in a line of exact analogy to the old Anglo-Saxon principle, all this appears in Christianity, but with a vast difference. Under Christ, all is regenerated and spiritualized."[92] Without the ameliorating effects of Christianity, Mullins warned, the Anglo-Saxon lust for freedom could result in a kind of Nietzschean nightmare of unbridled worship of power for its own sake. When yoked with Christian principles, however, Anglo-Saxon freedom—the same freedom, remember, that Mullins understood to have been bestowed by Jesus himself—produced "the moral and spiritual giants of history who, to the kingly elements of power, have always added the priestly elements of love and service."[93] The Christian faith plus political freedom, in other words, resulted in the ideal civilization. Herein lay the essential elements of Mullins's vision of Baptist democracy.

---

[89] Ibid.
[90] Ibid., 154.
[91] For a good, concise description of the "Anglo-Saxon constitution" tradition, see Shelton, *The Political Philosophy of Thomas Jefferson*, 26-27. The definitive work on the subject is J. G. A. Pocock, *The Ancient Constitution and the Feudal Law* (Cambridge: Cambridge University Press, 1957).
[92] Mullins, *The Axioms of Religion*, 154.
[93] Ibid., 155.

This vision received further clarification in chapter eleven, as Mullins elaborated upon his religio-civic axiom of "a free church in a free state." The axiom, "which states the American principle of the relationship between the Church and State," he wrote, "is so well understood and is accepted by the people of the United States so generally and heartily that it is unnecessary to spend time in pointing out at length what the axiom implies."[94] Despite the risk of seeming redundant, Mullins nevertheless offered a brief sketch of how the doctrine of the separation of church and state developed in both the United States and England. Then, in words that could easily have been borrowed directly from John Locke, he described the divergent functions of church and state. "The American view," Mullins began, "is based on fundamental facts of human society and the Gospel. The Church is a voluntary organization, the State compels obedience. One organization is temporal, the other spiritual. Their views as to penal offenses may be quite different, that being wrong and punishable in the Church which the State cannot afford to notice. The direct allegiance of the Church is to God, in the State it is to law and government. One is for the protection of life and property, the other for the promotion of spiritual life."[95]

Since church and state obviously served two different purposes in society, Mullins reasoned, their functions should never overlap. To illustrate, he cited three examples of potential conflict between church and state. One, the use of public tax money to support private religious schools, he believed flagrantly violated the principles of the religio-civic axiom.[96] A second, the practice of reading the Bible in the public schools could be considered wrong if done for the purposes of religious instruction, insofar as such instruction could violate the consciences of students. Bible verses used for moral teaching, however, "[are] not objectionable even to atheists. A moral text-book ... containing extracts from other works containing wholesome teaching, might be employed to advantage without violating any man's conscience."[97] The third example,

---

[94] Ibid., 185.
[95] Ibid., 195-196.
[96] Ibid., 197.
[97] Ibid., 198.

tax-exemptions for religious organizations, did not constitute a violation of the religio-civic axiom because, according to Mullins, the right to tax implied a sovereignty which the state could not exercise over the church.

Two critical points immediately stand out in this account of "a free church in a free state." The first is Mullins's now-familiar assertion that his position needed neither explication nor justification but, instead, may be taken for granted as conventional wisdom. Such a perspective reflects the relative security available to someone speaking comfortably within the mainstream of society. Whereas the dissenter must persuade a skeptical public to consider an alternative perspective, the insider simply appeals to existing prejudices. Compare, then, the nonchalance with which Mullins presented his axiom with the passionate, detailed, and often-exhausting arguments concerning church and state made by dissenters John Smyth, Thomas Helwys, Roger Williams, Isaac Backus, and even, to a large extent, John Leland, all of whom challenged long-standing cultural assumptions regarding state establishments of religion.[98]

As dissenters calling for religious liberty, they bore the burden of proving their arguments fully, insofar as none of their unorthodox positions could be taken for granted. Accordingly, they provided ample evidence from Scripture, theology, philosophy, and contemporary political theory to support their intellectually creative appeals. Mullins clearly does not belong in this Baptist tradition of dissent. Throughout *The Axioms of Religion*, he frequently professed no need to defend his ideas because they were so widely accepted by all Americans.[99] In the case of the religio-civic axiom, he proudly confessed to stating the

---

[98] Despite his vocal and enthusiastic support for the new American republic, Leland was an incurable agitator, a stubborn critic of religious establishments, and was widely considered scandalous by his contemporaries. See McLoughlin, *New England Dissent, 1630-1833*, vol. 2, 928-935.

[99] Mullins's intellectual and theological reliance upon the cultural assumptions of his day reflects the unfortunate legacy of what Mark Noll has called the "evangelical Enlightenment" of the eighteenth and nineteenth centuries in which evangelical Christians uncritically absorbed Enlightenment ideas about science, philosophy, politics, and economics and presumed that these new perspectives meshed perfectly with their Christian faith. See Noll, *The Scandal of the Evangelical Mind*, especially 83-107.

obvious. When Mullins wrote about "a free church in a free state," he did so as a Baptist completely at ease with the world around him.

The other aspect that deserves additional attention centers upon the relationship between the religio-civic axiom of religion and the American principle of the separation of church and state. Introducing the axiom, Mullins did not connect it with any theological rationale or specifically Baptist doctrine. Instead, he explicitly equated the religio-civic axiom with the *American* principle of church-state relations. For Mullins, in other words, the fifth axiomatic element of the Baptist faith came directly from American constitutional theory, with liberal democratic ideals defining the way Baptists properly understood their relationship with the state. Later, Mullins noted that the American view of church and state (which, apparently, doubled as the Baptist view of church and state) came from "the fundamental facts of human society and the Gospel," but the priority, as indicated by Mullins's heavy reliance on John Locke's brand of liberalism, clearly fell upon the former.[100]

Finally, Mullins's treatment of his sixth axiom, the social axiom, reflected his longstanding—though, as noted above, diplomatically expressed—reservations about the social gospel movement. Some Christians, he observed, "are asserting that individualism is a false teaching and that the gospel aims primarily at social results."[101] The churches undoubtedly bore a heavy responsibility for their collective failure to alleviate the many social problems of the day. But, Mullins insisted, "a mere social Christianity must fail, since it ignores the basal law of Christianity. To regenerate the individual is the sole condition of permanent moral progress in the social sphere."[102] To this end, the church must exert its influence as a force for good both through the conversion of individuals and as an advocate for more Christian social, economic, and political practices. By way of summary, Mullins then made an intriguing observation. "It is the essence of Christianity to send a man after his fellows," he wrote. "The Christian who understands the

---

[100] Mullins, *The Axioms of Religion*, 195-196.
[101] Ibid., 201.
[102] Ibid., 204. Note that Mullins falls into exactly the fallacy that so vexed Rauschenbusch, that of separating social Christianity from the rest of the Gospel message.

meaning of his religion, therefore, will be a force for civic, commercial, social, and all other forms of righteousness. *Thus Christianity in America will become the religion of the State, although not a State religion.*"[103] This distinction, though slight, suggested the implicit irony of Baptist democracy as articulated by Mullins, which insisted upon the institutional separation of church and state while, at the same time, both encouraging and celebrating the moral and ideological convergences between the two.

Having thus described in detail the six axioms of religion—Baptist ideas that served as the common "alphabet of the Christian religion"—Mullins turned to an examination of Baptist views about the proper relationships between local churches, ecumenism, and the ordinances of baptism and the Lord's Supper. Not surprisingly, as he dealt with each subject Mullins returned time and again to the themes of freedom and democracy. Commenting, for example, on the prospects for unity across the various Christian denominations, he noted that "the deeper tides of modern life are all setting toward democracy in Church and State," with the law of "spiritual gravitation" leading Christians around the world to discover the axiomatic principle of the individual soul's competency in religious matters.[104] Where the world was heading, Mullins believed, Baptists had already been standing for centuries.

Nowhere was this fact more apparent than in the United States, and in the penultimate chapter of *The Axioms of Religion*, Mullins finally turned his full attention to chronicling the contributions of Baptists to American civilization. To be sure, the notion that Baptist theology and America democracy shared a common heritage and a fraternal relationship had surfaced intermittently throughout the book. Now Mullins dropped all pretenses of subtlety. "We may regard American civilization as a Baptist empire," he declared, "for at the basis of this government lies a great group of Baptist ideals."[105] Building on this idea of America as a Baptist empire, Mullins contended that political and religious life traveled on parallel roads that never diverged greatly in

---

[103] Ibid., 207. Emphasis added.
[104] Ibid., 233-234.
[105] Ibid., 255.

direction or democratic orientation. "Religion is the ultimate fact of man, and civilization is the dim reproduction of religion," he wrote. "Baptists have furnished the sheaf of religious ideals around which the others have gathered and done obeisance; that those ideals have imparted their peculiar glory to our temporal and political organization; that they have fallen from heaven on the hard forms of earthly power and glorified them.[106] The mixture of Baptist theology and American democracy could hardly be more apparent.

Such a mixture, though, was not coincidental. Indeed, according to Mullins, American civilization owed its very soul to the Baptists and their democratic faith. Baptists, he wrote, "have furnished to American civilization the most spiritual interpretation of Christianity the world has ever seen."[107] The practice of believers' baptism cherished the right of individual self-determination in religion, and the Baptist polity of church government of, by, and for the people illustrated the Baptists' exclusive reliance on the Holy Spirit—not some petrified ecclesiastical hierarchy—for divine guidance. "Thus we hold up to civilization in doctrine and polity the burnished mirror of New Testament Christianity," observed Mullins, "in which it may study its own image to advantage and discover the spiritual basis of American institutions."[108] In the Baptist faith, he implied, America could see its true, best self revealed.

Moreover, Mullins claimed, through Baptist theology alone, American civilization gained a complete understanding of liberty. "The greatest fact of modern history was the discovery of the idea of liberty, and that discovery was made by the Baptists," he wrote. "The discovery of this idea is the spiritual analogue to the discovery of the New World by Columbus and its emancipation by Washington."[109] Mullins, in a fanciful but telling allegory, then imagined what a heroic sculpture of Liberty might look like. "I would have a perfect image of liberty carved from the purest marble," he began. "I would have Columbus, the intrepid navigator and explorer of the New World placing the pedestal

---

[106] Ibid., 257.
[107] Ibid., 261.
[108] Ibid., 263.
[109] Ibid., 269.

in position, and George Washington, the dauntless soldier, lifting the statue into place, and Roger Williams robing the image in the garments of righteousness and placing the chaplet of divine approval upon its brow."[110] If Mullins's sculptor should want to see what this grand image of Liberty looked like in the modern world, "he would have to search until he found it written in the earliest Confessions of Faith of the Baptists and embodied in their church life and political creed."[111]

Significantly, the nature of Liberty, as described in Mullins's remarkable allegory, remained constant for Columbus, Washington, and Williams—each of them made their own separate contributions toward bringing the same grand statue to completion. The liberty for which the American general Washington fought, in other words, was the liberty for which the (briefly) Baptist dissenter Williams agitated. They simply represented two important steps in the ultimate triumph of a monolithic ideal of liberty on American soil, a victory embodied in the faith and practice of Baptists in the United States. "It was no accident that a Baptist wrote our national anthem," wrote Mullins. "The Baptist heart was the native place of liberty, and when S. F. Smith wrote ["My Country 'Tis of Thee"] it was but the natural union of faith in God on the part of the Baptist preacher joined to patriotism in an American citizen. It was but the deep spring of religious liberty bubbling up and over into thrilling song through the lips of a loyal citizen of this greatest country on earth."[112] Baptists, liberty, faith in God, patriotism, America, citizenship—all blended into a seamless garment for Mullins.

Baptist theology and American democracy not only shared a common understanding of liberty, but a common identity as well. The former, stated Mullins plainly, supplied the moral and spiritual assumptions upon which the latter stands.[113] American democracy was the political expression of soul competency, the distinctive essence of the

---

[110] Ibid.
[111] Ibid., 270.
[112] Ibid., 270. "The Star Spangled Banner" did not become the official national anthem of the United States until 1931. Before that, a number of hymns, including "My Country 'Tis of Thee," were variously considered to be "national anthems."
[113] Ibid.

Baptist faith.[114] "Look into a New Testament [that is, a Baptist] church and then at the American government and insight discovers that the latter is the projection of the shadow of the former," Mullins maintained. "One might in a certain sense say that the primary election which determined whether or not there should be an American government was held two thousand years ago on the shores of the Mediterranean when the little Baptist democracies assembled to worship."[115] Simply put, the six Baptist axioms of religion corresponded perfectly with the political axioms of American democracy, both of them coming from the same source and moving toward the same goal.[116] According to Mullins:

> The Baptist axioms of religion are like a stalactite descending from heaven to earth, formed by deposits from the water of life flowing out of the throne of God down to mankind, while our American political society is the stalagmite with its base upon the earth, rising to meet the stalactite and formed by deposits from the same life-giving stream. When the two shall meet, then heaven and earth will be joined together and the kingdom of God will have come among men.[117]

Indeed, he concluded in a pithy summation of Baptist democracy, the intelligent Baptist "can yield to none in his patriotism, for his religious ideals are the bedrock of the [American] political fabric."[118]

***

---

[114] Ibid., 271.

[115] Ibid., 273.

[116] Ibid., 273-274. The theological axiom corresponded to the fact that the state recognizes God's sovereignty by granting the church its independence; the religious axiom with the idea that all men are created free and equal; the ecclesiastical axiom to the principle that the American government is of, by, and for the people; the moral axiom to the right to vote and the judicial system; and the social axiom to the belief in equal rights to all and special privileges to none. The religio-civic axiom worked equally well in the political as in the religious context, Mullins wrote, so it needed no translation.

[117] Ibid., 274.

[118] Ibid., 275. *The Axioms of Religion* concludes with a final chapter on "Baptists and World Progress," which advances the claim, since democracy is the progressive trend of the modern world and Baptists are the most democratic of all religious organizations, the axioms of religion proclaimed by Baptists and "derived from the gospel of Jesus Christ are fitted to lead the progressive civilization of the [human] race." (277)

Written relatively early in his academic career, *The Axioms of Religion* defined the trajectory for Mullins's later work. For the rest of his life, he would revisit and restate—but never revise—the ideas he set forth in his widely celebrated second book. The affinity Mullins identified in 1908 between Baptist theology and American democracy, an axiomatic relationship based on a shared commitment to freedom, continued to exert a strong influence upon his imagination. "Indulge me in a little fancy as we contemplate 'Old Glory,' the name we have learned most to love to describe our flag," Mullins wrote in a 1912 article titled "Baptist Bed-Rock Ideals":

> The stripes of continuous color across the flag tell of a homogenous American life, and being equal in width they tell of justice and equality; and the red, white, and blue in the color scheme tell of American variety and of unity in variety; and the cluster of stars in the flag, each star separate from the other stars, tells of the principles of autonomy and individualism which underlie our whole system; and they are the stars to show that those principles of freedom and individualism are the freedom of an ordered universe and not of chaos in the world.[119]

When the United States entered World War I, Mullins gladly lent his patriotic support to the cause.[120] Characteristically, Mullins read great theological significance into the war and endorsed the American military effort as, ultimately, a struggle for the Baptist ideals of freedom and democracy. "This war has been fundamentally a Baptist war," he wrote in November 1918. "It has been a conflict for the rights of the common man. The root principle out of which the war sprang was the value of the common man in the sight of God." A war fought to make the world safe for democracy must be a Baptist war, he continued, for "democracy is the expression in political life of the infinite worth of the common man in the sight of God," an axiomatic principle of Baptist faith and practice.[121] Victory for America, in Mullins's eyes, ultimately meant victory for the Baptist cause.

---

[119] *Baptist World*, 9 May 1912, 9.
[120] Beginning in the fall of 1917, he served as the religious director for the Y.M.C.A. outpost at Camp Taylor in Louisville. See Isla May Mullins, *E. Y. Mullins*, 158.
[121] *Baptist Standard*, 21 November 1918, 9.

If John Leland's individualistic understanding of religion decisively transformed the identity of Baptists in America, reinterpreting the principles of Baptist theology in harmony with those of liberal democracy and bringing Baptists into the mainstream of American culture, then it was Mullins who fully and systematically integrated the democratic ideals of individual sovereignty and absolute freedom into Baptist theology. His concept of "soul competency" enshrined the individual conscience as sacred and unassailable, and his ideas of church polity dovetailed nicely with democratic political theory. For Mullins, the Baptist faith and the American republic perfectly complemented one another, as they represented the purest expressions of freedom in the spiritual and political realms, respectively. "Our age beyond all others is the age of freedom," he wrote in 1913. "Absolute freedom in all spheres is the ideal."[122] As Mullins wrote about freedom, however, particularly religious freedom, the boundaries between church and state became less clear and the Baptist identity became more confused. Indeed, as articulated by Mullins, a moral identification of Baptist identity with American democracy thrived behind the thin veil of "religio-civic" institutional separation.

Mullins grounded his understanding of religious liberty in human nature, which he saw in distinctively modern terms. "Religious liberty rests upon a person's original creation in God's image... as a free and self-determining being," Mullins claimed. His idea of soul competency, the right of individuals to enjoy direct and unmediated access to God, logically followed from this view of creation. "A human being, as a person created in God's image, free and spiritual, [is] competent to deal directly with God."[123] Anything that interfered with individuals' abilities to make decisions concerning their religious beliefs, meanwhile, violated their sacred human rights. Mullins's conception of church governance reflected his convictions regarding individual freedom. He believed each church represented a spiritual democracy in which each believer enjoyed

---

[122] E. Y. Mullins, *Freedom and Authority in Religion* (Philadelphia: Griffith and Rowland Press, 1913) 11.
[123] E.Y. Mullins, "The Baptist Conception of Religious Liberty," in *Proclaiming the Baptist Vision: Religious Liberty*, 86-87.

equal stature and an equal hand in making congregational decisions. This was, Mullins claimed, the New Testament ideal. It was also, perhaps not coincidentally, the American way. The state represented a political expression of Christian ideals, the most significant of which was, of course, freedom.

The priority of the individual, the privatization of religion, the sovereignty of the conscience, the identification of absolute freedom as the greatest good—all these ideas, the fruits of the Enlightenment and the foundation of the liberal democratic state, had steadily been eroding historic understandings of Baptist faith and practice since the days of Leland. With Mullins, however, these ideas *became* the historic understandings of Baptist faith and practice. In his rendition, the modern, democratic state owed its very political and philosophical identity to the Baptists and their religious principles. Proof of the state's good faith and embrace of Baptist ideals rested securely in the First Amendment: by granting religious freedom to its citizens, the United States demonstrated its congruence with "true Christianity." The irony, of course, lay in the fact that Baptists like Mullins could insist so vehemently on a complete institutional separation of church and state, all the while triumphantly proclaiming Baptist identity and the ideals of American democracy to be intimately and organically connected.

E. Y. Mullins, in the name of freedom, thus wrote Baptist democracy into the theological orthodoxy of his denomination. Indeed, *The Axioms of Religion* did not vanish into academic obscurity upon publication. It became, rather, one of the basic textbooks for two generations of students at Southern Baptist seminaries. "Do you doubt," George Truett asked rhetorically at Mullins's silver anniversary gala, "that as the years pass on these axioms as stated by President Mullins will find favor everywhere?"[124] Likewise, Mullins was not a lonely voice crying out in the wilderness of Southern Baptist life. He served as president of the Southern Baptist Theological Seminary for twenty-five years, as president of the Southern Baptist Convention from 1921 to 1924, and almost single-handedly crafted the 1925 Southern Baptist Faith and Message statement. Long celebrated for his theological moderation,

---

[124]Truett, "A Quarter Century of World History," 61.

Mullins, during the first quarter of the twentieth century, stood in the center of Southern Baptist life, where Baptist theology and American democracy freely mixed.

4

George Truett and the Baptist Apology for Democracy

The Southern Baptist Convention had been meeting in the Washington, D.C., for several days when the delegates, or, in the Baptist vernacular, "messengers," assembled on the east side of the United States Capitol building for a public worship service on Sunday, 16 May 1920. The crowd of messengers, estimated to be more than 15,000, also included members of Congress, the Supreme Court, and President Wilson's Cabinet.[1] For many of the Southern Baptists in attendance, the occasion could hardly have been more momentous. "Presidents have been inaugurated on those historic steps, world leaders have walked up the marble stairway of our Capitol," gushed an editorial in the Baptist Standard, the Texas Baptist newspaper, "but we doubt if ever under the shadow of the Capitol there was ever held a more significant service."[2] It was, indeed, a momentous occasion. After all, before the throng stood George W. Truett, pastor of the First Baptist Church of Dallas and arguably the most famous Southern Baptist preacher of his generation, poised to deliver a sermon on "Baptists and Religious Liberty" from the symbolic center of American democracy.

The last notes of "My Country 'Tis of Thee" still lingered in the breeze as Truett began his address. By all accounts, what followed did

---

[1] Organizers of the event, well aware of Truett's popularity, moved the service from the indoor facility where the business meetings of the convention had taken place in order to accommodate the expected crowd. The most reliable estimate of the crowd seems to be 15,000, which appears in numerous sources, including Truett's earliest biographer, Powhatan W. James in *George W. Truett: A Biography* (New York: The MacMillan Company, 1939) 1. The numbers, however, do vary widely. E. W. Stephens, for example, wrote of "an assemblage of over 100,000 people," but since no other sources come close to that figure, Stephens's number is likely a misprint ("At Washington with the Southern Baptists," *The Baptist*, 29 May 1920, 627).

[2] *Baptist Standard*, 27 May 1920, 8.

not disappoint his expectant audience. "The setting, the subject, and the speaker combined to make this an historic event, about which our children and our children's children will read," continued the effusive *Baptist Standard* editorial. "Surely the preacher was surrounded by a great cloud of witnesses who in other years had helped make our country a refuge for men and women oppressed because of their religious beliefs."[3] Another *Baptist Standard* editorial offered a much more succinct appraisal: the Sunday afternoon that George Truett preached about religious liberty from the steps of the United States Capitol was "the greatest hour ever witnessed" by the Southern Baptist Convention.[4]

Perhaps no single event in the first quarter of the twentieth century better exemplified the intersection of Baptist theology and American democracy than this celebrated sermon from the Capitol steps. Just as E. Y. Mullins wrote the assumptions of "Baptist democracy" into the theological mainstream of his denomination, Truett gave them a powerful, public voice. It was, to be sure, an unmistakably *Baptist* voice. Truett championed an individual's freedom to believe or not to believe in God, a believer's freedom to fellowship directly with God, a church's freedom to conduct its affairs without interference from the state. Like other Baptists, both before and since, he embraced religious liberty and fiercely opposed any perceived institutional overlap between church and state. Truett's sermon eloquently stated these convictions in dramatic fashion—and because of that, it has become the stuff of legend for Baptist imaginations, a heroic address of epic proportion and, in the words of one Baptist historian, "one of the most often quoted Baptist statements on religious liberty of the twentieth century."[5]

But what, really, did Truett say? In the process of arguing for the necessity of a strict separation between church and state, he seamlessly wove Baptist theology and American democracy together to the point that the two were virtually indistinguishable. In the name of religious liberty, he assumed an essential harmony between church and state.

---

[3] Ibid.
[4] *Baptist Standard*, 20 May 1920, 1.
[5] Walter Shurden, *Proclaiming the Baptist Vision: Religious Liberty*, 5.

Truett, of course, was not alone among Baptists, before or since, in holding to such a view, and his interpretation of the relationship between church and state was in keeping with those of his fellow Baptists in the first quarter of the twentieth century. As a ringing declaration of church-state separation, then, George Truett's sermon from the Capitol steps was—and still is—popularly considered a powerful expression of the Baptist ideal. For this, it has become famous. As a celebration of the supposed harmony between Baptist theology and the American state, however, the sermon serves as perhaps the single most eloquent, and accurate, expression of "Baptist democracy" in the early twentieth century.

***

If the Southern Baptists wanted to make a public statement—and the decision to hold a worship service on the steps of the United States Capitol building suggests that they did—then George Truett was the right person to deliver it. As perhaps the best known Southern Baptist preacher in America, Truett represented the public face (and voice) of the denomination.[6] By May 1920, Truett had indeed traveled a great distance from his humble beginnings in the mountains of North Carolina. Born in 1867, two years after the end of the Civil War, he spent his formative years in the remote hills of Clay County, where his grandfather was a Baptist preacher in the area and his great uncle had gained a legendary local reputation as a fiery camp meeting evangelist.[7] Truett grew up

---

[6]Truett "was the most famous Southern Baptist preacher of his generation, and probably the greatest of all time," writes Baptist historian Leon McBeth. "He was the soul of Baptist statesmanship and in many ways was the unofficial spokesman for the entire denomination." See McBeth, "George W. Truett: Baptist Statesman," *Baptist History and Heritage* 32 (April 1997): 9.

[7]James, *George W. Truett*, 6-11. James's biography of Truett, while serving as a faithful record of the man's life and achievements, is somewhat colored by the fact that the author was both Truett's son-in-law and, as a fellow pastor, a longtime colleague in ministry. James's work is very helpful as a general introduction to Truett, particularly in the intimate details he offers about his subject's personality and family life. Nevertheless, it should be read primarily for what it is: a warm tribute to a greatly admired father-in-law. Keith E. Durso's more recent *Thy Will Be Done: A Biography of George W. Truett* (Macon GA: Mercer University Press, 2009) fills a puzzling gap in Baptist scholarship created by the lack of attention that historians have paid to Truett since his death more than fifty years ago. Durso's biography of the great preacher is welcome and far-too-long overdue.

familiar with both the language and the ethos of evangelical Southern Baptist faith, but he did not make a public profession of faith until he was nineteen, during a revival meeting in nearby Hayesville.[8] After graduating from high school, Truett crossed over the state line into north Georgia, where, along with a cousin, he founded Hiawassee Academy, a private Christian school.[9]

Truett taught at Hiawassee for only two years before his family, seeking more and better farmland, left the rocky soil of the North Carolina mountains in 1889 and moved to Texas. Truett entered Grayson College in Whitewright, intending to pursue a career in law. The members of Whitewright Baptist Church soon perceived that the young law student had undeniable gifts for teaching and preaching and so, at a Saturday evening church meeting in 1890, the congregation decided that Truett should be ordained into the gospel ministry.[10] Despite Truett's repeated appeals to the community to wait several months before taking such a momentous step, the church ordained him the next morning after a brief examination period.[11]

Almost immediately after his ordination, Truett's life took another unexpected turn, this time toward Baylor University in Waco, Texas. The Baptist school, like so many institutions of higher learning in the post-Reconstruction South, carried a debilitating amount of debt—in Baylor's case, a sum of $92,000 (more than $2 million in 2011 dollars, adjusted for inflation). Knowing that the university desperately needed fund-raising assistance, the pastor of Whitewright Baptist Church recom-mended Truett for the job, noting that "wherever he speaks, people do what he wants them to do."[12] Baylor hired Truett, who quickly confirmed Jenkins's confident assessment by raising enough money from Texas Baptists to erase the entire debt in less than two years. Having

---

[8] Ibid., 24.
[9] Ibid., 31ff. The school eventually became Truett-McConnell College, a coeducational Baptist junior college.
[10] Ibid., 45ff.
[11] Ibid., 49-50. Truett's own account of his call to ministry may be found in James, 47-50.
[12] Letter from R. F. Jenkins to B. H. Carroll, quoted in Peter Clarke MacFarlane, "The Apostle to the Texans," *Collier's* 50 (4 January 1913): 22.

spectacularly saved Baylor from financial ruin, the 26-year-old Truett enrolled there as a student in 1893 to complete his education.[13]

Three months after graduating from Baylor in June 1897, Truett became pastor of the First Baptist Church of Dallas, a position he held for the rest of his life. From the beginning, the match between church and pastor was a good one, despite a tragic hunting accident less than six months into Truett's long tenure there. On 4 February 1898, Truett was walking behind J. C. Arnold, the Dallas chief of police and a member of First Baptist, when his shotgun discharged and hit Arnold in the back of the leg. Arnold died a day later from the wound. Newspaper accounts of the incident described Truett as "prostrated with grief."[14] When he returned to his pulpit the next Sunday, "his eyes were sunken in dark hollows from the week's sleeplessness, and his sensitive face was marked with deep lines of suffering."[15] If anything, the traumatic event only strengthened the bond between Truett and his congregation, for in 1902, when Baylor University asked Truett to become its next president, he politely declined the invitation, saying "I have sought and found the shepherd heart of a pastor. I must remain at Dallas."[16]

The pastorate, Truett discovered, was his true calling in life. "The most virile, the most robust, the most challenging business in the world today is the preacher's calling," he told an interviewer in 1925. "He must be sincere above all things. A man is a ghastly falsehood if he does not speak and live the truth. He should be such an honest, genuine, sincere, benevolent man that his community would trust its life in his hands. When such men do enter the pulpit, the people hear him gladly."[17] By all accounts, Truett was just such a man, and Dallas responded accordingly. During his forty-seven years of service at First Baptist Church, the

---

[13] For an account of Truett's experience as a student at Baylor and pastor of East Waco Baptist Church, see James, 66ff.

[14] *Dallas Morning News*, 6 February 1898, 1.

[15] James, 88-89. James describes the accident and its devastating effect on Truett, 85-90. See also Craig Skinner, "The Bullet That Broke a Preacher's Heart," *Preaching* 14 (May-June 1999): 52-55.

[16] Truett, quoted in James, 95-96.

[17] Truett, quoted in George W. Gray, "Out of the Mountains Came This Great Preacher of the Plains," *The American Magazine* 100 (November 1925): 140.

congregation added more than seven thousand new members, most of them by baptism.[18] "He preaches for conversions," wrote one journalist, "and gets them at the close of every sermon. In his regular church services, he averages fifty to seventy-five conversions a month."[19] Under Truett's watch, First Baptist Church of Dallas became, as one admirer put it in 1923, "one of the mighty forces of the nation, both in numbers and in spiritual fruitfulness. There, as pastor, teacher, and evangelist, [Truett's] genius has shone for more than twenty years, where his name is a household word, and his fame is like a fragrance throughout the nation."[20]

Journalist George Gray agreed. "The whole city is his parish," he observed in a national magazine profile of Truett. "When he celebrated the twenty-fifth anniversary of his pastorate, [Dallas] merchants devoted their paid advertising space in the newspapers to felicitate him, and so many people desired to take part in the celebration that it was spread over a week. A Methodist bishop publicly said, 'The greatest asset the city of Dallas has is George Truett—more valuable than your skyscrapers, your railroads, your boasted industries, is this great preacher of God.'"[21] Crowds of people routinely packed the First Baptist Church sanctuary to hear Truett preach, many of them members of different churches and denominations. Everyone in Texas's largest city, it seemed, considered Truett a friend. "Dr. Truett can hate the sin and love the sinner and make the sinner understand that he feels both emotions," observed Peter Clark MacFarlane, author of another national magazine piece on the famous preacher. "Said some one to me: 'He makes the

---

[18] Skinner, 54. Baptist churches generally receive new members in two ways: by transfer of letter from another Baptist church, or by baptism. Though some Baptist churches now recognize the baptisms of other Christian denominations, many still do not and require adult Christians to be baptized by immersion before they may join the church. New believers, meanwhile, are baptized after making a public profession of faith. Church growth experts usually draw a direct relationship between a church's effectiveness at evangelism and the number of new members it receives by baptism; a high number of baptisms suggests a very active evangelism ministry.

[19] Gray, 140.

[20] Joseph Fort Newton, *Some Living Masters of the Pulpit: Studies in Religious Personality* (New York: George B. Doran Company, 1923) 217-218.

[21] Gray, 16.

strongest Prohibition speeches I have ever heard, but if he were to die, I think every saloon in town would close on the day of his funeral."[22] Truett, wrote Edgar DeWitt Jones in a book profiling thirty-two leading American preachers, "rarely speaks on civic affairs or takes part in meetings of a general interest, but when he does, it is an event, and Dallas listens."[23]

Further contributing to the luster of Truett's growing legend—especially in the eyes of the national media—was the fact that he spent a month every summer preaching to the cowboys of west Texas.[24] Though revered in Dallas as a "prince of the pulpit," Truett gained the hard-won respect of his cowboy congregation through his "earnest, simple, straight-forward preaching of the gospel of Jesus."[25] MacFarlane, in fact, felt compelled to invent a new word in order to express adequately his sense of awe upon meeting Truett, the Texas preacher. This, he wrote in the introduction to his *Collier's* magazine piece, "is the story of a *Texanic* personality. Even before going to Texas, the writer was informed that George W. Truett holds Texas in the hollow of his hand."[26] MacFarlane's experience in Dallas did nothing to change that assessment. Truett, he exclaimed, "is a mile-a-minute sort of person. He seems to have entered the world on the run and never to have slackened his pace."[27] The man preaches with a "tongue of fire," MacFarlane continued. "His sermons have come to be the sensations of the annual conventions of his communion. At Baltimore in 1909, his speaking place was filled, packed and jammed, two hours before the preaching hour. So every year as the place of these annual conventions is shifted over the country, people will stand in the aisles to hear the man."[28]

---

[22] MacFarlane, 21.
[23] Edgar DeWitt Jones, *American Preachers Today: Intimate Appraisals of 32 Leaders* (Indianapolis: Bobbs-Merrill Company, 1933) 294.
[24] See James, 98-114.
[25] Doyle L. Young, "Leadership that Motivates: A Study in the Life of George W. Truett," *Baptist History and Heritage* 20 (January 1985): 48.
[26] MacFarlane, 21. Emphasis added.
[27] Ibid.
[28] Ibid.

Truett soon became a very prominent figure in Southern Baptist life and beyond. In 1919, he led the first major fund-raising effort of the SBC, the "75 Million Campaign," and, from 1927 to 1929, he served three terms as the convention's president. Truett consistently lent his support to the various Baptist mission programs and, for five years in the 1930s, promoted the growth of Baptist churches around the world as president of the Baptist World Alliance. His non-Baptist peers from around the country recognized Truett's brilliance as well. He was one of twenty preachers personally invited by President Wilson to travel to war-torn Europe and, under the auspices of the American Y.M.C.A., preach to Allied soldiers and sailors in the autumn of 1918.[29] He appeared in numerous books about "masters of the pulpit" and, in 1925, a *Christian Century* survey of 90,000 ministers named Truett one of the twenty-five "greatest leaders" in American Protestantism.[30] "Dr. Truett is numbered among the small group of powerful preachers in America," noted Jones. "Some say he is the brightest star in the galaxy of sermonic geniuses among the Baptists."[31]

Truett's preaching abilities and his almost regal presence in the pulpit inspired breathless description from his contemporaries. "He looks a celebrity—large frame, broad-shouldered and rugged, with sensitive features, and a superb head crowned with gray hair," wrote George Gray. "His eyes are blue and deep-set, the brooding eyes of a mystic. His hands are restless."[32] Sometimes in these popular accounts of

---

[29] Truett was a vocal supporter of the American effort in World War I. In November 1917, he introduced a resolution at the Baptist General Convention of Texas pledging the full support of Texas Baptists in the ongoing struggle of "democracy against autocracy." See *Baptist Standard*, 29 November 1917, 14, 22. His pastoral activities in France were faithfully reported in the *Baptist Standard*, and his return to Dallas was a citywide event. As Truett entered the train station from the platform, friends lifted him onto their shoulders so the crowd could see him. It took ten minutes for him to get out of the building after which he still had to pass through the crowds lining the steps. See *Dallas Morning News*, 5 February 1919, 7. A dinner reception for Truett drew more than a thousand well-wishers (*Dallas Morning News*, 7 February 1919, 16) and the crowd for his first Sunday back in the pulpit of First Baptist Church spilled out onto the street (*Baptist Standard*, 13 February 1919, 7, 18).

[30] "Greatness in Preachers," *Christian Century* 42 (1925): 44-45.

[31] Jones, 293.

[32] Gray, 16.

Truett in the pulpit, the preacher assumed an almost superhuman character. Hyperbole flowed freely. "Like the fox in the Spartan's breast, he tears directly into the vitals of a man till his heart is laid bare to himself," claimed MacFarlane. "Once the man's oratorical passion has been aroused he attacks like a whirlwind. He comes on like a cavalry charge. You hear the beat of drums, the clatter of sabers, the huzzas of advancing hosts. The ground rocks and reels with the thunder and thud of ten thousand hoofs, and suddenly there in the midst of you is that figure with the burning cheek, the gleaming teeth, and the blazing eye, swinging high the sword of his flashing spirit and hacking his way into your heart."[33]

While Truett's preaching prowess repeatedly overwhelmed those who came to hear him, the pastor's personal qualities were no less legendary. His warm, generous spirit and strong commitment to humanity struck Edgar DeWitt Jones as especially noteworthy traits. Truett "belongs to the Church Universal," he wrote. "In times like the present it is refreshing to find so sturdy a defender of his own particular interpretation of Christianity, who at the same time finds something divine in every man, woman, and child, and is measurably helping to usher in the great consummation."[34] If Truett has any "weaknesses, foibles, or faults," Jones continued, "they are certainly not known to his congregation or his fellow ministers. Nor has he any critics worth noting, if we except an extreme individualistic fighting fundamentalist parson in the Lone Star State who has publicly attacked Truett for his 'modernism' of all things."[35] More than anything else, those who spent time talking to Truett and those who knew him came away impressed with his genuine passion for ministry. "Curious is it not, and praiseworthy altogether that

---

[33] MacFarlane, 22.
[34] Jones, 295.
[35] Jones, 300. The "parson" to whom Jones refers here is J. Frank Norris, the controversial preacher who was pastor of the First Baptist Church of Fort Worth, Texas, for many of the years that Truett was in Dallas, and was an early proponent of fundamentalism among Baptists in the South. Among Norris's more colorful epithets for Truett were "the Holy Father" and "his sanctimonious holiness." See Barry Hankins, *God's Rascal: J. Frank Norris and the Beginnings of Southern Fundamentalism* (Lexington KY: University Press of Kentucky, 1996). See also Leon McBeth, "John Franklyn Norris: Texas Tornado," *Baptist History and Heritage* 32 (April 1997): 23-38.

a man known throughout America as a preacher of unusual gifts, should be known best in his home city as a shepherd of souls, a friend of suffering human beings?" asked Jones. "And the explanation is at hand—the man, the man is greater than any sermons he ever preached."[36]

In typically humble fashion, Truett consistently refused to take personal credit for any of his success as either a preacher or a pastor. Anyone, he suggested, could do the job well if properly grounded in Scripture and a rich relationship with God. "Complex as civilization is," he said, "the preacher has these factors on his side: first, the human conscience; second, the Bible; and third, God. Your conscience drives you back to seek something beyond the mists. The appeal of the Bible is elemental and universal, and the book can never be superseded. And then—God is on our side, the Divine reaching down into human experience and working with man and for man. If the preacher will stay by the central truths of the Bible and will present them, with a life in consonance with his preaching, he will find a hearing."[37]

Truett's remarkable tenure as pastor of First Baptist, Dallas, lasted until his death in 1944 at age 77. Diagnosed with Paget's disease, a form of bone cancer, he spent several agonizing months undergoing treatment before dying on 7 July. The news hit Dallas hard. The *Dallas Morning News* ran his obituary on its front page, in bold type that overshadowed the latest war news from Europe, and over the next several days chronicled the various tributes to Truett that poured in from across the nation and around the world.[38] Truett's funeral on 10 July attracted almost 6,000 mourners to the First Baptist Church, with many more standing outside in the hot sun listening to the service via loudspeaker. "The Christian world bowed its head in tribute to the man whose words and deeds give him eternal life in the minds of man," reported the *Dallas Morning News* on page one. "In the war-torn corners of the earth, men turned from their duties to send tributes to the Dallas pastor whose

---

[36] Jones, 301.
[37] Gray, 140.
[38] *Dallas Morning News*, 8 July 1944, 1.

evangelistic fervor reared him to the stature that many compare to Spurgeon and St. Paul."[39]

***

During his long career, Truett stood squarely in the denominational mainstream of his day, and his public positions on major theological and political issues were consistent with those of his Baptist contemporaries. Questions about salvation, concerns about Roman Catholicism, and reflections on the virtues of democracy dominated Baptist conversations during the early years of the twentieth century and helped shape the denomination's identity, as well as the worldview of faithful Baptists like Truett.

Above all else, the issue of personal salvation preoccupied Baptists. Like his fellow Baptists, Truett rejected infant baptism as a legitimate means of salvation. "Salvation," he wrote, "is by a person, and that person is none other than the Divine Lord and Savior, Jesus Christ. Whoever receives Him to be his Savior is saved by Him. Whoever turns away from Him does not have spiritual life, but spiritual death."[40] Salvation required faith, and faith, ultimately, was a private matter. The crucial decision to accept or reject Jesus as savior, Truett believed, must be made by individuals acting alone and in keeping with their own consciences. No one could make that decision for another person, hence the illegitimacy of infant baptism. Truett's Baptist contemporaries echoed this position. "Fundamentally, Baptists hold that religion is individualistic, that it is something in the mind and heart," wrote one prominent Texas Baptist in 1920. "Therefore if one is not religious in his own mind and heart, he is not religious at all, and no outside pressure can make him so."[41] For this reason, Baptists insisted upon absolute religious freedom for everyone. "One must believe for himself, and repent for himself, and be baptized for himself, and pray for himself," Truett told the Baptist General Convention of Texas in 1916. "Therefore, no institution, whether church or state, and no person—whether parent,

---

[39] *Dallas Morning News*, 11 July 1944, 1.
[40] George Truett, "Preparation for Meeting God," in *A Quest for Souls*, ed. J. B. Cranfill (Dallas: Texas Baptist Book House, 1917) 91.
[41] *Baptist Standard*, 3 June 1920, 5.

or preacher, or pope, or priest—must dare to come between that soul and its divine Lord."[42]

Despite such lofty language of freedom, much of the Baptist rhetoric in support of religious liberty during Truett's day contained strong anti-Catholic sentiments. For Baptists, the Roman Catholic Church represented the epitome of false religion and stood for everything that Baptists despised—autocracy, creedalism, hierarchy, "proxy religion," and so forth.[43] Baptists consistently defended the right of Catholics to worship freely, but they made it clear that, in matters of faith and practice, they considered Catholics to be gravely mistaken. At the heart of this Baptist antipathy lay an uneasy suspicion that Catholics in America owed their true allegiance not to the United States, but to the pope and his designs for world domination. Behind every Catholic move, Baptists saw the potential for sabotage. In 1919, when the papal undersecretary of state personally delivered a friendly message from the pope to President Wilson, the *Baptist Standard* urged Americans to be wary "of this greeting from the autocrat of autocrats in which he ascribes to himself a love for the principles and noble ideals of freedom and justice." Clearly, the papal envoy's goodwill visit represented another piece of the pope's plan to "crush the good ship of democracy" by lulling the president and his advisors to sleep with flattering words.[44] J. B. Gambrell, an outspoken Texas Baptist leader and a colleague of Truett, claimed in 1921 that "the papacy claims universal dominion over every

---

[42] George Truett, "What We Preach," in *Sermons from Paul*, ed. Powhatan W. James (Grand Rapids MI: Eerdmans Publishing Company, 1947) 21.

[43] Creedalism and proxy religion are Baptist vernacular terms that perhaps require some explanation. Historically, Baptists have been notoriously independent and wary of corporate confessions or creeds, such as the Nicene or Apostles' Creed, that cannot be found in the Bible. As James Dunn has written, "Ain't nobody but Jesus going to tell me what to believe" nicely sums up the typical Baptist attitude regarding creeds. See James Dunn, "Yes, I Am a Baptist," in *Why I Am a Baptist*, ed. Cecil Staton (Macon GA: Smyth and Helwys, 1999) 47. Creedalism, then, refers to any attempt to prescribe certain beliefs as authoritative. "Proxy religion" refers primarily to the practice of infant baptism, in which a family or a church, on behalf of a baby, makes the decision to bring that baby into the fellowship of the church. Such "religion by proxy" undermines the Baptist conviction that church membership should be an expression of an individual's free will and religious experience.

[44] *Baptist Standard*, 23 January 1919, 10-11.

sphere of human existence and in all relations of life, over kings, emperors, and all the functionaries of government in every nation of the earth." Consequently, non-Catholics "are suspicious of Rome and are on the ground against her in politics. They have to be if they are to maintain their liberties."[45]

Perhaps the most serious (and certainly the most common) accusation Baptists leveled against the Catholic Church was that it was "anti-democratic," not just in its internal church polity but in its perceived hostility toward American ideals of freedom and equality. The very idea that a Catholic could potentially place allegiance to the church ahead of allegiance to the state both astounded and alarmed Baptists, who confidently asserted that nothing like that could ever happen with them. Indeed, the essential harmony between Baptist principles and American democracy, they claimed, rendered such a scenario simply implausible. "Baptists are, of all the religious bodies, the most democratic," wrote E. Y. Mullins in 1919. "The individual, the church, the district association, the state and general conventions, all seek to embody the free democratic principle."[46] Or, as Truett put it several years earlier, "the triumph of democracy, thank God, means the triumph of Baptists everywhere."[47]

To be sure, this equation of democracy and Christianity exerted a powerful influence on the imaginations of Truett and his fellow Baptists. Democracy, he wrote, "is the goal for this world of ours—both the

---

[45] *Baptist Standard*, 5 May 1921, 1. Baptists' reaction to John Kennedy as a presidential candidate in 1960 represents the most famous example of their anti-Catholic suspicions. Kennedy's speech to a group of anxious ministers in Houston, in which he assured them that his public decisions as president would be based upon the best interests of the United States and not the theological positions of the Vatican, is a classic of American politics. See *"Let the Word Go Forth": The Speeches, Statements, and Writings of John F. Kennedy, 1917-1963*, ed. Theodore Sorenson (New York: Laurel, 1988) 130-136, for the text of Kennedy's address. Even with this public assurance, however, some Baptists remained uneasy about having a Catholic in the White House. Closer to Truett's time, New York governor Al Smith, also a Catholic and the Democratic candidate for president in 1928, faced the same kind of suspicion Kennedy did, though he was less successful in combating them.
[46] E.Y. Mullins, "Wanted: A Baptist Demonstration," *Baptist Standard*, 2 January 1919, 5.
[47] George Truett, "God's Call to America," 19.

political goal and the religious goal."[48] In a sermon preached during the early months of the American participation in World War I, Truett expressed his firm confidence in the future of democracy. Democracy cannot fail, he argued, because it is of God. "It may be that other wars will have to be fought before true democracy can be established in all the earth," he declared, "but established it will be because its basic principles are the very essence of the Kingdom of God."[49] As such, the United States, the foremost voice of democracy in the world, had a special religious mission to perform. "The task of America," declared Truett on another occasion, using words reminiscent of Rauschenbusch, "is that she herself become thoroughly and truly Christian. Brethren, this mighty America can command the conversion of the world on one condition only, and that is that she be Christian through and through." The United States, he continued, "is to be Christian in her commerce, and in her politics, and in her art, and in her education, and in her literature, and in every phase and fiber of her social order."[50]

Nevertheless, Truett's own experience during the war as a member of President Wilson's hand-picked brigade of preachers taught him that America's mission to the world sometimes carried a heavy cost. Truett was deeply moved by the bravery and commitment of the Allied soldiers he met in the camps and on the battlefield. These men, he wrote to his wife, "are to face death when called, a death for the world's betterment, for its safety, for righteousness. If one can fortify them, to any degree, he feels he must."[51] When the armistice ending hostilities in Europe went into effect on 11 November 1918, Truett was in northwestern France near the town of Brest. "Today is probably the most notable day in all history, next to the day when Jesus died on Calvary," he wrote in his journal. "All France is a riot of joy. Never, ever did the world see the like before. Two flags everywhere were waving—the French and American flags....

---

[48] George Truett, "The Prayer Jesus Refused to Pray," in *Follow Thou Me* (Nashville: The Sunday School Board of the Southern Baptist Convention, 1932) 43.

[49] George Truett, "The Eagle and Her Nest," in *The Prophet's Mantle* (Nashville TN: Broadman Press, 1948) 80.

[50] Truett, "God's Call to America," 22-23.

[51] George Truett, letter to wife , 19 October 1918. In Truett Collection., File 1343, A. Webb Roberts Library, Southwestern Baptist Theological Seminary, Fort Worth, Texas.

Now may the victorious nations be humble, and obedient to the call of the highest. It is a time for prayer. God help us!"[52]

While touring the battle-scarred landscapes of France and Germany and visiting with victorious Allied soldiers, Truett pondered the significance of the war and tried to place the conflict, with its tremendous death toll and widespread misery, in a larger context. The war, he concluded, was a divine judgment upon Germany delivered by the Allied nations. "Now, may people everywhere be given to see that God's will must be followed, or all shall go wrong," he wrote on 10 December 1918. "Germany ignored God's will—forgot that nations are amenable to Him, to reap what they sow—forgot that their guns, submarines, and Zeppelins could not overturn His throne. The Lord reigneth—let all the earth rejoice."[53] As he considered God's hand in guiding the outcome of the war, Truett was particularly impressed by the pure motives that had compelled the United States into the conflict. In what may have been the outline for his standard sermon to the American troops in Europe, the preacher scribbled the following notes on the last two well-worn pages of his journal:

> Patriotism to be forever based on righteousness.... Whatever our national faults—I will confess that our history here and there puts us to blush, yet in this conflict, God is our record, we enter it with clean hands and a pure conscience.... For no selfish end did you unsheathe the sword, but to redeem your plighted word and to defend the weak. Justice and mercy are our guiding stars.... National greatness consists in these things. Home, religion, and the highest things to be given the highest place.[54]

In war as well as in peace, Truett firmly believed that God had given the United States a redemptive mission to perform in the world, a divine calling that suggested an intimate connection between the ideals of church and state: a shared sense of purpose and, perhaps, even a shared destiny.

Other Baptists echoed Truett's faith in America as a partner in the missionary endeavor. "Missions is the war behind this great war.

---

[52] George Truett, diary, 11 November 1918, Truett Collection, File 665.
[53] George Truett, diary, 10 December 1918, Truett Collection, File 665.
[54] George Truett, diary, No date (last two pages) Truett Collection, File 655.

Missions is the key to unlock the future of this world," wrote the *Baptist World*'s editors in 1918. "The only real safety for the New Testament faith is in spiritual democracy. The little, self-governing groups of regenerate men, called churches in the New Testament. They alone can truly make and keep democracy safe for the world."[55] American victories for democracy on the field of battle, it seemed, promised to bring with it success in the Baptist struggle to win souls for Jesus. "Without wishing to displace the soldier in the affection and loyal support of all lovers of justice and right," wrote another ardent advocate of evangelism, "I would place beside him the foreign missionary as equally worthy of the confidence and support of those who are truly determined to safeguard the democracy of the world."[56] Baptist foreign missionaries and American soldiers abroad, in other words, stood for the same thing—democracy, in its spiritual and political forms, respectively.

At home, too, Baptists understood their missionary work as essential to the success of the American way of life. As an advertisement for the SBC's Home Mission Board asked in 1920, "is America worth saving from radical socialists, bolshevists, the untempered teaching of unbelieving intellectuals, and the flagrant fleshly sins of misguided multitudes?" If so, the ad concluded, then Baptists should give generously to support home missions, for "next to the faith which binds men to Almighty God, the safety and preservation of this nation is today the most important thing in the entire world."[57] Such a fortuitous congruence of church and state seemed obvious to most Baptists: Baptists stood for freedom in the spiritual realm, America stood for freedom in the political realm. This shared commitment to freedom bound the two, church and state, together. Indeed, for Baptists in America, the state was not a rival to the church, but an ally. A threat to one posed a threat to the other, as the great liberal Baptist preacher Harry Emerson Fosdick noted in *The Challenge of the Present Crisis* (1918). "Your country needs you," he appealed during World War I. "The

---

[55] *Baptist World*, 13 June 1918, 4.
[56] *Baptist Standard*, 23 January 1919, 12.
[57] Advertisement in the *Baptist Standard*, 19 October 1920, 17. The Home Mission Board was the agency responsible for overseeing Southern Baptist missionary activity in the United States.

Kingdom of God on earth needs you," he wrote. "The cause of Christ is hard tested and righteousness is having a heavy battle in the earth—they need you."[58]

Shaped by the Baptist theology of his day, steeped in the Baptist understanding of the world, and conversant in the Baptist language of democracy, Truett spoke for the large majority of Baptists in America when he stepped to the lectern on the Capitol steps that Sunday afternoon in Washington, D.C. His celebrated sermon, therefore, must be understood in this context. Truett's invocation of the Baptist ideals of religious liberty and the separation of church and state rested largely on the assumption that Baptists shared a common goal with the American state in promoting freedom around the world. The possibility of a disjunction between a theological understanding of freedom—as understood, for example, by the early Baptists in England to be both freedom *from* the power of sin and death and freedom *for* obedience to God—and a liberal democratic concept of freedom as a virtue in and of itself seems to have concerned neither Truett nor his contemporaries. At the time, such a breach between Baptist theology and American democracy was inconceivable. After all, wrote Truett, "democracy is the goal toward which all feet must travel... both in government and in religion."[59]

***

The rhetorical link between Baptists and America is evident from the very start of Truett's famous 1920 sermon. Southern Baptists, he began, "count it as one of life's highest privileges to be citizens of our one great, united country." Having established Baptists comfortably in the mainstream of the American present, Truett then placed securely alongside the great names of the American past. Let us look back, he said, "to the days of Washington and Jefferson and Madison, back to the days of our Baptist fathers, who have paid such a price, through the long generations, that liberty, both religious and civil, might have free course

---

[58] Harry Emerson Fosdick, *The Challenge of the Present Crisis* (New York: Association Press, 1917) 98-99.
[59] Truett, "The Prayer Jesus Refused to Pray," 43.

and be glorified everywhere."[60] By drawing this parallel between Baptists and the American founders, Truett made it clear that the Baptist vision has always been consistent with the purest of American ideals; from the very start, Baptists and America had been moving in the same direction of freedom. Indeed, Truett continued, "the supreme contribution of the new world to the old is the contribution of religious liberty. This is the chiefest contribution that America has thus far made to civilization. And historic justice compels me to say that it was pre-eminently a Baptist contribution." Baptist ideals, in other words, lay at the very heart of American democracy.

Truett then elaborated upon what Baptists meant by religious liberty. "It is the consistent and insistent contention of our Baptist people, always and everywhere," he said, "that religion must be forever voluntary and uncoerced, and that it is not the prerogative of any power, whether civil or ecclesiastical, to compel men to any religious creed or form of worship, or to pay taxes in support of a religious organization to which they do not belong and in whose creed they do not believe."[61] This conviction, Truett claimed, inevitably grew out of the fundamental principles of Baptist theology, foremost of which, of course, was the absolute lordship of Jesus Christ over the life of a believer. Closely connected with the lordship of Jesus was the ultimate authority of Scripture as the word of God. Baptists "ask only one question concerning all religious faith and practice, and that question is, 'What saith the Word of God?' Not traditions, nor customs, nor councils, nor confessions, nor ecclesiastical formularies, however venerable and pretentious, guide Baptists, but simply and solely the will of Christ as they find it revealed in the New Testament."[62] With Jesus as their king, the Bible their only authority, and individuals able to interpret Scripture for themselves through the power of the Holy Spirit, Baptists discovered a freedom of religion unable to be circumscribed by human institutions.

---

[60] George Truett, "Baptists and Religious Liberty," reprinted in *Baptist History and Heritage* 33 (Winter 1998) 66.
[61] Truett, "Baptists and Religious Liberty," 67.
[62] Ibid., 68.

Having thus established Baptists as both the quintessential representatives of the American character and the champions of religious freedom, Truett made a revealing rhetorical move. "The Baptist message and the Roman Catholic message are the very antipodes of each other," he declared, in keeping with the prevalent Baptist worldview in 1920.[63] To be sure, Truett maintained, "a Baptist would rise at midnight to plead for absolute religious liberty for his Catholic neighbor, and for his Jewish neighbor, and for everybody else." Nevertheless, Baptists and Catholics remained irreconcilably polarized in their understanding of religion, and in Truett's description of this polarization, his understanding of what it meant to be an American began to take shape.

Truett first pointed to the Baptist emphasis on the ability of individuals to approach God directly, without the aid of a priestly intermediary. "For any person or institution to dare to come between the soul and God," he declared, "is a blasphemous impertinence and a defamation of the crown rights of the Son of God."[64] He then discussed the illegitimacy of infant baptism as just such an interposition between the soul and God. Baptists "solemnly believe that infant baptism, with its implications, has flooded the world, and floods it now, with untold evils." Chief among these evils, Truett claimed somewhat ironically, given his enthusiastic identification of Baptist theology and American democracy, was the "secularizing of the church and ... the blurring of the line of demarcation between the church and the unsaved world."[65] Indeed, having made this point about infant baptism, Truett proudly proclaimed that "to Baptists, the New Testament clearly teaches that Christ's church is not only a spiritual body but is also a pure democracy, all its members being equal, a local congregation, and cannot subject

---

[63] Ibid., 69. More contemporary Baptists, uncomfortable with the sermon's anti-Catholic sentiment have tried to isolate Truett's defense of religious liberty from his opinions about Roman Catholicism. Such revisionism clearly misrepresents Truett's understanding of religious freedom, which was inextricably bound up with his perception of Catholicism as the very antithesis of freedom. See Shurden, *Proclaiming the Baptist Vision*, 6, and the editor's notes on the sermon text in *Baptist History and Heritage*, 85, for two attempts to decontextualize Truett's remarks in the name of ecumenism.
[64] Ibid., 70.
[65] Ibid., 71.

itself to any outside control." Because of this independent, democratic nature of the New Testament church, a nature most faithfully exemplified in the practices of Baptist congregations, Truett confidently declared that, "never, anywhere, in any time, has a true Baptist been willing, for one minute, for the union of church and state, not for a moment."[66]

Following this often-quoted remark, Truett expanded upon what he meant by the union of church and state. Not surprisingly, his comments focused exclusively upon the Roman Catholic Church and its claims of "world supremacy." History, Truett said, records that by the medieval period, the pope "assumed to be monarch of the world, making the astounding claim that all kings and potentates were subject to him." The pope lorded his authority "over parliaments and council chambers, having statesmen to do his bidding, and creating and deposing kings at his will."[67] In Truett's view, the fact that the pope, on behalf of the Church, claimed the ultimate allegiance of all Catholics worldwide represented an intolerable state of affairs. Any church that demands priority over the state, he implied, violated the basic principles of religious freedom. In the papacy, Truett saw the worst form of autocracy and the most implacable foe of democracy, "and until the principle of democracy, rather than the principle of autocracy, shall be regnant in the realm of religion, our mission [as Baptists] shall be commanding and unending."[68] The Catholic Church, with its pretensions to authority over both worldly governments and individual believers, embodied for Truett the kind of autocratic impulse that led to the institutional union of church and state. Baptists, with their commitment to democracy, offered an alternative.

American history, Truett contended, bore out this assertion. Recalling the names of Baptists who suffered financial and physical hardships for the sake of religious freedom, Truett argued that Baptists were responsible for keeping the flame of freedom burning brightly through the dark ages of religious establishment in the colonies. "They

---

[66] Ibid., 72.
[67] Ibid., 74.
[68] Ibid., 75.

dared to be odd, to stand alone, to refuse to conform, though it cost them suffering and even life itself," he said.[69] Baptists, Truett continued, "offered their protests and remonstrances and memorials, and, thank God, mighty statesmen were won over to their contention... until at last it was written into our country's Constitution that church and state must in this land forever be separate and free, that neither should ever trespass upon the distinctive functions of the other. It was pre-eminently a Baptist achievement." The presumed ideological intimacy here between Baptists and the American founders is striking as Truett once again made certain that his listeners did not forget the fundamental harmony between Baptist ideals and American democracy.

Having thus established the theological and historical affinities between Baptists and America, Truett finally turned his attention to the concerns of his own era. "And now, my fellow Christians, and fellow citizens," he asked, "what is the present call to us in connection with this priceless principle of religious liberty?" The most obvious obligation was to serve unfailingly the American state that had been so generous in its guarantee of religious freedom. "There comes the clarion call to us to be the right kind of citizens," Truett said. "Happily, the record of our Baptist people toward civil government has been a record of unfading honor. Their love and loyalty to country have not been put to shame in any land. In the long list of published Tories in connection with the Revolutionary War there was not one Baptist name."[70] The end of freedom, Truett continued, resided in the creation of a righteous society; as the champions of freedom, Baptists must work to make America virtuous. "The people, all the people, are inexorably responsible for the laws, the ideals, and the spirit that are necessary for making a great and enduring civilization," he argued. "Every man of us is to remember that it is righteousness that exalteth a nation, and that it is sin that reproaches and destroys a nation."[71] America, if true to its mission to serve humanity, could be a beacon of light in the world.

---

[69] Ibid., 77. Truett is wrong here in saying that the struggle for religious freedom cost some Baptists in America "even life itself." No Baptists were ever killed on American soil on account of their religious beliefs.
[70] Truett, "Baptists and Religious Liberty," 78.
[71] Ibid., 79.

As such, Truett noted, American ideals represented a cause worth dying for. "The integrity of one's country is worth dying for," he claimed. "And, please God, the freedom and honor of the United States of America are worth dying for."[72] This observation became particularly significant in light of the two other things Truett considered worthy of the supreme sacrifice: the sanctity of womanhood and the safety of childhood. Strangely, this evangelical Baptist preacher did not include the Christian faith in his list. One way of looking at this omission is simply as an oversight, that Truett certainly believed Christianity a cause worthy of martyrdom but, for whatever reason, neglected to mention it here. Another, more problematic interpretation, however, is that, after naming the freedom and honor of America as a worthy cause, Truett felt that adding the Christian faith—which, for Baptists, was all about freedom and democracy—to the list would be superfluous.

Nevertheless, Truett clearly believed that the preservation of American ideals required the active involvement of Christians in civil affairs. As "a citizen and as a Christian teacher," he called upon Congress to ratify the United States's proposed membership in the League of Nations and praised the work of those "moral and religious forces" that brought about Prohibition.[73] The American heritage of liberty, Truett continued, "calls us imperiously to be the right kind of Christians. Let us never forget that a democracy, whether civil or

---

[72] Ibid., 80. One remarkable observation by Truett deserves additional comment. Calling for Americans to extend the virtues of Christian unselfishness to other nations, he says that "the world is now one big neighborhood.... National isolation is no longer possible. The markets of the world instantly register every commercial change. An earthquake in Asia is at once registered in Washington City.... Every one of us is called to be a world citizen, and to think and act in world terms." Globalization tends to be thought of as primarily a twenty-first-century idea. The fact that a Southern Baptist preacher was saying these things in 1920 is quite prescient.

[73] Ibid., 81. Like many Baptists, Truett included, J. B. Gambrell considered the League of Nations to be an application of Baptist principles to international affairs. "Baptists insisted on the principle of open discussion and liberty for every soul to act for itself in religion," he wrote in the *Baptist Standard*. "We have had 140 years of it in America with the result that America has enlightened the world." Not even the framers of the League of Nations covenant, chief among them Woodrow Wilson, "knew how closely they were following the matchless principles of the New Testament." See "Concerning the League of Nations," *Baptist Standard*, 20 February 1919, 11, 19.

religious, not only has its perils, but also has its obligations." Again, Truett spoke of the responsibilities of church and state in the same breath. "A democracy calls for intelligence," he said, and Christian schools represented the best hope for educating citizens rightly. "A democracy needs more than intelligence, it needs Christ." In the aftermath of the Great War, Truett predicted that the educational center of the world "will henceforth be in this New World of America. We must build here institutions of learning that will be shot through and through with the principles and motives of Christ, the one Master over all mankind."[74] Only this sort of Christian education, he maintained, could adequately produce citizens capable of governing themselves in keeping with the principles of democracy.

After linking this endorsement of Christian education with a call for Baptists around the world to get on with the work of evangelism, Truett concluded his sermon with one last appeal to the selfless example of Baptist heroes of the past. In so doing, he neatly articulated the prevailing Baptist understanding of church and state in the early part of the twentieth century, weaving together the images of cross and Capitol to create "a cloud of witnesses" of undetermined identity. "If we are to be in the true succession of the... mighty days and deeds of our Baptist fathers in later days, then selfish ease must be utterly renounced for Christ and his cause and our every gift and grace and power utterly dominated by the dynamic of his Cross," declared Truett. "Standing here today in the shadow of our country's Capitol, compassed about as we are with so great a cloud of witnesses, let us today renew our pledge to God, and to one another, that we will give our best to church and to state, to God and to humanity, by his grace and power, until we fall on the last sleep."[75]

Truett's sermon thus ended just as it began, with a mixture of Christianity and democracy, Baptist theology and patriotism. Did the cloud of witnesses assembled in the shadow of the Capitol refer to "our Baptist fathers in later days"? Did it refer to those American leaders who labored beneath the Capitol to preserve, protect, and defend democracy?

---

[74]Ibid., 82.
[75]Ibid., 84.

In the end, given the implications of Truett's sermon, such specificity matters little. For Truett and the crowd of Baptists on the east lawn of the Capitol building, either referent would have been appropriate, for both embodied a heritage of freedom. Indeed, by giving their best "to church and to state," Baptists in America ultimately understood themselves to be serving the same end—the victory of religious and political freedom over the constrictive forces of autocracy around the world.

***

Truett's peers immediately recognized his sermon as a *tour de force* performance, both as a faithful exposition of Baptist theology and a compelling appropriation of American democracy. "Never did any man in the history of our nation appear more like a prophet of God than did Pastor Truett that hour when, with unerring precision and unswerving devotion to the facts of history, he laid bare the errors and weaknesses of Roman Catholicism," declared the *Baptist Standard*. "He unrolled the scrolls of the past and revealed the marvelous contribution Baptists had made to religious liberty."[76] One prominent Texas Baptist preacher wrote of his experience on the Capitol lawn, listening to Truett's speech beside a Roman Catholic priest. His comments reflect the extent to which Baptists intimately associated the principles of their church with the ideals of their state. "I told [the priest] more, and something of the billows upon billows of the simple, great multitudes who loved liberty and Christ in the South, and of their uncontaminated Americanism," the Baptist minister wrote, "and went on until he seemed conscious of the contrast I was not stating but implying. In a little while George [Truett] was hot on the trail of the [Catholics], and my Catholic friend shifted away from me."[77] The contrast this preacher meant to imply by his talk of freedom and Americanism, of course, was the familiar one between Baptists and Catholics, democracy and autocracy. Love of liberty and uncontaminated Americanism seemed naturally to go together, and Baptists in 1920 considered themselves to be the purest religious manifestation of this harmony and George Truett its most eloquent champion.

---

[76] "Some Impressions of the Convention," 8.
[77] Ibid.

More than eighty years later, the influence of Truett's sermon on the Baptist imagination continues to be strong. It has become, for many Baptists, the definitive statement of the Baptist understanding of religious freedom. Truett himself, largely by virtue of this one address, now stands among the foremost proponents of church-state separation in the Baptist tradition, and contemporary Baptists supporters of separation frequently enlist him as their ally. "Strict separation has been maintained by every major Baptist advocate of religious liberty from Thomas Helwys, through Roger Williams, John Clarke, Isaac Backus, and John Leland, to the twentieth-century giants E. Y. Mullins, George Truett, and J. M. Dawson," writes one Baptist historian.[78] Certainly a casual reading of the sermon from the Capitol steps provides ample evidence to support Truett's reputation as a strict separationist. Indeed, Truett decisively and dramatically rejected any institutional overlap between church and state as autocratic and inconsistent with individual freedom.

Baptists today vigilantly monitor the activities of both church and state against just such institutional overlap in matters of public funding for religious organizations and charity work, religious displays on government property, and religious activities in public schools.[79] For Baptist watchdogs of church-state separation, these kinds of political issues represent the battlegrounds upon which the struggle for religious liberty continues to be fought. Baptists take seriously their mission to patrol the constitutional watchtowers against those who would undermine the precious American tradition of freedom. Truett, they claim, understood this responsibility explicitly.[80]

---

[78] Jim Spivey, "Separation No Myth: Religious Liberty's Biblical and Theological Bases," *Southwestern Journal of Theology* 36 (1994): 15.

[79] See, for example, James Dunn, "Church and State in Contemporary United States: A Wall of Separation?" *Baptist History and Heritage* 33 (Winter 1998): 36.

[80] "If Truett were alive today, he would say that the defense and propagation of [church-state separation] is why the Baptists of America need a Baptist Joint Committee on Public Affairs," wrote Stan Hastey, former executive director of the Alliance of Baptists. See Hastey, "The History and Contributions of the Baptist Joint Committee," *Baptist History and Heritage* 20 (July 1985): 43. The Baptist Joint Committee on Public Affairs (now the Baptist Joint Committee for Religious Liberty) is an advocacy organization funded by numerous Baptist groups in the United States, headquartered in Washington, D.C., and dedicated to defending religious liberty and the separation of church and state.

Such a claim involves two assumptions: that an essential harmony exists between the ideals of Baptist theology and those of American democracy, and that the preservation of religious freedom depends upon the continued integrity of the Constitution, particularly the principles of the First Amendment. The freedom of the church, according to this perspective, rests in the hands of the state. Herein lies both the irony of the Baptist tradition of religious freedom and the most enduring legacy of Truett's famous sermon: Baptists today may stridently reject any overlap between church and state, but their language—the very way they articulate their identity and express themselves theologically—is completely saturated with the rhetoric of American democracy. The cherished wall of separation functions less like a barrier than a mirror. When Baptists look at America, they see their own reflection and proudly point out the resemblances. In his sermon, Truett, like other Baptists before and since, self-consciously positioned Baptists in the American mainstream, both historically and ideologically, and clearly equated the goals of the church with those of the state. What Baptists bring to the religious world, he said, the United States brings to the political realm—democracy and the promise of freedom.

Nobody has articulated this understanding of the Baptist identity better than George Truett that spring day in Washington. Seamlessly weaving together the principles of Baptist theology and American democracy, Truett articulated what it meant to be Baptist in the early years of the twentieth century. As such, his sermon rightly deserves its legendary status, but not for the traditional reasons. Perhaps no other Baptist, before or since, has captured the irony of the Baptist identity in America so perfectly as did Truett in May 1920 when he stood in the shadow of the Capitol and proclaimed religious freedom. His words still ring today, the echoes of Baptist democracy.

5

Baptists and the Subtle Snares of Freedom

Despite their collective confidence that the world would continue its steady march toward an increasingly bright, democratic, and Christian future, E. Y. Mullins, Walter Rauschenbusch, and George Truett, and their generation of Baptists lived in the twilight of American Christendom.[1] Born into Baptist families within seven years of one another in the 1860s, these three men all came to maturity in a world still largely shaped by the ethos of evangelical Protestantism and its guiding assumption that religion—specifically, Protestant Christianity—provided the necessary moral foundation for a stable and virtuous nation.[2] In such an environment, the perceived goals of church and state frequently overlapped: what was considered good for the one was, more often than not, considered good for the other. Certainly the sweepingly optimistic, and largely uncritical, identification of Baptist principles with the ideals of American democracy that consistently appeared in the works of Rauschenbusch, Mullins, and Truett between 1900 and 1925 reflected their implicit understanding that the United States was, at its core, a Christian civilization.

---

[1] See McClintock, "Walter Rauschenbusch," 491. Regarding the end of American Christendom, historian William Lee Miller has observed that "establishment by law ended in the nineteenth century. Establishment by cultural domination ended in the twentieth." See Miller, *The First Liberty*, 350. Handy argues that "the Protestant era in American life had come to its end by the mid-thirties" in *A Christian America*, 213. Ahlstrom locates the end of Protestant cultural hegemony in America in the 1960s. See Ahlstrom, 1079ff. For a good, concise account of how Protestantism's grip on American culture slipped in the twentieth century, see James Davison Hunter, *Culture Wars: The Struggle to Define America* (New York: Basic Books, 1991) especially 67-106. See also Rodney Clapp, *A Peculiar People: The Church as Culture in a Post-Modern World* (Downers Grove IL: Intervarsity Press, 1996) 16-32; and Robert Linder and Richard V. Pierard, *Twilight of the Saints: Biblical Christianity and Civil Religion in America* (Downers Grove IL: Intervarsity Press, 1978) 77-86.
[2] See Goen, "Baptists and Church-State Issues in the 20th Century," 226ff.

Baptists, they maintained, could be loyal Americans without conscientious reservation because, ultimately, the United States represented the political expression of distinctively Baptist theological convictions. These convictions could be, and often were, reduced to a single, unifying concept: democracy. During the early years of the new American republic, the fiery John Leland had passionately proclaimed a self-consciously democratic gospel that, in content, often seemed to be as much "American" as it was "Baptist." Preaching boldly the virtues of democracy almost a century later, Rauschenbusch, Mullins, and Truett each offered a more refined echo of Leland's evangelical patriotism and, in doing so, helped to construct a Baptist identity that proved equally at home on either side of the rhetorical divide between church and state. A fervent devotion to the idea of democracy in all its various incarnations formed the core of this identity.

Fervent devotion, however, did not necessarily bring clear definition to the idea of democracy in the works of Rauschenbusch, Mullins, and Truett. Despite their frequent invocations of "democracy," the three offered slightly different interpretations of the word.[3] Rauschenbusch tended to talk about democracy prophetically in terms of social justice, the dignity of the common man, and an equality of economic opportunity. The relative righteousness of American democracy, he insisted, must always be measured against the standard of true democracy expressed in the Kingdom of God's ethical imperative. In America's willingness to legitimize greed, corruption, and oppression of the poor in the name of capitalism, Rauschenbusch found democracy as practiced in the United States tragically, even sinfully, flawed. His solution, however, was not to discard American democracy but, rather, to transform it by bringing the Christian (and thus democratic) ideals of mutual love and selfless service to bear on all aspects of society. Only

---

[3] See, for example, Stanley Hauerwas's comments about Rauschenbusch in "The Democratic Policing of Christianity," 219ff. Rauschenbusch, writes Hauerwas, "was as enthusiastic about democracy as he was unclear about its nature." The same could be said of both Mullins and Truett. For a good general overview of the era's ambiguous, but powerful, faith in the spiritual unity of democracy and Christianity, see Jan Dawson, "The Religion of Democracy in Early Twentieth Century America," *Journal of Church and State* 27 (1985): 47-68.

when thoroughly "christianized" could the United States begin to realize its potential as a true democracy for all people. In contrast to Rauschenbusch's prophetic stance, meanwhile, Mullins and Truett shared a more "priestly" understanding of American democracy, celebrating its essentially Christian (and Baptist) origins and character.[4] Far removed from the injustices of the industrialized cities that plagued Rauschenbusch's conscience, neither Mullins nor Truett expressed any reservations about the intrinsic goodness of a society that rejected hierarchies of all kinds and promoted the exercise of individual freedom (this despite the inescapable racial inequality and discrimination that characterized life in cities of the old Confederacy such as Louisville and Dallas during the early 1900s). As the political expression of New Testament religious principles, American democracy to them seemed a plain manifestation of God's will for humanity and an example for the world to emulate.

Regardless of the different aspects of democracy they chose to emphasize, though, all three of these Baptists drew inspiration from the same vague, though compelling, lexicon of liberal democratic ideals and its vocabulary of freedom, equality, individualism, choice, autonomy, inalienable rights, and the common man. Likewise, all three believed that the language of democracy conveyed the highest aspirations of both church and state. As such, Rauschenbusch, Mullins, and Truett found that their religious commitments as Baptists perfectly complemented their temporal loyalties as Americans. This basic assumption, that being a Baptist and being an American represented two expressions of the same democratic ideal, lay at the very center of an understanding of Baptist identity that may be called "Baptist democracy."

---

[4]Martin Marty has made a distinction between the "priestly" and the "prophetic" understandings of American civil religion. The priestly interpretation claims that the United States enjoys a unique relationship with God, and with that relationship comes a special blessing. Moreover, as a blessed nation, the status quo reflects God's will. The prophetic understanding, meanwhile, argues that, as a nation to whom much has been given, the United States will be held to a high standard of accountability before the judgment seat of God. Complacency in the face of social injustice risks incurring the wrath of God. See Marty, "Two Kinds of Two Kinds of Civil Religion," in *American Civil Religion*, eds. Russell E. Richey and Donald G. Jones (New York: Harper and Row, 1974) 139-157.

As expressed in the works of Rauschenbusch, Mullins, and Truett, the idea of Baptist democracy rested upon several critical, related assertions. The first of these assertions was that the New Testament church functioned as a democracy and, therefore, democracy represented the most Christian form of government. A second key assertion of Baptist democracy maintained that the democratic practices of local Baptist churches collectively provided the most faithful modern manifestation of the New Testament church. "Baptist churches in their very constitution approximate Christian principles of organization and give a fair chance to any Christian community to form a Christian social life," claimed Rauschenbusch in 1906. "They trust the people with self-government and form Christian democracies."[5] The third assertion upon which the claims of Baptist democracy rested was that the United States, as a democracy, was founded upon Baptist (and, by extension, New Testament) religious principles adapted for political use. Indeed, as Mullins confidently wrote in *Axioms of Religion*, "one might in a certain sense say that the primary election which determined whether or not there should be an American government was held two thousand years ago on the shores of the Mediterranean when the little Baptist democracies assembled to worship."[6] Finally, the fourth central assertion of Baptist democracy insisted that the institutional separation of church and state reflected the New Testament ideal and, thus, represented a necessary feature of any truly Christian society.

This last assertion served as particularly compelling evidence for Baptists who joyously proclaimed the sweet harmony of Baptist faith and American democracy. One only had to read the First Amendment, they reasoned, to discover the extent to which Baptist principles had influenced the ideals of the United States. Moreover, the fact that the nation's founding documents acknowledged the necessity of religious liberty and the separation of church and state revealed America's essentially Christian character. The principles of religious liberty and the separation of church and state, then, cast a doubly illuminating light

---

[5] Walter Rauschenbusch, "Why I Am a Baptist," *Rochester Baptist Monthly*, January 1906, 108.

[6] E. Y. Mullins, *The Axioms of Religion*, 273.

upon the basic claims of Baptist democracy, which made American democracy appear consistent with Baptist theology even as they confirmed Baptists as undeniably American.

While proclaiming an essential harmony between Baptist principles and American democracy, however, Rauschenbusch, Mullins, and Truett all took particular care to emphasize that, as Baptists, they believed fervently that the institutions of church and state should always be kept separate, with no overlap between them. It was, after all, the fact that the United States had affirmed the cherished Baptist principle of religious liberty in its founding documents that first secured for American democracy its exalted position in the imaginations of Baptists such as John Leland and his spiritual descendants. Starting with this shared commitment to religious liberty, many Baptists in America soon perceived other attributes of the American state that seemed consistent with their understanding of the Christian faith and, along with Mullins, they confidently asserted that "the intelligent Baptist can yield to none in his patriotism, for his religious ideals are the bed-rock of the political fabric."[7]

Unlike earlier generations of Baptists, both in Britain and in colonial America, who understood themselves primarily as religious dissenters whose Christian convictions of conscience had placed them at odds with the established church, the coercive state, and the culture formed by the nexus between these two institutions, Baptists in the United States during the early years of the twentieth century identified themselves comfortably and closely with the state and felt invested in its success.[8] Rauschenbusch, Mullins, and Truett certainly did. For them and other

---

[7] Ibid., 275.

[8] As George Marsden has observed, more conservative Baptists, particularly in the North, began to gravitate toward fundamentalism and its pessimistic view of American culture in the aftermath of World War I. At the same time, however, they nevertheless maintained a strong sense of patriotic devotion to the ideal of a Christian America. See Marsden, *Fundamentalism and American Culture*, 153-164. John Roach Straton, a prominent Baptist fundamentalist in New York City, was a good example of this juxtaposition. Straton, wrote Marsden, "never quite made up his mind whether the United States was Babylon or the New Israel. Perhaps he thought of New York City as Babylon in the midst of Israel. At any rate, despite his non-stop prophecies of doom, he remained a full-fledged patriot" (162).

Baptists of that age, the separation of church and state began and ended at the institutional level, and even then it served primarily as a means to prevent Roman Catholics from using public tax money to fund their parochial schools.[9] Underneath this formal, institutional separation, however, the moral claims of church and state blended together to create a seamless garment of Baptist democracy.

Indeed, the sense of moral and ethical separation from the state that John Smyth and Thomas Helwys experienced—the sense that church and state operated according to very different standards, with very different priorities, and under very different authorities—simply did not factor into the worldview of Rauschenbusch, Mullins, and Truett. Just as their strong faith in democracy made them enthusiastic patriots committed to the preservation of the American ideals and prestige, it also made a divergence between the goals of Baptists and those of the American state difficult, if not impossible, to imagine. As Truett proclaimed in 1911, "the triumph of democracy means the triumph of Baptists everywhere," and no nation symbolized the promise of democracy more grandly than the United States.[10] Accordingly, then, historian Rufus Spain's assessment of Southern Baptists in the late nineteenth century applies equally well to the champions of Baptist democracy in the first years of the 1900s. "The conclusion must be that Baptists conformed to the society in which they lived," wrote Spain.

---

[9] For an excellent example of how Baptists in the early- to mid-twentieth century understood Roman Catholicism as the primary, if not the only, threat to the separation of church and state in America, see J. M. Dawson, *Separate Church and State Now* (New York: Richard R. Smith, 1948) 32-73. The classic Baptist expression of anti-Catholic sentiment from the nineteenth century is William Cathcart, *The Papal System: From Its Origin to the Present Time* (Philadelphia: The American Baptist Publication Society, 1872). Cathcart's assessment of the Roman Catholic Church as a superstitious and anti-democratic corruption of New Testament Christianity not only reflected the attitudes of his contemporary Baptists but also strongly influenced subsequent generations. Indeed, a general suspicion of Catholicism as a subversive element in American society runs throughout much of the Baptist literature of the twentieth century. See also John Clifford, "The Attitude of Baptists to Catholicism—Roman and Greek," *Review and Expositor* 8 (1911): 331-344. For a concise historical survey of Baptist views on Catholicism, see Torbet, *A History of the Baptists*, 490-492.

[10] George Truett, "God's Call to America," 19.

"Their importance as a social force was in supporting and perpetuating the standards prevailing in society at large."[11]

Paradoxically, then, the celebrated notion that Baptist principles shared common ground with the ideals of American democracy began with—and, throughout the work of Rauschenbusch, Mullins, and Truett, continued to be rooted in—the conviction that, between the distinctive realms of church and state, no common ground existed.

This ironic nature of Baptist democracy has created a problematic legacy for Baptists in America, particularly those who identify themselves as theological "moderates" (in opposition to the self-described conservatives who currently dominate the Southern Baptist Convention). Though lacking the sometimes exaggerated rhetorical flourishes found in earlier champions of Baptist democracy, contemporary moderate Baptists nonetheless remain self-consciously faithful to the examples set by Rauschenbusch, Mullins, and Truett in the first decades of the twentieth century, insisting upon the rigorous separation of church and state while at the same time proclaiming a rich harmony between Baptist principles and the ideals of American democracy.

Contemporary Baptist interpretations of religious liberty and the separation of church and state begin at this point. The professed Baptist ideal may be a kind of institutional separation between church and state, but beneath this ideal lies a blend of religion and politics, theological conviction and democratic principle as familiar today as it was in the early 1900s. Consider the manner in which James Dunn, a long-time Baptist campaigner for the separation of church and state, has described the valuable, ongoing work of the Baptist Joint Committee for Religious Liberty. The public advocacy and educational organization, he wrote, is "Bible based, doctrinally rooted in Baptist distinctives, and passionately dedicated to conserving the values of the Constitution and the Bill of Rights."[12] Such a description assumes a fundamental consistency between Scripture, Baptist identity, and the founding documents of American democracy. From this perspective, then, defending the

---

[11] Spain, *At Ease in Zion*, 214.
[12] James Dunn, "Reflections," *Report from the Capital*, 28 January 1996, 3.

Constitution of the United States becomes tantamount to defending biblical truth and Baptist principles of faith.

This assumption is a dangerous one for Christians to make—especially Christians who, at least historically, have understood themselves to be wary of the state and its coercive power. The danger here is that, while carefully guarding the front door of the church against obvious violations of the First Amendment, Baptists will not only welcome Caesar in through the back door but invite him to make himself at home as well. That is precisely what the ambiguous language of Baptist democracy, in which theology slides easily, imperceptibly, into ideology, encourages. The church, in the name of religious freedom, adopts the vocabulary and values of the state. Baptists, in the spirit of church-state separation, become patriotic apologists for America. The end result is that Baptists lose their ability to define either themselves or their witness to the world in distinctively biblical, theological language.

Insofar as the mindset of Baptist democracy has persevered long beyond the twilight years of American Christendom in which it originally flourished, love of liberty and uncontaminated Americanism still seem to be naturally compatible with Baptist faith and practice. Understanding this mindset (and its attendant moral and spiritual hazards) presents a challenge, especially for Baptists who have been profoundly shaped by its assumptions. Even among moderates who cherish academic freedom, Baptist conversations about the Baptist past tend to take place within a Baptist echo chamber. In order to see themselves clearly, Baptists sometimes need assistance from Christians who are outside the Baptist family. Accordingly, then, the insights of theologians John Howard Yoder and Stanley Hauerwas provide a helpful framework within which to explore the implications of Baptist democracy as an enduring influence upon Baptist faith and practice. While neither of these thinkers stand within the Baptist tradition (though Yoder, a Mennonite, did belong to the larger, free church tradition), their reflections upon the nature of the liberal democratic state and its effects upon the life and witness of the Christian community illuminate the concept of Baptist democracy as championed by Rauschenbusch, Mullins, and Truett and, perhaps more significantly, its problematic legacy for contemporary Baptists who understand themselves primarily as ardent, even prophetic, defenders of religious liberty and the separation of church and state.

***

The rise of Baptist democracy announced a dramatic departure from the early Baptist tradition of dissent and self-conscious separation from the powers of the world. It was indeed a remarkable turnabout, especially in light of the Baptists' historically troubled relationships with temporal government. By the early 1900s, Baptists in America no longer considered the state a threat to their religious freedom. Instead, they embraced it as an ally in the effort to "Christianize" society at home and abroad through the spread of democracy and other "Christian" principles. Firmly convinced that the principles behind both Baptist theology and American democracy flowed from the same divine source, Baptists emerged from the nineteenth century a transformed people. The spiritual descendants of the erstwhile dissenters of the seventeenth and eighteenth centuries became ardent defenders of the American state in the twentieth, earnestly devoted to its welfare and deeply identified with its values—all in the name of religious liberty and the separation of church and state.[13]

Though not specifically writing about Baptists, the late Anabaptist theologian John Howard Yoder addressed the tendency of rigorous separationist rhetoric to accompany decidedly harmonious relations between the ideals of church and state in an essay titled "The Constantinian Sources of Western Social Ethics."[14] Yoder began with what he called the original "Constantinian shift," or the process by

---

[13] For an excellent account of how the ethos of the liberal democratic state and its provision of religious liberty poses as an attractive rival to the Christian salvation story, see Cavanaugh, "The City: Beyond Secular Parodies" in *Radical Orthodoxy*. "In the modern age," writes Cavanaugh, "Christians have tended to succumb to the power of the state soteriology," and they have done so based on Christian ideals. In the separation of the church from the state, "many Christians have seen the God of peace emancipated from captivity to the principalities and powers; and in national unity, despite religious pluralism, many have glimpsed the promise of the original Christian quest for unity and peace" (190).

[14] See John Howard Yoder, "The Constantinian Sources of Western Social Ethics," 135-147, in John Howard Yoder, *The Priestly Kingdom: Social Ethics as Gospel* (Notre Dame IN: University of Notre Dame Press, 1984).

which Christians adjusted their theological and ethical convictions to conform to the new religious and political realities after the Roman emperor Constantine's conversion to Christianity in 313. Whereas before Constantine, Christians frequently experienced persecution as a minority religious sect, after Constantine their faith soon became the official faith of the Roman Empire, with the government assuming responsibility for defining orthodoxy and suppressing heresy.[15] When Caesar entered the church, Yoder argued, the character of the church changed forever. Rather than insist that, in order to become a Christian, Caesar had to change his behavior to conform with Christian standards of conduct, the church instead simply changed its ethical standards in such a way that allowed Caesar to continue acting like Caesar—waging war, suppressing dissent, coercing allegiance, collecting taxes, and so forth—only now with the blessing of the church.[16]

While this "Constantinian shift" toward a fusion of church and state may seem like an ancient issue long since reversed by the tides of history, Yoder warned that its influence continues to shape Christian ethics in the contemporary Western world. As evidence, he described several enduring variations of the Constantinian relationship between God and Caesar. The first of these variations arose in the aftermath of the Protestant Reformation as independent nation-states began to emerge in Europe. With each state having its own established church—or, in the case of Catholic states such as France and Spain, an officially-recognized church—the pursuit of national interest and the celebration of national identity became more important than preserving the unity of an international church. In other words, being French or Dutch or Swiss or English mattered more than being Christian. Under this "neo-

---

[15] In response to the controversy over Arianism, Constantine organized the First Ecumenical Council of Christian bishops in Nicea. The Arians believed that Jesus the Son was not of one substance with God the Father and that there had been a time when Jesus did not exist. The church leaders meeting in Nicea not only declared these ideas heretical but also produced a statement (which became known as the Nicene Creed) intended to serve as a comprehensive summary of orthodox Christian beliefs. For a concise account of the First Ecumenical Council, the theological controversy that sparked it, and the political factors behind Constantine's decision to convene it, see Kenneth Scott Latourette, *A History of Christianity*, vol. 1, *Beginnings to 1500* (San Francisco: HarperCollins, 1975) 153ff.

[16] Yoder, "The Constantinian Sources of Western Social Ethics," 137-138.

Constantinian" arrangement, wrote Yoder, "one can now have wars, even holy wars, against other Christian nations. No longer can a bishop call a king to Canossa, for the bishop is the creature of the king."[17] In this variation of Constantinianism, then, church and state remained intimately related to one another, but the freedom of the former was circumscribed—and, in truth, its essential character defined—by the latter.

The second of these variations that Yoder described, "neo-neo-Constantinianism," emerged in the aftermath of the Enlightenment and the American Revolution. "Religious liberty and disestablishment bring it about progressively that church and state as *institutions* become less linked," Yoder wrote. "Each has greater autonomy over against the claims of the other. Yet even with this shift, the moral identification changes little, as the U. S. especially demonstrates." Once Christians come to understand the separation of church and state as a theological good, then "a society where this separation is achieved is not a pagan society but a nation structured according to the will of God." In other words, Yoder argued, "moral identification of the church with nation remains despite institutional separation."[18] In substance if not in style, neo-neo-Constantinianism, despite its strident rhetoric in support of strictly separating church and state, in fact preserves the moral and ethical overlap between church and state that characterized earlier stages of Christendom.

With the help of Yoder, the problematic legacy of Baptist democracy (and its unmistakably neo-neo-Constantinian character) becomes easier to appreciate. Rauschenbusch, Mullins, and Truett, as did Leland before them, all operated on the assumption that, in Yoder's words, the

---

[17] Ibid., 141. Yoder here refers to the conflict between Pope Gregory VII and the Holy Roman Emperor, Henry IV, over the question of who had the right to appoint bishops and other church officials. Henry refused to recognize Gregory's authority to name bishops within the Holy Roman Empire and denounced him as pope. Gregory responded by excommunicating Henry and deposing him as emperor. The conflict ended in January 1077 with Henry traveling to Canossa to beg the pope's forgiveness, which Gregory granted (after, legend has it, allowing the king to stand barefoot in the snow for three days). See Latourette, 470-473.

[18] Ibid., 142.

separation of church and state was both theologically desirable and indicative of a nation structured according to God's will. Insofar as the First Amendment had legally separated the institutions of church and state in America, Baptists happily recognized the United States as a godly nation worthy of unqualified support.[19] Indeed, if the Kingdom of God was, in fact, a democracy, then surely the United States offered a glimpse of God's ultimate will for all people, for not only did the American government follow the New Testament church's democratic model, but it provided for religious liberty as well. Such a felicitous, though superficial, convergence of Baptist principles with American democracy suggested the possibility of a deeper moral resonance between church and state. Baptists reasoned that, as long as the United States continued to protect freedom, democracy, and God-given human rights at home while promoting their expansion abroad, they could hardly fail to pledge their steadfast allegiance to America. By supporting the state, in other words, Baptists understood themselves to be affirming at some level their most cherished religious convictions.

Building upon Yoder's work, theologian Stanley Hauerwas has described the false sense of security that the state's promise of religious liberty can produce in Christians, particularly those in the United States who have been shaped by the assumptions of liberal democracy. Freedom of religion, he writes, "has tempted Christians in America to think that democracy is fundamentally neutral and, perhaps, even friendly toward the church."[20] As a result, Hauerwas continues,

---

[19] Rauschenbusch, it must be noted, refused to lend his support to the American war effort in World War I. While certainly concerned about the future of democracy in Europe and eager to see democratic values triumphant on a global scale, Rauschenbusch nonetheless had reservations about war as an instrument of foreign policy. At the same time, however, he proudly cited his son's participation in the war as a member of the ambulance service. See Sharpe, 388.

[20] Stanley Hauerwas, *After Christendom? How the Church is to Behave if Freedom, Justice, and a Christian Nation are Bad Ideas* (Nashville TN: Abingdon Press, 1991) 70. Although he is skeptical of the claim that democracy is the form of government best suited to Christianity, Hauerwas acknowledges that, commendably, democracies tend to be less oppressive than other kinds of states. See "A Christian Critique of Christian America," in *Christian Existence Today: Essays on Church, World, and Living In Between* (Durham NC: The Labyrinth Press, 1988) 180ff. In this, Hauerwas echoes Yoder, "The Christian Case for Democracy," 151-171, in *The Priestly Kingdom*. These qualified endorsements of democracy represent a departure

"American Christians... have thought that their primary religious duty to the state was and is to provide support and justification for the state that guarantees freedom of religion."[21] In performing this duty, Christians have subordinated the Gospel to the interests of the state and its exigencies, allowing the needs of the state to determine the priorities of the church. Despite the New Testament's non-violent ethic of peacemaking, for example, Christians will quickly cite "national security" or the defense of national ideals as sufficient justification for their endorsement of, and participation in, the violence of war.[22]

Pragmatism thus replaces truth as the standard for Christian conviction, a lingering effect of what Hauerwas (again, following Yoder's line of argument) calls the Constantinian habit of thought that says Christians must "rule, if not the government, then at least the ethos

---

from the prevailing opinion among Christian ethicists in the mid-twentieth century that, for various reasons, democracy was the most Christian political system possible. "Democracy is the best way of life," wrote Elton Trueblood, "not because all men are virtuous and reasonable, but because all men are greedy. The government exists primarily to curb the wanton exercise of power, either in any faction or in any individual man. *Democracy is necessitated by the fact that all men are sinners; it is made possible by the fact that we know it.* See Trueblood, *Foundations for Reconstruction* (New York: Harper and Brothers Publishers, 1946) 104-105, emphasis in original. Reinhold Neibuhr's *The Children of Light and the Children of Darkness* (New York: Charles Scribner's Sons, 1944) remains the classic apology for democracy as the form of government most consistent with Christianity.

[21] Ibid.

[22] The late Baptist theologian James McClendon wryly observed that the task of most contemporary Christian ethics revolves around finding and justifying exceptions to presumed Christian standards of morality. See James McClendon, *Systematic Theology*, vol. 1, *Ethics* (Nashville TN: Abingdon Press, 1986) 47-55. For an extended account of the New Testament narrative as normative for (as opposed to suggestive of) Christian ethics, see John Howard Yoder, *The Politics of Jesus: Vicit Agnus Noster* (Grand Rapids MI: Eerdmans Publishing Company, 1994). A typical example of how Christians adjust their ethical convictions to rationalize the actions of the state may be found in a 2003 essay by Southern Baptist Theological Seminary president Albert Mohler. After acknowledging that Jesus' statement, "Blessed are the peacemakers" (Matt. 5:9), serves as an unambiguous "basis for any Christian understanding of war and its morality," Mohler proceeds to explain why and when Christians may justifiably kill others in order to defend the state. "Respect for human life sometimes requires the taking of human life," he writes. "Those who fight for life and liberty deserve our gratitude, our support, and our prayer." See "Fighting for Peace," *The Southern Seminary Magazine* 71 (Spring 2003) inside cover, 9.

of America."[23] In the name of supporting democracy and their vested interest in its maintenance, he argues, "Christians police their own convictions to insure that none of those convictions might cause difficulty in making democracy successful."[24] Under such circumstances, Hauerwas contends that the Christian witness becomes "captured by practices and narratives that are more constitutive of that entity called America than that community called Church. Indeed, the confusions of these narratives have made it impossible for us to rightly be proclaimers and hearers of the Word."[25]

The root of the problem does not lie primarily with the state. The fault, instead, resides with well-intentioned Christians and their willingness to align themselves uncritically with the national interest, even at the expense of undermining their own shared identity as disciples of Jesus. "We thus fail to remember that the question is not whether the church has the freedom to preach the gospel in America," insists Hauerwas, "but rather whether the church in America preaches the gospel as truth. The question is not whether we have freedom of religion and a corresponding limited state in America, but whether we have a church that has a people capable of saying no to the state."[26] For Christians, he maintains, the ability to say no to the state is an acquired skill, developed gradually through participation in baptism, communion, and other concrete practices of the church that bear witness to the fact that Christians claim Jesus, not Caesar, as Lord and the Gospel as the church's foundational story.[27] Without the moral resources nurtured

---

[23] Hauerwas, "A Christian Critique of Christian America," 183.

[24] Hauerwas, "The Democratic Policing of Christianity," 228.

[25] Stanley Hauerwas, *Unleashing the Scripture: Freeing the Bible from Captivity to America* (Nashville TN: Abingdon Press, 1993) 43.

[26] *After Christendom?* 71.

[27] See also Herbert Richardson, "Civil Religion in Theological Perspective," 161-184, in *American Civil Religion*, eds. Russell E. Richey and Donald G. Jones (New York: Harper and Row, 1974). In this essay, Richardson maintains that the only true limitation on the state's tendency to absolutize itself comes not from theological doctrine or religious belief. "There is nothing the church (or anyone else) believes that cannot be woven into the state's mythology," he writes. Instead, "the real limitation on the power of the state is its citizens' loyalty to and participation in groups whose membership, goals, and procedures are not isomorphic or consistent with the membership, goals, and procedures of the state" (182). For an excellent account of how the practices of the church provided Catholics in Chile

by such participation in a community that understands itself as an alternative to the state—that is, a community organized and sustained by a story that transcends the narrow boundaries of the nation—Hauerwas doubts that Christians can develop the perceptive skills needed both to distinguish the truth of the Gospel from the false claims of the state, and to resist the temptation to confuse the two.[28]

Some Baptists recognize the problem and have attempted to offer constructive solutions. Baptists "thought they had finally liberated Christian faith from all political entanglements by agreeing to the institutional separation of church and state proposed by the leading figures of the Enlightenment," writes theologian Barry Harvey. What went largely unnoticed in this arrangement was that "the formal separation of these institutions took place under the auspices of a social arrangement that sanctioned a moral and cultural identity between mainline Protestant Christianity and the liberal nation-state."[29] The results of this moral harmony between church and state, claims theologian Mikeal Broadway, have been disastrous for the church. "Like so many sheep, American churches offer thanks for their bounty and dare not trouble the waters of prosperity," he observes. "In appreciation for religious liberty, they return loyalty, pledging to the American flag as an act of piety, even if they eschew bowing before the crucifix. The world

---

with the moral resources with which to resist the violence of the Pinochet regime, see Cavanaugh, *Torture and Eucharist.*

[28] Stanley Hauerwas, *A Community of Character: Toward a Constructive Christian Social Ethic* (Notre Dame IN: University of Notre Dame Press, 1981) 72-86. Barry Harvey has suggested that the Jews may serve as a useful example of a people who have developed the moral practices and skills needed to survive as a distinctive, though minority, religious community scattered throughout the various states of the world. See Harvey, *Another City,* 157ff. Along these same lines, Reinhold Neibuhr once observed that the alleged moral superiority of the Jews resides in the fact that "they stand slightly on the outside, as a minority, and the critical detachment of their status gives them a resource which saves them from their traditionalism in accepting the standards of their community." See Neibuhr, *Pious and Secular America* (New York: Charles Scribner's Sons, 1958) 94.

[29] Harvey, *Another City,* 85. See also Barry Harvey, "Round and Round About the Town: The Ecclesial Dimensions of Living In the Truth," *Perspectives in Religious Studies* 25 (1998): 107.

is in the church, and the church cannot figure out how or whether to mark out any independent identity."[30]

The problem, ultimately, resides in the way Baptists understand themselves—or fail to understand themselves, as the case may be—as a gathered community of believers, called out from the world as a sign of God's grace. The church, writes Harvey, "serves as a school for the formation of the kinds of persons who can embody before the world an alternative way of living."[31] The success or failure of this formative process depends largely upon the integrity of the church's character and sense of mission, a reality recognized by Baptist historian C. C. Goen. "Given the loss of understanding about what it means to be church and the consequent melding of private piety with public religion," he has observed, "the struggle to maintain a relationship between church and state that is both theologically sound and socially/politically viable often seems to be a lonely rear-guard action."[32] Baptists find it hard to remember that their spiritual ancestors formed their religious identity "primarily as a counter-cultural movement in cultures whose pretensions to be 'Christian' they condemned as phony," Goen continues. As a result, "they may be unwilling to risk the consequences of rejecting the blandishments of social respectability and political power. They may not be able to commit themselves to become a church fully obedient to God, pursuing its mission faithfully out of the resources that God alone supplies."[33]

---

[30]Mikeal Broadway, "The Ways of Zion Mourned: A Historicist Critique of Church-State Relations" (Ph.D. diss., Duke University, 1993) 1. James McClendon perhaps saw more clearly than most Baptist theologians the need to develop skills of theological discernment. The struggle of theology, he wrote, "begins with the humble fact that the church is not the world." The temptation to blur the distinctions between church and world in a way that enables the former to conform to the latter's expectations and priorities always exists, but if Christians conspire "to conceal the difference between church and world, we may in the short term entice the world, but we will do so only by betraying the church." See McClendon, "What is a 'baptist' Theology?" *American Baptist Quarterly* 1 (1982): 16ff.

[31]Harvey, "Round and Round About the Town," 113.

[32]Goen, 250.

[33]Ibid.

At one time, the need for a Christian identity independent of the state and its ideology would have been obvious to dissenters such as Smyth, Helwys, and their fellow non-conforming Baptists in Britain. Almost by definition, these early Baptists, who self-consciously gathered as communities of believers set apart from the world, collectively represented a moral alternative to the state. By contrast, as the examples of Rauschenbusch, Mullins, and Truett demonstrate, during the first decades of the twentieth century, the deliberate cultivation of a Christian identity that was distinctly separate from the state seemed unnecessary to Baptists in America, where the cherished Baptist principles of democracy and religious liberty had long been written into the very law of the land.

Ironically, however, the neo-neo-Constantinian moral identification of church with state that animated Baptist democracy left Baptists without the theological resources they needed to define themselves as Christians set apart by God to bear witness to the world that Jesus, not Caesar, is Lord. Instead, by baptizing the language of liberal democracy and adopting Caesar's vocabulary as their own, Baptists lost the one skill that every dissenting community requires: the ability to say no. If the Baptist faith simply represented a spiritualized version of American democracy—or, conversely, if American democracy provided a political expression of the Baptist faith—then how could there possibly be any conflict between church and state, or anything from which Baptists might feel compelled to dissent? If the Kingdom of God was a democracy, then how could the church possibly offer a legitimate alternative to the state? Simply put, the more Baptists identified themselves with America, the less free they were to identify themselves clearly as Christians called by God to form new communities of redeemed, regenerate believers, visible manifestations of the body of Christ in the world charged with proclaiming in word and deed God's reign over all temporal powers. Bound to America by the promise of religious liberty, Baptists willingly entered theological captivity in the land of the free. That, ultimately, is the problematic legacy of Baptist democracy.

Conclusion

Despite its fundamental, albeit largely unacknowledged, challenge to the integrity of Baptists' ongoing theological witness, the triumphant blend of Baptist theology and American democracy continues to exert a powerful influence upon Baptist identity. To be sure, Baptists have proudly advertised their patriotism ever since the days of Leland.[1] The enduring legacy of Baptist democracy, however, goes deeper than mere patriotic observances. Beyond the standard examples of religiously-tinged patriotism that many Baptists share with their fellow Christians in the United States—the display of American flags in worship spaces, for example, or God and country celebrations in connection with national holidays—there lies a more subtle, but far more significant contemporary manifestation of Baptist democracy in the way that theologically moderate Baptists understand and describe both themselves and their religious convictions.[2] Indeed, more than fifty years after the last member of the trio died, moderate Baptists still faithfully, even tenaciously, maintain the neo-neo-Constantinian assumptions that Rauschenbusch, Mullins, and Truett shared regarding religious liberty and the proper relationship between church and state. As such, it may be that moderate Baptists in the South represent the last surviving embers of American Christendom.

Consider the work of leading moderate Baptist scholars and activists in the aftermath of the intramural theological and political conflicts that

---

[1] See, for example, W. Morgan Patterson, "The Americanization of Baptists," in *Baptists and the American Experience*, ed. James E. Wood, Jr. (Valley Forge PA: Judson Press, 1976) 141ff.

[2] Conservative Southern Baptists, it must be noted, freely express their patriotism without apology. See, for example, "Bush Blesses Baptists," *Baptist Standard*, 17 June 2002, 1. Moderates frequently consider such overt celebrations of God and country as further evidence that conservatives have failed to uphold the Baptist principle of church-state separation. After describing the dangers in confusing piety with patriotism, Walter Shurden writes that "there are indications in the last several years that the lines between church and state are becoming seriously confused, even among some Baptists." See Shurden, *The Baptist Identity*, 52.

divided the Southern Baptist Convention during the closing decades of the twentieth century. Self-consciously adopting the stance of prophetic dissent that once defined their Baptist ancestors in England and colonial America, moderates portrayed themselves as defenders of the *authentic* Baptist identity, over against those who charted a more socially and theologically conservative course for the Southern Baptist Convention. Moderates, explained historian Walter Shurden, "are not revising, amending, or altering the Baptist heritage that they consider so crucial to expressing their faith. They are preserving, safeguarding, and proclaiming that heritage."[3] To that end, Shurden and his fellow moderates identified various "Baptist distinctives" as a means of defining their theological witness.[4] Of these distinguishing marks of Baptist identity, one consistently took precedence over the others. The Baptist tradition, Shurden argued, simply could not be understood apart from its overarching commitment to freedom. "I am convinced," he wrote, "that the one word that comes closer than any other to capturing the historic Baptist identity is the word 'freedom.'"[5] James Dunn put the matter much more simply. A passion for freedom, he insisted, "burns in the innards of every true Baptist."[6]

It is at this point that the moderates' theological argument begins to leak. The problem is that both Shurden and Dunn have defined the allegedly distinctive Baptist idea of freedom in a way that is not, in fact, distinctively Baptist—at least not in a way that John Smyth, Thomas Helwys, and other pre-Enlightenment Baptists would have recognized. The Baptist understanding of freedom, wrote Shurden, affirmed "the sacredness of individual choice" and, as such, it reflected the Baptist

---

[3] Walter B. Shurden, foreword to *Defining Baptist Conviction*, 9. Since Shurden's comments, the Southern Baptist Convention has twice revised the 1963 Baptist Faith and Message Statement to include more conservative language regarding the inspiration of the Bible, the role of women in the church, pastoral authority, family relationships, and a number of social issues. A full text of the 2000 Baptist Faith and Message statement may be found in *The Baptist Faith and Message: A Statement Adopted by the Southern Baptist Convention, June 14, 2000* (Nashville TN: Southern Baptist Convention, 2000).
[4] See Shurden, *The Baptist Identity*, 1ff.
[5] Ibid., 55.
[6] James Dunn, "Religious Liberty and Church/State Separation Go Hand in Hand," 71.

understanding of human nature.[7] "Baptists assert that each individual is created in the image of God," he noted. "Each individual, therefore, is competent under God to make moral, spiritual, and religious decisions. Not only is the individual privileged to make those decisions, the individual alone is *responsible* for making those decisions."[8] The Baptist commitment to religious freedom followed from this view of human nature: if people are essentially free to make their own choices about who and what they will be, then they must have the liberty to worship God (or not) according to the dictates of individual conscience, and the institutional separation of church and state represented the best way to safeguard that liberty.[9]

For Dunn, meanwhile, this notion that all individuals are absolutely free and autonomous to make their own decisions regarding spiritual matters was an axiomatic theological principle, a self-evident truth for which no proof is necessary.[10] Because individuals must be free, Dunn argued, church and state must be completely separate. Any form of religious coercion violated the sanctity of private conscience, where the individual will jealously guards its autonomy. Dunn agreed with Shurden in locating this expansive Baptist understanding of individual freedom in the creation story. "Soul freedom and the concept of free moral agency from the Baptist point of view finds our volitional capacity written into our being," he observed. "We are programmed to be choosers."[11] God did not make puppets, Dunn wrote, but men and women in the divine image; therefore, "one simply argues by assertion that the biblical estimate of humankind is the starting point for understanding religious liberty. If one presupposes creatures made somehow like God—persons, deciders, choosers—then precisely that construction demands freedom."[12] Made in the image of God, then, humans are like God precisely in their ability to exercise free will. This

---

[7] Walter B. Shurden, *The Baptist Identity*, 23. See also Shurden, "How We Got That Way," 13-30, in *Proclaiming the Baptist Vision*.
[8] Ibid., 24, emphasis in original.
[9] Ibid., 55
[10] James Dunn, "Church, State, and Soul Competency," 66.
[11] James Dunn, "The Baptist Vision of Religious Liberty," 32.
[12] Ibid.

understanding of freedom, insisted Dunn, is the traditional Baptist point of view.

He is partly correct. This understanding of freedom has indeed been the traditional Baptist point of view since the days of John Leland, when Baptists in the young American republic enthusiastically embraced the political ideals of Jefferson and Madison and proudly called them their own. It is wrong, however, to argue that this individualistic understanding of freedom—derived from John Locke and his fellow philosophers in the age of Enlightenment—reflects a theological tradition that stretches back to the earliest Baptists in seventeenth-century England. While John Smyth and Thomas Helwys did, undoubtedly, have a passion for freedom, they understood this freedom to be a gift of God through the grace of Jesus Christ. Specifically, they believed the freedom of a Christian to be the freedom not to sin—the freedom, in other words, to obey God rather than the corrupted (and corrupting) instincts of a fallen human nature. The very idea that the freedom of a Christian was somehow intrinsic to human nature would have struck these early Baptists as a theological impossibility—or, as Helwys once put it, a "most damnable heresy."[13] Simply put, seventeenth-century English Baptists did not understand Christian freedom in the same way as their moderate Baptist descendants do four hundred years later.

Nevertheless, the moderate argument from history still insists that the Baptist understanding of freedom has remained consistent since the early 1600s. It also insists that their commitments to religious liberty and individual freedom distinguish Baptists from their fellow Christians while at the same time marking them as intrinsically American. "That which made the American Revolution both unique and lasting was the Constitution and the Bill of Rights," wrote Baptist historian William Estep. "At every point in the struggle for religious freedom in the colonies, the Baptists led the way. They and those who joined them in the final phase of the battle shaped a nation of freedom."[14] As a result of the Baptist struggle for American freedom, he continues, the nation "has

---

[13] Thomas Helwys, *An Advertisement or Admonition*, 91.
[14] William R. Estep, *Revolution Within the Revolution: The First Amendment in Historical Context, 1612-1789* (Grand Rapids MI: Eerdmans Publishing Company, 1990) 178.

become the refuge for the persecuted of the earth, as well as a center for missionary outreach unprecedented in the history of Christianity."[15] Religious liberty serves as the historical link between Baptists and American democracy, observed James E. Wood, Jr., one of the leading Baptist scholars of the twentieth century regarding issues of church and state. "No theme is more central to Baptists and the American experience than religious liberty, which on the one hand has long been regarded as the most distinctive feature of American political and religious life, and on the other hand has been the most conspicuous principle of Baptist faith and practice," he writes. Religious liberty "was fundamental in the development of this nation and is widely regarded as America's greatest contribution to world civilization. To this, it must be said, Baptists made a distinct and notable contribution."[16]

In order to preserve this Baptist heritage of freedom, champions of the moderate cause urge committed Baptists, as Dunn put it, to "study history, the Constitution, and the Bill of Rights. Know how we got the documents of democracy and why. If we do not understand why we have these safeguards for freedom, we are not likely to defend them."[17] Authentic, freedom-loving Baptists, it has been said, bear a moral responsibility "to participate responsibly in the political process, and thereby help safeguard the health of American democracy."[18] As Rauschenbusch, Mullins, and Truett did in years past, contemporary moderate Baptists understand American democracy to be reflective of their most distinctive religious convictions and, at least partially, a result of their spiritual ancestors' courageous insistence upon freedom for all. To be sure, there are plenty of good reasons why Christians both in the United States and around the world should be concerned about (and contributing to) the health and well-being of their respective countries. In Jeremiah 29:7, for example, God tells His people that, while exiled in Babylon, they should "seek the welfare of the city where I have sent you

---

[15] Ibid.

[16] James E. Wood, Jr., introduction to *Baptists and the American Experience*, 20. See also Dawson, *Baptists and the American Republic*.

[17] Dunn, "Religious Liberty and Church/State Separation Go Hand in Hand," 76.

[18] Stan Hastey, "The New Christian Right: Retrospect and Prospect," *American Baptist Quarterly* 6 (1987) 271.

into exile and pray to the Lord on its behalf, for in its welfare you will find your welfare." To argue, however, that Baptists in the United States have a responsibility to safeguard the health of American democracy because American democracy somehow represents a political expression of Christian truth is an argument that borders on idolatry.

Meanwhile, moderates insist that the conservative Southern Baptist leadership has little respect for, and even less commitment to, the American constitutional principles that nourish the freedom cherished by every true Baptist.[19] Indeed, the perceived threat to religious liberty and the separation of church and state posed by conservative Baptists allied with the "Christian Right" and bent on mandating religious practices in the public schools and financing religious institutions with public money looms large for moderates.[20] "Misguided, but extremely

---

[19] Such a charge may be a misrepresentation of the Southern Baptist position. The conservative leadership of the Southern Baptist Convention has tended toward what may be called an accommodationist stance on church-state issues in recent years, adhering to the traditional Baptist principle of religious liberty for all, but opposing strict separationist policies (such as an absolute ban on public school prayer) as too restrictive of the free exercise of religion. Will Dodson, of the Ethics and Religious Liberty Commission of the Southern Baptist Convention, describes his organization's interpretation of religious liberty and its proper application in public life in "Church and State in Contemporary United States: Toward a Greater Union: The Accommodation Position," *Baptist History and Heritage* 33 (Winter 1998): 43-53. For a good scholarly overview of the current Southern Baptist stance and its origins, see Barry Hankins, "The Evangelical Accommodation of Southern Baptist Conservatives," *Baptist History and Heritage* 33 (Winter 1998): 54-65. See also Hankins, *Uneasy in Babylon*, 139ff.

[20] The phrase "Christian Right" has proven over time to be fairly elastic, useful primarily for polemical, rather than descriptive, purposes. Ideas associated with Baptist ministers Jerry Falwell, a pastor and founder of the now-defunct Moral Majority, and Pat Robertson, founder of the Christian Coalition, frequently appear in moderate Baptist literature as indicative of the new direction taken by the conservative leadership of the Southern Baptist Convention. Moderates tend to portray conservative Baptists as a subset of the Christian Right. See, for example, Hastey, "The New Christian Right," 264-272. Barry Hankins, however, rightly notes that Southern Baptist conservatives describe their relationship with the Christian Right as limited and issue-dependent. See Hankins, *Uneasy in Babylon*, 107-114. Indiscriminate assertions that conservative Southern Baptists blindly endorse the agenda of the "Christian Right" must be considered with a fair degree of skepticism. Nevertheless, for an interesting examination of the ethos of the "religious right" written by two former associates of Falwell, see Cal Thomas and Ed Dobson, *Blinded By Might: Why the Religious Right Can't Save America* (Grand Rapids MI: Zondervan Publishing House, 1999).

dangerous," writes Shurden, "these people want to eliminate the First Amendment either by Constitutional convention or by reinterpretation."[21] In a sense, the specter of the religious right in the contemporary moderate Baptist imagination closely resembles the danger that Roman Catholics represented to Baptists in the early 1900s: a threat to the strict, *institutional* separation of church and state, focused mainly on issues related to public and private education.

Appropriately enough, then, it is in their response to this perceived threat that moderate Baptists most vividly reveal their continued dependence on the same neo-neo-Constantinian ethos of Baptist democracy that animated their spiritual ancestors in the first decades of the twentieth century. The assumptions of American Christendom, with its fusion of Christian faith and liberal democracy, persevere. Vigilantly patrolling the ramparts of American society for violations of the institutional separation of church and state, moderates fail to recognize the extent to which *their very identity as Baptists* has been shaped by their moral investment in the state. As articulated by moderate Baptists, the "distinctives" of Baptist theology—specifically, religious liberty and the separation of church and state—fully overlap with the ideals and philosophical underpinnings of American democracy, with fidelity to the First Amendment serving as the litmus test of authentic Baptist identity. Despite their strident (and sometimes shrill) rhetoric of separation, moderate Baptists seem unable to tell their story without reference to the story of American democracy; in order to distinguish themselves as a church, moderates need the state.

Remarkably, moderate Baptists continue to understand themselves as prophetic non-conformists in American culture because of their commitment to religious liberty and the separation of church and state. "Many denominations in America are eager to embrace and bless the powers that be, but I assume and trust that Baptists are not among them," wrote historian Edwin Gaustad, for in the past, Baptists "have played the vital role of the outsider, the social critic, the political

---

[21]Shurden, *The Baptist Identity*, 46. See also 51ff.

watchdog."[22] Apart from the vestigial memories of seventeenth- and eighteenth-century Baptist dissenters in Britain and colonial America, however, the basis of this ongoing self-perception cannot be easily discerned, given that moderates have self-consciously and explicitly defined themselves as staunch defenders of the Constitution, the Bill of Rights, and the American tradition of freedom. Preserving this tradition of freedom is certainly important and noble work, but doing so makes one neither a non-conformist nor a prophet.[23]

Nonetheless, moderates frequently warn against the confusion of citizenship and discipleship they perceive at work in the agenda of the "Christian Right." Christians, writes Shurden, "have to work hard at distinguishing between pietism and patriotism, assessing critically where one begins and the other ends.... Nationalism is not the faith of Christians. Baptists especially have insisted that the state is always subordinate to the Lordship of Jesus Christ."[24] Aside from their persistent agitation against school prayer and public subsidies for religious education, however, little evidence exists to suggest that moderate Baptists themselves perceive any real conflict between the goals of church and state. Indeed, under what circumstances would a moderate Baptist in America resist the state in obedience to the Lordship of Jesus Christ?[25] Moderates offer few clues.

---

[22]Edwin Gaustad, "U. S. Baptists and Modernity: Great Dissenters, Lousy Conformists," *Baptist History and Heritage* 36 (Winter/Spring 2001): 110. See also, for example, Estep, "Respect for Nonconformity Permeates the Baptist Conscience," and Shurden, "How We Got That Way," 13-31.

[23]As Richard John Neuhaus has noted, the "prophetic" challenge of the church "is not significant when the church merely endorses existing positions that challenge other existing positions. Significant challenge means throwing all positions into question." See *The Naked Public Square: Religion and Democracy in America* (Grand Rapids MI: Eerdmans Publishing Company, 1984) 224-225.

[24]Shurden, *The Baptist Identity*, 52.

[25]Killing in the name of the state, for example, has not been an insurmountable moral challenge for Baptists, moderate or conservative, in the past. See Ken Sehested, "Conformity or Dissent: Southern Baptists on War and Peace Since 1940," *Baptist History and Heritage* 28 (April 1993): 3-18. J. Bradley Creed wrote in "Freedom For and Freedom From: Baptists, Religious Liberty, and World War II," *Baptist History and Heritage* 36 (Summer/Fall 2001): 28-43, that "Baptists viewed World War II as a fight of freedom for democracy and from tyranny and that religious liberty was the source, stability, and

***

To be sure, Baptists by all accounts have flourished through their relationship with American democracy, but at what price has this success been bought? The cost is largely hidden, but it is high. Simply put, Baptists in America have lost their ability to bear a distinctive witness to the world. The language of democracy has infiltrated Baptist culture to the point that Baptists, particularly self-described theological moderates, have no other vocabulary with which to express themselves. Once Baptist principles presumably became incorporated into the political framework of the nation, once the language of the Baptist faith became part of the American vernacular and religious freedom a measure of democracy, Baptists no longer felt the need to explain their beliefs on their own terms and in their own words. Nowhere has this sad reality been more evident than in the transformation of religious liberty from radical Baptist theology into conventional patriotic mythology. The redemptive work of God has thus effectively disappeared from Baptist rhetoric, and religious liberty itself, easily the most visible of Baptist principles, has been absorbed into the vast melting pot of American freedoms. It has become—like freedom of speech, freedom of the press, freedom of assembly—an end to itself, a political right guaranteed by the First Amendment to be enjoyed by every citizen.

What, then, of the theological testimony that Baptists once embodied by their refusal to let their Christian convictions be compromised in order to meet the expectations of the state? Once Baptists conflate their distinctive identity as the church with the ideals of American democracy, how do they offer a moral alternative to the state that testifies to God's reign over the powers of the world? These questions linger unanswered—and, in many cases, unasked—in the wake of Baptist democracy and the enduring legacy of Walter Rauschenbusch, E. Y. Mullins, and George Truett.

In order to recover their distinctive identity, Baptists in America must relearn the countercultural ethic of Christian community embodied

---

foundation of democratic freedom" (29). A notable exception to this rule regarding Baptists and war-making has been the ongoing witness of the Baptist Peace Fellowship of North America.

in the faith and practices of their early English ancestors. To do so, they must also unlearn the deeply ingrained habits of Baptist democracy and reconsider the assumptions regarding church and state that, for more than two hundred years, have shaped their collective understanding of themselves. Indeed, Baptists have not always claimed freedom and democracy as the distinctive marks of their Christian identity. There was a time when Baptists understood themselves primarily as people who had come to faith in Jesus Christ, followed him in baptism, and then, under the guidance of the Holy Spirit and Holy Scripture, sought to make their lives conform to the pattern of his life, death, and resurrection. The Baptist past has given the Baptist present a compelling view of the Christian life, a powerful witness to offer the world. For the sake of their theological integrity, it is time that Baptists in the United States begin, finally, to separate their story as church from the star-spangled ideals of the state.

Bibliography

Primary Materials
Augustine. *Confessions*. Translated by Rex Warner. New York: Mentor, 1963.
The Baptist Faith and Message: A Statement Adopted by the Southern Baptist Convention, June 14, 2000. Nashville TN: Southern Baptist Convention, 2000.
The Baptist Hymnal. Nashville, TN: Convention Press, 1991.
Baptist Standard (Dallas TX)
Baptist World (Louisville KY)
Batten, Samuel Zane. *The Christian State: The State, Democracy, and Christianity*. Philadelphia: The Griffith and Rowland Press, 1909.
Biblical Recorder *(Raleigh NC)*
Brackney, William H. *Baptist Life and Thought: A Source Book*. Rev. ed. Valley Forge PA: Judson Press, 1998.
Christian Index (Atlanta GA)
Dallas *(TX)* Morning News
Fosdick, Harry Emerson. *The Challenge of the Present Crisis*. New York: Association Press, 1917.
Helwys, Thomas. *An Advertisement or Admonition, Unto the Congregations Which Men Call the New Freylers, in the Low Countries*. N.p.p.: n.p., 1611.
_____. *A Short Declaration of the Mystery of Iniquity*. Edited by Richard Groves. Macon GA: Mercer University Press, 1998.
Hobbes, Thomas. *Leviathan*. New York: The Liberal Arts Press, 1958
Kennedy, John F. *"Let the Word Go Forth": The Speeches, Statements, and Writings of John F. Kennedy, 1917-1963*. Edited by Theodore Sorenson. New York: Laurel, 1988.
Leland, John. *The Writings of John Leland*. Edited by L. F. Greene. New York: G. W. Wood, 1845. Reprint, New York: Arno Press, 1969.
Locke, John. "A Letter Concerning Toleration." In *"A Letter Concerning Toleration" in Focus*, edited by John Horton and Susan Mendus, 12-56. New York: Routledge, 1991.
_____. *Second Treatise of Government*. Edited by C. B. Macpherson. Indianapolis: Hackett Publishing Company, 1980.
Luther, Martin. *Luther's Works*. Edited by Jaroslav Pelikan. 55 vols. St. Louis: Concordia Publishing House, 1955-1986.
Lumpkin, William L. *Baptist Confessions of Faith*. Valley Forge PA: Judson Press, 1959.
Mathews, Shailer. *The Church and the Changing Order*. New York: The MacMillan Company, 1907.

_____. *The Social Gospel*. Philadelphia: Griffith and Rowland Press, 1910.

_____. *The Spiritual Interpretation of History*. Cambridge MA: Harvard University Press, 1917.

Mullins, E. Y. *The Axioms of Religion: A New Interpretation of the Baptist Faith*. Philadelphia: Judson Press, 1908.

_____. "The Baptist Conception of Religious Liberty." In *Proclaiming the Baptist Vision: Religious Liberty*, ed. Walter B. Shurden, 85-94. Macon GA: Smyth and Helwys, 1997.

_____. *Baptist Beliefs*. Philadelphia: American Baptist Publication Society, 1912.

_____. "Baptists in the Modern World," *Review and Expositor* 8 (1911): 345-352.

_____. *The Christian Religion in its Doctrinal Expression*. Philadelphia: Roger Williams Press, 1917.

_____. *Christianity at the Crossroads*. Nashville TN: The Sunday School Board of the Southern Baptist Convention, 1924.

_____. *Faith in the Modern World*. Nashville TN: The Sunday School Board of the Southern Baptist Convention, 1930.

_____. *Freedom and Authority in Religion*. Philadelphia: Griffith and Rowland Press, 1913.

_____. "Is Jesus Christ the Author of Religious Experience?" *The Baptist Review and Expositor* 1 (1904): 55-70.

_____. "A Message of the Baptist World Alliance to the Baptist Brotherhood, to Other Christian Brethren, and to the World." *Review and Expositor* 21 (1924): 19-30.

_____. "The Test of Christian Experience." In *The Fundamentals: A Testimony to the Truth*. Vol. 3, 76-85. Chicago: Testimony Publishing Company, 1917.

_____. "Wanted: A Baptist Demonstration." *Baptist Standard*, 2 January 1919, 5.

_____. "Why I Am a Baptist." *Forum* 75 (1926): 725-733.

_____. *Why Is Christianity True?* Philadelphia: American Baptist Publication Society, 1905.

Rauschenbusch, Walter. *Christianity and the Social Crisis*. New York: MacMillan and Company, 1907.

_____. *Christianizing the Social Order*. New York: MacMillan and Company, 1912.

_____. "The Church and Social Crises." In *The Baptist World Alliance: Second Congress Record of Proceedings*, 373-376. Philadelphia: Harper and Brother, 1911.

_____. "The Kingdom of God." In *The Social Gospel in America*, ed. Robert T. Handy, 264-267. New York: Oxford University Press, 1966.

_____. *Prayers of the Social Awakening*. Boston: Pilgrim Press, 1910.

_____. *A Theology for the Social Gospel*. New York: The MacMillan Company, 1917.

_____. "The True American Church." *The Congregationalist*, 23 October 1913, 562.

_____. "What is a Christian Nation?" *The Standard*, 23 February 1907, 5-6.

_____. "Why I Am a Baptist." *Rochester Baptist Monthly*. November 1905, 203; December 1905, 85-88; January 1906, 106-108; February 1906, 134-136; March 1906, 156-159.

"Re-Envisioning Baptist Identity: A Manifesto for Baptist Communities in North America." *Perspectives in Religious Studies* 24 (1997): 303-310.

Report from the Capital (Washington DC)

Rousseau, Jean-Jacques. *On the Social Contract*. Edited by Roger D. Masters. Translated by Judith R. Masters. New York: St. Martin's Press, 1978.

Smith, Gerald Birney. *Social Idealism and the Changing Theology*. New York: The Macmillan Company, 1913.

Smyth, John. *The Complete Works of John Smyth*. Edited by W. T. Whitley. 2 vols. Cambridge: Cambridge University Press, 1915.

Truett, George. "Baptists and Religious Liberty." *Baptist History and Heritage* 33 (Winter 1998): 66-85.

_____. *God's Call to America*. New York: George H. Doran Company, 1923.

_____. *Follow Thou Me*. Nashville TN: The Sunday School Board of the Southern Baptist Convention, 1932.

_____. *The Prophet's Mantle*. Nashville TN: Broadman Press, 1948.

_____. "A Quarter Century of World History." *Review and Expositor* 22 (1925): 49-67. _____. *A Quest for Souls*. Edited by J. B. Cranfill. Dallas: Texas Baptist Book House, 1917.

_____. *Sermons from Paul*. Edited by Powhatan W. James. Grand Rapids MI: Eerdmans Publishing Company, 1947.

U.S. Bureau of the Census. *Historical Statistics of the United States: Colonial Times to 1970*. Pt. 1. Washington DC: GPO, 1975.

U. S. Congress. Senate. Senator Beveridge of Indiana speaking for the Joint Resolution on United States policy in the Philippines. S.R. 53. 56th Cong., 1st sess. *Congressional Record* 33, pt. 1 (9 January 1900).

Whitsitt, William H. *A Question in Baptist History: Whether the Anabaptists of England Practiced Immersion Before the Year 1641?* Louisville KY: Chas. T. Dearing, 1896. Reprint, New York: Arno Press, 1986.

Williams, Roger. *The Bloudy Tenent of Persecution for the Sake of Conscience*. Edited by Richard Groves. Macon GA: Mercer University Press, 2001.

Wilson, Woodow. *The Papers of Woodrow Wilson*. 69 vols. Edited by Arthur S. Link. Princeton NJ: Princeton University Press, 1966-1994.

Secondary Material

Adams, Henry. *The Degradation of Democracy*. New York: Peter Smith, Inc., 1949.

Ahlstrom, Sydney. *A Religious History of the American People*. New Haven CT: Yale University Press, 1972.

Allen, Frederick Lewis. *Only Yesterday: An Informal History of the 1920s*. New York: Harper and Row, 1931.

Ammerman, Nancy. *Baptist Battles: Social Change and Religious Conflict in the Southern Baptist Convention*. New Brunswick NJ: Rutgers University Press, 1990.

Aquinas, Thomas. *Summa Theologica*. Translated by the Dominican Fathers of the English Province. 19 vols. London: R. & T. Washbourne, 1911-1922.

Atkins, Gaius Glenn. *Religion in Our Times*. New York: Round Table Press, Inc., 1932.

Ayers, Edward. *The Promise of the New South: Life After Reconstruction*. New York: Oxford University Press, 1992.

Beckley, Harlan. *Passion for Justice: Retrieving the Legacies of Walter Rauschenbusch, John A. Ryan, and Reinhold Neibuhr*. Louisville KY.: Westminster/John Knox Press, 1992.

Bellah, Robert. *The Broken Covenant: American Civil Religion in Time of Trial*, 2nd ed. Chicago: University of Chicago Press, 1992.

Bloom, Harold. *The American Religion: The Emergence of the Post-Christian Nation*. New York: Simon and Schuster, 1992.

Boles, John B. *The Great Revival: Beginnings of the Bible Belt*. Rev. ed. Lexington KY: University Press of Kentucky, 1996.

Brackney, William H. *The Baptists*. New York: Greenwood Press, 1988.

_____. *Christian Voluntarism in Britain and North America: A Bibliography and Critical Assessment*. Westport CT: Greenwood Press, 1995.

Broadway, Mikael. "The Ways of Zion Mourned: A Historicist Critique of Church-State Relations." Ph.D. dissertation, Duke University, 1993.

Brown, Meg Lota. *Donne and the Politics of Conscience in Early Modern England*. Leiden, The Netherlands: E. J. Brill, 1995.

Burrage, Champlain. *The Early English Dissenters, in the Light of Recent Research (1550-1641)*. Vol. 1, *History and Criticism*. Cambridge: Cambridge University Press, 1912.

Butterfield, Herbert. *The Whig Interpretation of History*. London: G. Bell and Sons, 1963.

Cathcart, William. *The Papal System: From Its Origin to the Present Time*. Philadelphia: The American Baptist Publication Society, 1872.

Cavanaugh, William T. "The City: Beyond Secular Parodies." In *Radical Orthodoxy*, edited by John Milbank, Catherine Pickstock, and Graham Ward, 182-200. New York: Routledge, 1999.

_____. *Theopolitical Imagination: Discovering the Liturgy as a Political Act in an Age of Global Consumerism.* New York: T. & T. Clark, 2002.

_____. *Torture and Eucharist: Theology, Politics, and the Body of Christ.* Malden MA: Blackwell Publishers, 1998.

Clapp, Rodney. *A Peculiar People: The Church as Culture in a Post-Modern World.* Downers Grove IL: Intervarsity Press, 1996.

Clifford, John. "The Baptist Attitude to Catholicism—Roman and Greek." *Review and Expositor* 8 (1911): 331-344.

Coggins, James. *John Smyth's Congregation: English Separatism, Mennonite Influences, and the Elect Nation.* Waterloo OT.: Herald Press, 1991.

_____. "The Theological Positions of John Smyth." *The Baptist Quarterly* 30 (1984): 247-264.

Coker, Joe L. "Sweet Harmony vs. Strict Separation: Recognizing the Distinctions Between Isaac Backus and John Leland." *American Baptist Quarterly* 16 (1997): 241-250.

Creed, J. Bradley. "Freedom For and Freedom From: Baptists, Religious Liberty, and World War II." *Baptist History and Heritage* 36 (Summer/Fall 2001): 28-43.

_____. "John Leland, American Prophet of Religious Individualism." Ph.D. dissertation, Southwestern Baptist Theological Seminary, 1986.

Curti, Merle. *The Growth of American Thought.* New York: Harper and Brothers Publishers, 1943.

Curtis, Susan. *A Consuming Faith: The Social Gospel and Modern American Culture.* Baltimore: The Johns Hopkins University Press, 1991.

Davis, Derek H. *Religion and the Continental Congress, 1774-1789.* New York: Oxford University Press, 2000.

Dawson, J. M. *Baptists and the American Republic.* Nashville TN: Broadman Press, 1956.

_____. *Separate Church and State Now.* New York: Richard R. Smith, 1948.

Dawson, Jan. "The Religion of Democracy in Early Twentieth Century America." *Journal of Church and State* 27 (1985): 47-68.

DeWeese, Charles B., ed. *Defining Baptist Convictions: Guidelines for the Twenty-first Century.* Franklin TN: Providence House Publishers, 1996.

Dilday, Russell H., Jr. "The Apologetic Method of E. Y. Mullins." Th.D. dissertation, Southwestern Baptist Theological Seminary, 1960.

_____. "Mullins the Theologian." *Review and Expositor* 96 (1999): 75-86.

Dodson, Will. "Church and State in Contemporary United States: Toward a Greater Union: The Accommodation Position." *Baptist History and Heritage* 33 (Winter 1998): 43-53.

Driesbach, Daniel L. "Mr. Jefferson, a Mammoth Cheese, and the 'Wall of Separation Between Church and State': A Bicentennial Commemoration." *Journal of Church and State* 43 (2001): 725-745.

Dunn, James. "Church and State in Contemporary United States: A Wall of Separation?" *Baptist History and Heritage* 33 (Winter 1998): 31-42.
_____. "Church, State, and Soul Competency." *Review and Expositor* 96 (1999): 61-73.
_____. "Yes, I Am a Baptist." In *Why I Am a Baptist*, ed. Cecil Staton, 43-48. Macon, Ga.: Smyth and Helwys, 1999.
Durso, Keith E. *Thy Will Be Done: A Biography of George W. Truett*. Macon GA: Mercer University Press, 2009.
Eberts, Henry William. "The Legacy of Walter Rauschenbusch." *Religion in Life* 37 (1968): 382-400.
Eighmy, John L. *Churches in Cultural Captivity: A History of the Social Attitudes of Southern Baptists*. Knoxville TN: University of Tennessee Press, 1972.
Ellis, William E. *"A Man of Books and a Man of the People": E. Y. Mullins and the Crisis of Moderate Southern Baptist Leadership*. Macon GA: Mercer University Press, 1985.
Ely, Richard T. *Social Aspects of Christianity*. New York: Thomas Y. Crowell and Company, 1889.
Eskew, Harry, and Hugh T. McElrath. *Sing With Understanding: An Introduction to Christian Hymnology*. Nashville TN: Broadman Press, 1980.
Estep, William R. *Revolution Within the Revolution: The First Amendment in Historical Context, 1612-1789*. Grand Rapids MI: Eerdmans Publishing Company, 1990.
_____. "Thomas Helwys: Bold Architect of Baptist Polity on Church-State Relations." *Baptist History and Heritage* 20 (July 1985): 24-34.
Fishburn, Janet. *The Fatherhood of God and the Victorian Family*. Philadelphia: Fortress Press, 1981.
Fortin, Ernest. "The Political Implications of St. Augustine's Theory of Conscience." In *Classical Christianity and the Social Order*, edited by J. Brian Benestad, 65-84. Lanham MD: Rowman and Littlefield, 1996.
Freeman, Curtis. "Can Baptist Theology Be Revisioned?" *Perspectives in Religious Studies* 24 (1997): 273-302.
_____. "E. Y. Mullins and the Siren Songs of Modernity." *Review and Expositor* 96 (1999): 23-42.
_____. "A New Perspective On Baptist Identity." *Perspectives in Religious Studies* 26 (1999): 59-65.
Gaustad, Edwin. "The Backus-Leland Tradition." *Foundations* 2 (1959): 131-152.
_____. *Liberty of Conscience: Roger Williams in America*. Grand Rapids, MI: Eedrmans Publishing Company, 1991.
_____. "Religious Liberty: Some Fine Distinctions." *American Baptist Quarterly* 6 (1987): 215-225.
_____. "U. S. Baptists and Modernity: Great Dissenters, Lousy Conformists." *Baptist History and Heritage* 36 (Winter/Spring 2001): 101-112.

George, Timothy, and David Dockery. *Baptist Theologians*. Nashville, TN: Broadman Press, 1990.

Goen, C. C. "Baptists and Church-State Issues in the 20th Century." *American Baptist Quarterly* 6 (1987): 226-253.

Graves, Thomas. "Baptist Identity in the 20th Century." *Baptist History and Heritage* 35 (Summer/Fall 2000): 7-23.

Gray, George W. "Out of the Mountains Came This Great Preacher of the Plains." *The American Magazine*, November 1925, 16-17, 134-147.

"Greatness in Preachers." *Christian Century* 42 (1925): 44-45.

Grenz, Stanley. *Isaac Backus—Baptist and Puritan*. Macon GA: Mercer University Press, 1983.

Haight, Roger. "The Mission of the Church in the Theology of the Social Gospel." *Theological Studies* 49 (1988): 477-497.

Hall, Timothy. *Separating Church and State: Roger Williams and Religious Liberty*. Urbana IL: University of Illinois Press, 1998.

Handbook to The Baptist Hymnal. Nashville TN: Convention Press, 1992.

Handy, Robert T. *A Christian America: Protestant Hopes and Historical Realities*. New York: Oxford University Press, 1984.

———. *A History of the Churches in the United States and Canada*. Oxford: Oxford University Press, 1976.

———. *The Social Gospel in America, 1870-1920*. New York: Oxford University Press, 1966.

Hankins, Barry. "The Evangelical Accommodation of Southern Baptist Conservatives." *Baptist History and Heritage* 33 (Winter 1998): 54-65.

———. *God's Rascal: J. Frank Norris and the Beginnings of Southern Fundamentalism*. Lexington KY: University Press of Kentucky, 1996.

———. *Uneasy in Babylon: Southern Baptist Conservatives and American Culture*. Tuscaloosa AL: University of Alabama Press, 2002.

von Harnack, Adolf. *What is Christianity?* Translated by Thomas Bailey Saunders. New York: G. P. Putnam and Sons, 1901.

Harvey, Barry. *Another City: An Ecclesiological Primer for a Post-Christian World*. Harrisburg PA: Trinity Press International, 1999.

———. *Politics of the Theological: Beyond the Piety and Power of a World Come of Age*. New York: Peter Lang, 1990.

———. "Round and Round About the Town: The Ecclesial Dimensions of Living In the Truth." *Perspectives in Religious Studies* 25 (1998): 105-114.

Harvey, Paul. "'Yankee Faith' and Southern Redemption: White Southern Baptist Ministers, 1850-1890." In *Religion and the American Civil War*, edited by Randall Miller, Harry Stout, and Charles Reagan Wilson, 167-186. New York: Oxford University Press, 1998.

Hastey, Stan. "The History and Contributions of the Baptist Joint Committee." *Baptist History and Heritage* 20 (July 1985): 35-43.

_____. "The New Christian Right: Retrospect and Prospect." *American Baptist Quarterly* 6 (1987): 264-272.

_____. "Reconstructing the Revolution: Religion's Rightful Role." *Review and Expositor* 97 (2000): 39-48.

Hatch, Nathan. *The Democratization of American Christianity*. New Haven CT: Yale University Press, 1989.

Hauerwas, Stanley. *After Christendom? How the Church is to Behave if Freedom, Justice, and a Christian Nation are Bad Ideas*. Nashville TN: Abingdon Press, 1991.

_____. *Christian Existence Today: Essays on Church, World, and Living In Between*. Durham NC: The Labyrinth Press, 1988.

_____. *A Community of Character: Toward a Constructive Christian Social Ethic*. Notre Dame IN: University of Notre Dame Press, 1981.

_____. "The Democratic Policing of Christianity." *Pro Ecclesia* 3 (1994): 215-231.

_____. *Unleashing the Scripture: Freeing the Bible from Captivity to America*. Nashville TN: Abingdon Press, 1993.

Hays, Richard B. *The Moral Vision of the New Testament: A Contemporary Introduction to New Testament Ethics*. San Francisco: Harper Collins, 1996.

Herberg, Will. *Protestant-Catholic-Jew: An Essay in American Religious Sociology*. Garden City NY: Doubleday, 1955.

Hewitt, T. Furman. "Mining the Baptist Tradition for Christian Ethics: Some Gems." *Perspectives in Religious Studies* 25 (1998): 72-76.

Higgins, Paul L. *Preachers of Power: Henry Ward Beecher, Phillips Brooks, and Walter Rauschenbusch*. New York: Vantage Press, 1950.

Hinson, E. Glenn. "Baptist Contributions to Liberalism." *Baptist History and Heritage* 35 (2000): 39-54.

_____. "E. Y. Mullins as Interpreter of the Baptist Tradition." *Review and Expositor* 96 (1999): 109-122.

Hofstadter, Richard. *The Age of Reform: From Bryan to FDR*. New York: Vintage Books, 1955.

Hopkins, Charles Howard. *The Rise of the Social Gospel in American Protestantism, 1865-1915*. New Haven CT: Yale University Press, 1940.

Hostetler, Michael J. "Liberty in Baptist Thought: Three Primary Texts, 1614-1856." *American Baptist Quarterly* 15 (1996): 242-256.

Hovey, Alvah. *A Memoir of the Life and Times of the Rev. Isaac Backus, A.M.* Boston: Gould and Lincoln, 1859.

Hudson, Winthrop S. Introduction to *Walter Rauschenbusch: Selected Writings*. New York: Paulist Press, 1984.

_____. *Religion in America: An Historical Account of the Development of American Religious Life*, 3rd ed. New York: Scribner, 1981.

_____. "Walter Rauschenbusch and the New Evangelism." *Religion in Life* 30 (1961): 412-430.

Hunter, James Davison. *Culture Wars: The Struggle to Define America.* New York: Basic Books, 1991.

Hutchinson, William. *The Modernist Impulse in American Protestantism.* Durham, NC: Duke University Press, 1992.

Irons, Charles F. "Believing in America: Faith and Politics in Early National Virginia." *American Baptist Quarterly* 22 (2002): 346-412.

Jaehn, Klaus Juergen. "Formation of Walter Rauschenbusch's Social Conscience as Reflected in His Early Life and Writings." *Foundations* 16 (1973): 294-326; 17 (1974): 68-85.

James, Powhatan W. *George W. Truett: A Biography.* New York: The MacMillan Company, 1939.

James, William. *The Varieties of Religious Experience: A Study in Human Nature.* New York: New American Library, 1958.

Jones, Edgar DeWitt. *American Preachers Today: Intimate Appraisals of 32 Leaders.* Indianapolis: Bobbs-Merrill Company, 1933.

Koch, Adriene. *Jefferson and Madison: The Great Collaboration.* New York: Alfred A. Knopf, 1950.

Larson, Edward J. *Summer For the Gods: The Scopes Trial and America's Continuing Debate Over Science and Religion.* New York: Basic Books, 1997.

LaTourette, Kenneth Scott. *A History of Christianity.* Vol. 1, *Beginnings to 1500.* San Francisco: HarperCollins, 1975.

Lee, Jason K. *The Theology of John Smyth: Puritan, Separatist, Baptist, Mennonite.* Macon GA: Mercer University Press, 2003.

Leonard, Bill J., ed. *Dictionary of Baptists in America.* Downer's Grove IL: Intervarsity Press, 1994.

_____. *God's Last and Only Hope: The Fragmentation of the Southern Baptist Convention.* Grand Rapids MI: Eerdmans Publishing Company, 1990.

Linder, Robert, and Richard V. Pierard. *Twilight of the Saints: Biblical Christianity and Civil Religion in America.* Downers Grove IL: Intervarsity Press, 1978.

Link, Arthur S. *Woodrow Wilson and the Progressive Era, 1900-1917.* New York: Harper, 1954.

_____., and Richard McCormick. *Progressivism.* Wheeling IL: Harlan Davidson, Inc., 1983.

Lucas, Sean Michael. "Christianity at the Crossroads: E. Y. Mullins, J. Gresham Machen, and the Challenge of Modernism." *The Southern Baptist Journal of Theology* 3 (Winter 1999): 58-78.

MacFarlane, Peter Clarke. "The Apostle to the Texans." *Collier's*, 4 January 1913, 21- 22.

Maddox, Timothy D. F. "E. Y. Mullins: Mr. Baptist for the 20th and 21st Century." *Review and Expositor* 96 (1999): 87-108.

Manis, Andrew. "Regionalism and a Baptist Perspective on the Separation of Church and State." *American Baptist Quarterly* 2 (1983): 213-227.

Marsden, George. *Fundamentalism and American Culture: The Shaping of Twentieth Century Evangelicalism, 1870-1925.* New York: Oxford University Press, 1980.

_____. *Religion and American Culture.* Fort Worth TX: Harcourt College Publishers, 2001.

Marsh, Charles. *God's Long Summer: Stories of Faith and Civil Rights.* Princeton NJ: Princeton University Press, 1997.

Marty, Martin E. *Righteous Empire: The Protestant Experience in America.* New York: Dial Press, 1970.

_____. "Two Kinds of Two Kinds of Civil Religion." In *American Civil Religion*, eds. Russell E. Richey and Donald G. Jones, 139-157. New York: Harper and Row, 1974.

Maston, T. B. *Isaac Backus: Pioneer of Religious Liberty.* London: James Clarke & Co., 1962.

McBeth, H. Leon. *The Baptist Heritage: Four Centuries of Baptist Witness.* Nashville TN: Broadman Press, 1987.

_____. "English Baptist Literature on Religious Liberty." Th.D. dissertation, Southwestern Baptist Theological Seminary, 1961.

_____. "George W. Truett: Baptist Statesman." *Baptist History and Heritage* 32 (April 1997): 9-22.

_____. "John Franklyn Norris: Texas Tornado." *Baptist History and Heritage* 32 (April 1997): 23-38.

McClendon, James. *Systematic Theology.* Vol. 1, *Ethics.* Nashville TN: Abingdon Press, 1986.

_____. "What is a 'baptist' Theology?" *American Baptist Quarterly* 1 (1982): 16-39. McClintock, David Alan. "Walter Rauschenbusch: The Kingdom of God and the American Experience." Ph.D. dissertation, Case Western Reserve University, 1976.

McLoughlin, William. *Isaac Backus and the American Pietistic Tradition.* Boston: Little, Brown, and Company, 1967.

_____. "Isaac Backus and the Separation of Church and State in America." *American Historical Review* 73 (1968): 1392-1413.

_____. *New England Dissent, 1630-1833.* 2 Vols. Cambridge MA: Harvard University Press, 1971.

_____. *Soul Liberty: The Baptists' Struggle in New England, 1630-1833.* New Hanover NH: University Press of New England, 1991. McMahone, Martin. "Liberty More Than Separation: The Multiple Streams of Baptist Thought on Church-State Issues." Ph.D. dissertation, Baylor University, 2001.

Mead, Sidney E. *The Lively Experiment: The Shaping of Christianity in America.* New York: Harper and Row, 1963.

Miller, Perry. *Roger Williams: His Contribution to the American Tradition.* Indianapolis: The Bobbs-Merrill Company, 1953.
Miller, William Lee. *The First Liberty: Religion and the American Republic.* New York: Alfred A. Knopf, 1996.
Mims, Edwin. *The Advancing South: Stories of Progress and Reaction.* Garden City, NY: Doubleday, Page, and Company, 1927. Minus, Paul. *Walter Rauschenbusch: American Reformer.* New York: Macmillan, 1988.
Mohler, Albert, Jr. "Baptist Theology at the Crossroads: The Legacy of E. Y. Mullins." *The Southern Baptist Journal of Theology* 3 (Winter 1999): 4-23.
_____. "Fighting for Peace," *The Southern Seminary Magazine,* Spring 2003, inside cover, 9.
Moore, LeRoy. "Roger Williams and the Historians." *Church History* 32 (1963): 432- 451.
Moore, Russell and Gregory Thornberry. "The Mystery of E. Y. Mullins in Contemporary Baptist Historiography." *The Southern Baptist Journal of Theology* 3 (Winter 1999): 44-57.
Morgan, David. *The New Crusades, the New Holy Land: Conflict in the Southern Baptist Convention, 1969-1991.* Tuscaloosa AL: University of Alabama Press, 1996.
Morgan, Edmund S. *Roger Williams: The Church and the State.* New York: Harcourt, Brace and World, Inc., 1967.
Mowry, George E. *The Era of Theodore Roosevelt, 1900-1912.* New York: Harper, 1958.
Mullins, Isla May. *E. Y. Mullins: An Intimate Biography.* Nashville TN: The Sunday School Board of the Southern Baptist Convention, 1929.
Neely, Alan, ed. *Being Baptist Means* Freedom. Charlotte NC: Southern Baptist Alliance, 1988.
_____. "Denominationalism, Centralization, and Baptist Principles: Observations by a Somewhat Perplexed Baptist." *American Baptist Quarterly* 21 (2002): 484-498.
Nettles, Thomas J. "E. Y. Mullins—Reluctant Evangelical." *The Southern Baptist Journal of Theology* 3 (Winter 1999): 24-42.
Neuhaus, Richard John. *The Naked Public Square: Religion and Democracy in America.* Grand Rapids MI.: Eerdmans Publishing Company, 1984.
Newton, Joseph Fort. *Some Living Masters of the Pulpit: Studies in Religious Personality.* New York: George B. Doran Company, 1923.
Nichols, Robert Hastings. "The Influence of the American Environment on the Conception of the Church in American Protestantism." *Church History* 11 (1942): 181-192.
Niebuhr, H. Richard. *The Kingdom of God in America.* Chicago: Willett, Clark, and Company, 1937.

Niebuhr, Reinhold. *The Children of Light and the Children of Darkness.* New York: Charles Scribner's Sons, 1944.

_____. *Moral Man and Immoral Society: A Study in Ethics and Politics.* New York: Charles Scribner's Sons, 1932.

_____. *Pious and Secular America.* New York: Scribner, 1958.

_____. "Walter Rauschenbusch in Historical Perspective." *Religion in Life* 27 (Autumn 1958): 527-536.

Noll, Mark A. *A History of Christianity in the United States and Canada.* Grand Rapids MI: Eerdmans Publishing Company, 1992.

_____., Ed. *The Princeton Theology, 1812-1921: Scripture, Science, and Theological Method from Archibald Alexander to Benjamin Breckinridge Warfield.* Grand Rapids MI: Baker Book House, 1983.

_____. *The Scandal of the Evangelical Mind.* Grand Rapids MI: Eerdmans Publishing Company, 1994.

_____., George M. Marsden, and Nathan O. Hatch. *The Search for a Christian America.* Colorado Springs CO: Helmers and Howard, 1989.

Numbers, Ronald L. *The Creationists.* New York: A. A. Knopf, 1992.

Olcott, Charles S. *The Life of William McKinley.* 2 vols. Boston: Houghton, Mifflin, and Company, 1910. Oxnam, G. Bromley. *Personalities in Social Reform.* New York: Abingdon-Cokesbury Press, 1950.

Patterson, W. Morgan. "The Americanization of Baptists." In *Baptists and the American Experience,* edited by James E. Wood, Jr., 137-152. Valley Forge PA: Judson Press, 1976.

Phillips, Stephen. "Thomas Helwys and the Idea of Religious Liberty." Ph.D. dissertation, Baylor University, 1998.

Pleasants, Phyllis. "E. Y. Mullins: Diplomatic Theological Leader." *Review and Expositor* 96 (1999): 43-60.

Pocock, J. G. A. *The Ancient Constitution and the Feudal Law.* Cambridge: Cambridge University Press, 1957.

Porter, Henry Alfred. "An Interpretation, One Among a Thousand." *Review and Expositor* 22 (1925): 11-26.

Poteat, Edwin McNeill. "Religion in the South." In *Culture in the South,* edited by W. T. Couch, 248-269. Chapel Hill NC: University of North Carolina Press, 1935.

Proclaiming the Baptist Vision: Religious Liberty. Edited by Walter B. Shurden. Macon GA: Smyth and Helwys, 1997.

Ritschl, Albrecht. *The Christian Doctrine of Justification and Reconciliation.* Edited by H. R. Mackintosh and A. B. Macauley. Edinburgh: T. & T. Clark, 1900.

Robertson, A. T. "A Sketch of the Life of President Mullins." *Review and Expositor* 22 (1925): 7-10.

Ramsay, William. *Four Modern Prophets: Walter Rauschenbusch, Martin Luther King, Jr., Gustavo Gutierrez, and Rosemary Radford Reuther.* Atlanta: John Knox Press, 1986.

Richardson, Herbert. "Civil Religion in Theological Perspective." In *American Civil Religion,* edited by Russell E. Richey and Donald G. Jones, 161-184. New York: Harper and Row, 1974.

Schneider, Carl. "The Americanization of Karl August Rauschenbusch, 1816-1899." *Church History* 24 (1955): 3-14.

Sehested, Ken. "Conformity or Dissent: Southern Baptists on War and Peace Since 1940." *Baptist History and Heritage* 28 (April 1993): 3-18.

Sharpe, Dores Robinson. *Walter Rauschenbusch.* New York: The MacMillan Company, 1942.

Sheldon, Garrett Ward. *The Political Philosophy of Thomas Jefferson.* Baltimore: The Johns Hopkins University Press, 1991.

Shurden, Walter B. *The Baptist Identity: Four Fragile Freedoms.* Macon GA: Smyth and Helwys, 1993.

_____. "The Baptist Identity and the Baptist *Manifesto.*" *Perspectives in Religious Studies* 25 (1998): 321-340.

_____. *The Life of the Baptists in the Life of the World: 80 Years of the Baptist World Alliance.* Nashville TN: Broadman Press, 1985.

_____. *Not a Silent People: Controversies That Have Shaped Southern Baptists.* Macon GA: Smyth and Helwys, 1995.

Silber, Nina. *The Romance of Reunion: Northerners and the South, 1865-1900.* Chapel Hill NC: University of North Carolina Press, 1993.

Singal, Daniel J. *The War Within: From Victorian to Modernist Thought in the South, 1919-1945.* Chapel Hill NC: University of North Carolina Press, 1982.

Skinner, Craig. "The Bullet that Broke a Preacher's Heart." *Preaching* 14 (1999): 52-55.

Slosson, Preston William. *The Great Crusade and After, 1914-1928.* New York: The MacMillan Company, 1937.

Smith, Gary Scott. "To Reconstruct the World: Walter Rauschenbusch and Social Change." *Fides et Historia* 23 (1991): 40-63.

Smucker, Donovan E. *The Origins of Walter Rauschenbusch's Social Ethics.* Montreal: McGill-Queen's University Press, 1994. Spain, Rufus. *At Ease in Zion: Social History of Southern Baptists, 1865-1900.* Nashville TN: Vanderbilt University Press, 1967.

Spivey, Jim. "Separation No Myth: Religious Liberty's Biblical and Theological Bases." *Southwestern Journal of Theology* 36 (1994): 10-16.

Stackhouse, Max L. "The Continuing Importance of Walter Rauschenbusch." In *The Righteousness of the Kingdom,* ed. Max L. Stackhouse, 13-59. Nashville: Abingdon Press, 1968.

_____. "The Formation of a Prophet: Reflections on the Early Sermons of Walter Rauschenbusch." *Andover Newton Quarterly* 9 (January 1969): 137-159.

Steltze, Charles. "The Workingman and the Church." *The Outlook* 68 (1901): 717-721.

Stoeffler, F. Ernest. *The Rise of Evangelical Pietism*. Leiden, The Netherlands: E. J. Brill, 1965.

Sullivan, Mark. *Our Times: The United States, 1900-1925*. 6 vols. New York: Scribners, 1926-1932.

Sundquist, Steven. "The Kingdom of God and the Theological Ethics of Walter Rauschenbusch." *American Baptist Quarterly* 22 (March 2003): 77-98.

Szasz, Ferenc Morton. *The Divided Mind of Protestant America, 1880-1930*. University AL: University of Alabama Press, 1982.

Thomas, Cal, and Ed Dobson. *Blinded By Might: Why the Religious Right Can't Save America*. Grand Rapids MI: Zondervan Publishing House, 1999.

Thompson, Philip. "A New Question in Baptist History: Seeking a Catholic Spirit Among Early Baptists." *Pro Ecclesia* 8 (1999): 51-72.

_____. "Religious Liberty, Sacraments, God's Image, and the State in Two Periods in Baptist Life and Thought." Paper presented at the Catholic Theological Society / National Association of Baptist Professors of Religion conference, Villanova University, 4 June 2000.

de Tocqueville, Alexis. *Democracy in America*. 2 Vols. Ed. Phillips Bradley. New York: Alfred A. Knopf, 1945.

Torbet, Robert G. *A History of the Baptists*. Valley Forge PA: Judson Press, 1963.

Trueblood, Elton. *Foundations for Reconstruction*. New York: Harper and Brothers Publishers, 1946.

Walker, Williston, and Richard A. Norris, David W. Lotz, Robert T. Handy. *A History of the Christian Church*, 4th ed. New York: Charles Scribner's Sons, 1985.

Wamble, Hugh. "Baptist Contributions to the Separation of Church and State." *Baptist History and Heritage* 20 (July 1985): 3-13, 30.

Wardin, Albert, Jr. "Contrasting Views of Church and State: A Study of John Leland and Isaac Backus." *Baptist History and Heritage* 33 (1998): 12-20.

White, B. R. *The English Baptists of the Seventeenth Century*. London: The Baptist Historical Society, 1983.

Whitley, W. T. *A History of British Baptists*. London: Charles Griffin & Company, 1923.

Wiebe, Robert. *The Search for Order, 1877-1920*. New York: Hill and Wang, 1967.

Wilson, Charles Reagan. *Baptized In Blood: The Religion of the Lost Cause, 1865-1900*. Athens GA: University of Georgia Press, 1980.

Wood, James E, Jr. "Baptists and Religious Liberty." *Southwestern Journal of Theology* 6 (April 1964): 38-59.

_____. "Biblical Foundations of Church-State Relations." In *Church and State in Scripture, History, and Constitutional Law*, eds. James E. Wood, Jr., E. Bruce Thompson, and Robert T. Miller, 11-54. Waco TX: Baylor University Press, 1985.

_____. Introduction to *Baptists and the American Experience*. Valley Forge PA: Judson Press, 1976.

Woodward, C. Vann. *Origins of the New South, 1877-1913*. Baton Rouge LA: Louisiana State University Press, 1951.

_____. *The Strange Career of Jim Crow*. New York: Oxford University Press, 1955.

Wright, Jonathan. "The World's Worst Worm." *The Sixteenth Century Journal* 30 (1999): 113-133.

Yoder, John Howard. *The Politics of Jesus: Vicit Agnus Noster*, 2nd ed. Grand Rapids MI: Eerdmans Publishing Company, 1994.

_____. *The Priestly Kingdom: Social Ethics as Gospel*. Notre Dame IN: University of Notre Dame Press, 1984.

Young, Doyle L. "Leadership that Motivates: A Study in the Life of George W. Truett." *Baptist History and Heritage* 20 (January 1985): 45-51.

Zachman, Randall C. *The Assurances of Faith: Conscience in the Theology of Martin Luther and John Calvin*. Minneapolis: Fortress Press, 1993.

Index

American Revolution, 7-9, 40-42, 44-50; and the spirit of Democracy, 44-4; Baptist participation in 7-9: effects on religion, 49-50, 163.
A Theology for the Social Gospel, 55, 63-65, 78-84.
Aquinas, Thomas, 17-18.
Augustine, 17-18.
The Axioms of Religion, 91-92, 97, 107-126, 156.
Backus, Isaac, 38-40.
Baptists, 14-16, 29, 35-37, 169, 172; and the "Christian Right," 175-177; and the moderate-conservative controversy, 3-5, 171, 175-177; during the American Revolution, 7-9, 49-50; in England, 15-16, 20-23, 29-31, 35-37, 157, 169, 173; in the South, 3, 158.
Butterfield, Herbert, 14-15.
Conscience, 16-20, 27-28, 32-35; Enlightenment views of, 16-17, 38-44; Luther's understanding of, 18-19; Pre-modern understanding of, 17-20, 27-28, 32-35.
Dunn, James, 159-160, 172-173, 174.
First Amendment, 9, 46-48, 108, 156, 167, 173; Baptist influence on, 9, 46-48, 173; significance for Baptists, 49-50, 157, 167, 173, 175-176.
Freedom, 4-5, 155-169; as a "moderate" virtue, 4-5, 159, 170-177; Baptist views of, 5, 14-16, 35-37, 155-159, 164-169, 171-177.
Hauerwas, Stanley, 164-167.

Helwys, Thomas, 16, 28-36; and *A Short Declaration of the Mystery of Iniquity,* 32-34; and the origins of the Baptist movement, 29; return to England, 29; understanding of free will, 29-32.
Leland, John, 2, 37-49; and religious liberty, 44-49; political involvement of, 46-48; understanding of Baptist theology, 40-46, 154.
Locke, John, 16-17.
Mullins, Edgar Young (E.Y.), 12-13, 88-126; and fundamentalism, 102; and soul competency, 92, 109-111, 124; and *The Axioms of Religion,* 91-92, 97, 107-126; and the controversy over evolution, 96, 99-102; And World War I, 123; as a pastor, 95; as a theologian, 105; at the Southern Baptist Theological Seminary, 87-89, 95; early life, 93-94; education, 94; emphasis on individualism, 92, 109-114, 125; understanding of Baptist identity, 95-97, 103-105; views on democracy, 92, 109-11, 123-125, 155; views on modernism, 90, 96, 103-104.
Perkins, William, 19-20; and conscience, 19-20.
Progressivism, 65-67; and the social gospel, 65-67.
Rauschenbusch, Walter, 12-13, 52-65, 68-87; and *A Theology for the Social Gospel,* 55, 63-65, 78-84; and the Kingdom of God, 55, 61-

65, 68-84; and the social gospel, 54-55, 61-65, 68-84; and the idea of a Christian Nation, 68-69, 71-84; and World War I, 52-54, 64-65; as a pastor, 58-59, 61; at Rochester Theological Seminary, 55, 57, 62-63; early life, 56-57; education, 57; influences on, 62-64, 85-87; understanding of Baptist theology, 69-71; views on democracy, 69-84, 154-155; views on sin, 73, 78-84.

Roman Catholicism, 33, 138-139, 145-146; anti-democratic nature of, 138-139, 145-146; Baptist suspicions of, 138-139.

Shurden, Walter, 10, 171-172, 176, 177.

Smyth, John, 14, 16, 21-28; and the Bible, 22-26; and *The Character of The Beast*, 22-23, 26; and the origins of the Baptist movement, 22-23; arguments against infant baptism, 21-25; early life, 21; relations with the Mennonites, 21-22.

Social gospel, 54-55, 59-84; and the idea of a Christian nation, 68-69, 71-84; origins of, 59-61, 65-67; overlap with Progressivism, 65-67.

Truett, George W., 12-13, 89-90, 127-151; and World War I, 140-143; as a preacher, 131-137; at First Baptist Church of Dallas, 131-133, 136-137; early life, 129-130; education, 130; reaction to sermon at the U.S. Capitol, 128-129, 150-151; sermon at U.S. Capitol, 127-129, 143-151; stature among Southern Baptists, 134; understanding of Baptist theology, 137-143; views about democracy, 144-150, 155.

Williams, Roger, 37-39.

Yoder, John Howard, 160-164.